I0821831

Herodotus and the Philosophy of Empire

Herodotus and the Philosophy of Empire

Ann Ward

BAYLOR UNIVERSITY PRESS

Cover Design by Stephanie Blumenthal
Cover Images: Map of Greece and Bust of Herodotus. Used by permission of The Granger Collection, New York.

Library of Congress Cataloging-in-Publication Data

Ward, Ann, 1970-
Herodotus and the philosophy of empire / Ann Ward.
p. cm.
Includes bibliographical references and index.
ISBN 978-1-60258-007-7 (hbk. : alk. paper)
1. Herodotus. History. 2. History, Ancient. 3. Greece--History--To 146 B.C. I. Title.

D58.H7W37 2008
930--dc22

2008014378

Printed in the United States of America on acid-free paper

For Lee

teleios philos

Contents

Acknowledgments

The present work stems from the support and inspiration that I received from teachers to whom I owe a special debt of gratitude. My teacher and mentor Mary Nichols has provided me her friendship, patience, and wisdom throughout my studies and career, and without her this book would not have been possible. I also wish to give special thanks to my teachers Michael Davis and Michael Zuckert for all of their effort and assistance, which has made this a deeper and richer study of Herodotus. My gratitude is also owed to my editor at Baylor University Press, Carey Newman. His careful reading of my manuscript and his unstinting support, advice, and guidance allowed me to bring this project to completion. I would also like to thank the anonymous reviewers for their insightful comments on my work. All remaining shortcomings and errors are, of course, my own.

I would like to take this opportunity to thank many other people, too numerous to name individually, who have inspired my ideas and encouraged my academic aspirations. In particular, I wish to acknowledge my friends from my graduate program at Fordham University, my former colleagues at the University of Nevada, Las Vegas, and my present colleagues at Campion College, University of Regina. Above all I would like to thank David Fott for his collegial mentorship and Ted Jelen for believing in me and my work on Herodotus. I also wish to thank Campion College for its generous financial support of my research. I would like to acknowledge my former students at the University of Nevada, Las Vegas, and my current students at the University of Regina. They have been a joy to teach, and I have gained, and continue to gain invaluable insights from them in our discussions of Herodotus and classical political philosophy. I would also like to take this opportunity to thank my research assistant, Kristopher Schmaltz, graduate student in the Program for Social and Political Thought at the University of Regina, for his helpful and timely assistance in composing the index for this book. I would also like to acknowledge Diane Smth of Baylor University Press for her help and patience in preparing the manuscript for publication.

Finally, I wish to thank my mother, Patricia, my father, Mark, and my brother, Joseph Allen, for their love and support over the years. Growing up in a family that had excitement and interest in astronomy, history, and politics first gave me the idea when young that I would like to write a book. That this book has come to be an exploration of the *Histories*, I hope, proves worthy of their enthusiasm for all things intellectual. My deepest thanks and gratitude are for my husband and colleague Lee Ward. Like Herodotus, he has brought the world alive to me, and his love has made me know and feel the truth of Aristotle's teaching that without friends, life would not be worthwhile even if we had all other goods.

Regina, August 2007
Ann Ward

Chapter 1

Introduction

Athenian Democracy and the Problem of Empire

In the *Histories*, Herodotus offers a political science that combines freedom for thought with action and deliberation and culminates with Athens' manifestation as the best regime. Herodotus' defense of Athenian democracy occurs within the context of his transcultural system of regime analysis, including Egyptian theocracy, Scythian nomadism, Persian monarchy, and Spartan aristocracy, in which democratic Athens stands at the peak of the political possibilities that he explores. Herodotus' positive portrayal of democratic Athens is moderated, however, by his simultaneous critique of its inclination towards empire.

The portrait of Athenian democracy, I argue, also comes to light against the background of Herodotus' discussion of the founding of political regimes. In book 1 of the *Histories*, Herodotus investigates the origins of political power or the founding of such regimes as existed in Athens, Sparta, and Media. The stories of these regimes suggest that at the same time laws or regimes are founded, a notion of divinity behind the law arises that obscures the rational human agency involved. This leads to the discrepancy between what people say of the regime, that it is divinely inspired, and what actually operates in its creation, human reason or will. Herodotus illustrates the political dangers of founding myths in his story of Pisistratus, in which Athenian belief in divine support of their law left them susceptible to tyranny.

Herodotus turns to the question of why a notion of divine support arises when the regime is founded in the story of Deioces' founding of tyranny in Media. In his account of the rise of Deioces, Herodotus suggests that human beings are hard to govern because they are jealous of their freedom and equality and because they quickly conspire against any other human being whom they see trying to rule them. Political power is only possible if some men become like gods and other men become like beasts, and thus is inevitably based on a radical inequality and distortion of what is human. Herodotus therefore identifies the problem at the origin of the regime as the difficulty of combining freedom and equality with the need for political power and government.

In book 5, which is a new beginning to the *Histories*, the Athenian democracy is founded anew. Within his account of this new founding, Herodotus shows the movement from a divine to a secular foundation of government. Athenians no longer support the regime because they believe it to be a product of the divine, but because they believe the regime is theirs; patriotism, as it were, is at the origin of the new democracy. Athenians believe the democratic regime is theirs, Herodotus indicates, in two ways. First, because the regime is Athenian, or native, and second, being characterized by the equality of speech, all share equally in deliberation, and thus all, it is thought, participate equally in its decisions. The Athenians themselves are the regime. Thus, Herodotus indicates that Athens managed to combine equality with government by instituting self-government. Also, that patriotism replaces divine support for the regime means that what people say of the regime, that "it is ours," and what it actually is, a product of human agency, come closer together. This ability to capture what the regime actually is in speech allows the Athenians to internalize their regime. They believe it to be something within themselves and not a product of something outside of themselves, and thus possess a sense of wholeness rather than alienation. The regime, as it were, is in their hearts and minds. This internalization leads to their willingness, before the battle of Salamis, to forsake their city walls and therewith Athens' physical location and take to their ships, defeating Xerxes and saving Greece.

Athens, I argue, is also the most successful regime in taking account of the whole of human nature, both body and soul, thus making possible a life according to our highest human potential, the life of the mind. The Athenian integration of the desires of the body with the pursuits of the soul is illustrated when Herodotus says: "It is not only in respect of one thing but of everything that equality and free speech are clearly a good; take the case of Athens . . . when held in subjection [Athenians] would not do their best, for they were working for a task master, but, when freed, they sought to win, because each was trying to achieve for his very self" (V.78).[1] In this famous passage Herodotus indicates that the community of speech, reflecting the soul and shared by all, allowed each and was used by each to pursue his own private advantage. However, the pursuit of private material gain coincided with the public good only when conquering other cities. Thus, when Herodotus suggests that Athens makes possible a life according to humanity's higher nature or the mind, he suggests a potentiality of the regime, not its inevitable or permanent condition. Herodotus, I suggest, observing that Athens reflects the whole of human nature, seeks to place the regime on a more rational foundation than its patriotic or nativistic one.

Herodotus believes that the appeal to reason is possible because the Athenians understand the complexity of speech and the reality that speech is supposed to represent. Thus, for the Athenians, I argue, both human and divine speech is a mean between what Herodotus identifies as Egyptian "lying" and Persian "truth telling."[2] For instance, in his interpretation of oracles the Athenian Themistocles understands that the words of the god require interpretation because they can spawn a variety of meanings; they can conceal the truth or "lie," as it were. However, Themistocles also understands that words have one true meaning underlying the variety of meanings that they spawn; they can, as it were, be "truthful." Thus, not only is interpretation necessary, but there is also a correct interpretation.

The Athenian understanding of the complexity of speech—that words can both lie and tell the truth at the same time—makes them open and responsive, I argue, to the speech and thought of Herodotus.[3] Athens, therefore, has the potential to move in the direction of philosophy.[4] However, if Athens has the potential to be open to philosophy, it also has the potential to become imperial; the best regime, for Herodotus, can also become the worst.[5]

The imperialist impulse in Athens is reflected in the type of courage it possesses in contrast to that of the Spartans. According to Herodotus, Athenians and Spartans possess two different types of courage and fight for two different reasons. Spartan courage is defensive and is characterized by a type of spiritedness that is turned in on itself and seeks to defend its boundaries and what is its own. Also, Spartans fight not to win, but to achieve honor, largely through noble death, as shown by their "stand" at Thermopylae. While certainly worthy of praise, they lose sight of the end for which they are fighting. The Athenians, on the other hand, due to an intellectual inclination toward the universal, possess an aggressive type of courage shown by their "run" at Marathon, which is characterized by a type of spiritedness directed outwards and leads to the attempt to transcend boundaries, or to look on what is foreign or other. Athenians fight to win, and in doing so, tend to keep the end for which they are fighting in sight. Herodotus, I argue, although indicating that Athenian courage is higher, believes it to pose the danger that Athens will become as tyrannical as Persia or come to desire the universal empire that Persian king Xerxes did. In so doing, the Athenians will move from what I call the Herodotean perspective of contemplating the new and other, to the Persian extreme of trying to possess this other, politically or through conquest. The problem of imperialism in Athens, or the best regime, is one of the fundamental political problems Herodotus identifies in his *Histories*.

Our current international situation, which I will address in the epilogue, makes classical sources such as Herodotus—who provides a theoretical account of the politics of democracy and empire—especially relevant. However, contemporary political theorists and actors have tended to reach back not to Herodotus but to Thucydides for guidance. Thucydides' *War of the Peloponnesians and Athenians* attracts such interest because one of its main themes is the imperialism of democratic Athens. For instance, Michael Palmer argues that Thucydides' work brings to light the conflict between Athenian imperial policy and the principles that underlie and justify the Athenian democratic regime. Pericles, Athens' most prominent democratic leader at the outbreak of the war with Sparta, seeks to inspire in her citizens a love of the glory of Athens in order to overcome their fear of death and love of gain without having to "rise above . . . love of [their] own."[6] Yet the glory of Athens rested on the glory of her empire, which, Palmer argues, was both unjust and spawned the problem of Alcibiades, whom Thucydides regarded as the "outstanding representative of the post-Periclean generation of prominent Athenians." With Alcibiades, the tyranny of empire is introduced domestically, as Alcibiades wished to predominate internally in Athens as Athens wished to dominate externally other Greeks. The fruit of domestic tyranny is civil war, the worst of all political events. Thucydides' work thus stands as a warning against the dangers of imperialism to democratic regimes; the extinction of freedom abroad can lead to the disappearance of freedom and even chaos at home. Yet Thucydides, according to Palmer, suggests a solution to the immoderation of empire. Fear of the gods or traditional piety as displayed by Sparta is for Thucydides the source of political moderation and care for the common good. Palmer goes further, claiming, "Thucydides teaches that piety is an essential ingredient of all successful political life."[7]

Clifford Orwin and Steven Forde agree with Palmer that, for Thucydides, Alcibiades is the nexus uniting imperialism in international politics with the desire of ambitious statesmen to rule in domestic politics. Orwin argues that the "Athenian thesis"—that necessity or the natural demands of self-preservation and self-interest compel cities to rule over other cities—is correct "in theory," as Thucydides reveals that "[a]mong citizens as among cities, not virtue but necessity is the force to be reckoned on . . . the ultimate exigencies are those of the body; and the city's success in normal times depends on enlisting these in its behalf."[8] Moreover, in time of war, dedication to the "common good" only emerges "in opposition to a common enemy" who threatens the political and hence ultimately physical self-preservation of all. Yet, Orwin claims that the introduction of the "Athenian thesis" into the domestic affairs of Athens itself is "[in] practice . . . disastrous" (195). The problem is that no city can publicly admit its foundation in necessity or what is physically expedient, as its citizens expect their domestic life to be characterized by freedom, justice, and piety. Thucydides, Orwin asserts, believes "[t]he good of the city demands a healthy dose of hypocrisy so scorned by the noblest Athenians and by Alcibiades in particular" (195). It is Sparta, not Athens, therefore, which is Thucydides' best regime, as it publicly dedicates itself to the demands of justice and piety but privately adheres to the demands of its own self-interest. Thus, Orwin argues that, for Thucydides, the solution to the immoderation of Athens, manifested in its progressive public impiety in connection with its progressive imperial expansion, is a return to the "hypocrisy" of Spartan adherence to conventional virtue and piety, if not to its actual virtue and piety as Palmer suggests.[9]

Forde argues, on the other hand, that the problem of Alcibiades in Thucydides' account is not that he is an explicitly impious political cynic, as Palmer and Orwin maintain, but rather that Alcibiades is a "political idealist"; he believes in the ultimate convergence of all political interests between both cities and individuals alike.[10] For example, Alcibiades proposes that Athens together with Sparta exercise hegemony over the entire Greek world, not tyrannically but "voluntarily and without force, by good will" (196). Moreover, Alcibiades openly declares that his ambition to rule and his city's interests are one, and attempts to secure the consent of the Athenian citizens to dominate the public life of the city. Yet Thucydides, according to Forde, reveals that political interests do in fact diverge. Force and violence cannot be taken out of empire, and Alcibiades' willingness to betray Athens and serve her enemies shows not the unity of interests between the city and its greatest political leaders, but the subordination of the political community to Alcibiades' own ambitions for power and glory. Thucydides, however, does not point us in the direction of a return to the traditional virtues of piety and patriotism represented by Sparta, but rather suggests that politics is cyclical; according to Forde, "Thucydides offers no solution" to the dangers of imperialism that Alcibiades represents (210). Thucydides shows that the peak of political life, represented by Athenian equality, freedom, and "deliberate public speech," naturally culminates in empire which in turn throws forth men like Alcibiades, whose natural superiority to their fellow citizens means that the city's political life would end the moment they possessed it (210). The ambitions of Athens and Alcibiades, therefore, are doomed to fail yet doomed to be repeated throughout history.[11]

Like Forde, Gregory Crane argues that politics is cyclical; Thucydides' Athenians have switched places with the Persians as the former are now the imperialists rather than the freedom fighters they were in Herodotus. According to Crane, Thucydides' account of the Melian Dialogue between Athens and the tiny city of Melos inverts the stance that Herodotus, in book 8 of his *Histories*, attributes to Athens when it rejects an offer of friendship from imperial Persia. After the Athenian victory against the Persians in the battle of Salamis, Persia sends an offer of terms to Athens, claiming that the latter should not oppose overwhelming force, that they have no long term prospects for success, that there is no dishonor in yielding to a greater power, and that opposition at this point is not virtue but stupidity. The Athenians however rebuff the Persians asserting that the gods will be on the side of the just. Moreover, according to Crane, the Athenians decide to remain loyal to their understanding of a common Hellenic civilization that they would be betraying if they went over to the Persians, as well as to their feelings of their own self-worth and the value they place on freedom even over life itself.[12] Yet, Crane argues that in the Melian Dialogue two generations later, Thucydides' Athenians make arguments similar to those of Herodotus' Persians, and Thucydides' Melians reject them for the same reasons as Herodotus' Athenians. Moreover, Athens' assertion in the Melian Dialogue that the law for both gods and human beings is that the strong either dominate or destroy the weak, undermines, according to Crane, an older moral principle held by most Greeks that justice or restraint toward weaker powers was in the interests of the great. The imperial ambitions of the Athenians, Crane argues, drove them to forsake their Greek identity, or to become, as it were, Persian.[13]

Laurie M. Johnson argues that the Athenian thesis at Melos, that the strong dominate or destroy the weak by natural necessity, was a popular form of political rhetoric in imperial Athens unrepresentative of Thucydides' own views. To this extent, according to Johnson, Thucydides, contrary to a vast body of scholarship that claims otherwise, adheres neither to the realist nor the neo-realist understanding of international relations. Realists and neo-realists, according to Johnson, argue that all human beings are compelled to act by the natural passion of self-preservation and the pursuit of self-interest. The implications for the international system of this understanding of human nature is that all states, like the individuals that compose them, try to ensure their own security by constantly seeking to increase their power over other states. War and conquest of weaker powers by stronger ones is thus an inevitable feature of the relations between states; the cause of war and imperialism is the instability and competition for power within the international system itself.[14] Yet Thucydides, Johnson argues, indicates that none of the passions compel human beings to act, and hence denies the Athenian and realist claim that violence is natural, necessary, and thus blameless. Rather, Thucydides points to national and individual character as independent factors determining the relations between states in the international system. For instance, in contrast to Sparta's reticence and caution, Athens' national traits of daring, innovation, and the desire for glory—all motivations beyond self-interest—moved Thucydides' Athenians, according to Johnson, to acquire their empire and wage war against Sparta to preserve it. Moreover, Thucydides presents the decisions of individuals such as Themistocles and Pericles as essential to the acquisition and maintenance of the Athenian empire, and it was, for Thucydides, the failure of leadership, and not Athens' capabilities or lack thereof, that was the cause of her ultimate demise. Differences in individual character, therefore, between Pericles and future leaders, Johnson argues, led to the eventual decline and defeat of Athens.[15]

Jack Riley shares the view that for Thucydides the character of political leaders is crucial in understanding the actions and fate of states in the international system. According to Riley, Thucydides' account of the successful statesmanship of men such as Brasidas, Hermocrates, and Diodotus, points to the possibility that political freedom, stability, and empire can be combined. Riley indicates therefore, in contrast to most commentators, that Thucydides does not oppose but rather approves of imperialism. For instance, according to Riley, Thucydides shows that only with the rise of the Cretan empire and the rigid imposition of order that it brings, does pre-Hellenic Greece progress out of its chaotic, precivilized condition in which it was politically, economically, culturally, and morally enfeebled. Moreover, contrary to Palmer, Orwin, and Forde, Riley argues that Thucydides never links the Athenian imperial project—with Alcibiades as its most prominent exponent and the Sicilian expedition as its most ambitious expansion—with the fear of domestic tyranny and factional conflict within Athens that threatens civil war. Rather, the cause of factional conflict and the eventual downfall of Athens was an outburst of "frenzied piety" among the people during the Sicilian campaign, spawned by Alcibiades' "unconventional private habits" and manner of life (145, 143). In contrast to Palmer and Orwin, Riley claims, "[i]t was not the abandoning of piety, but in this case at least the retention of piety that caused the suspicion of Alcibiades, his removal from the command, and the downfall of the city" (143).[16] The problem with Athens, therefore, is not her imperial ambitions but the excessive piety of her people that does not permit Athens to act on her ambitions properly. Thus, for Riley, Thucydides shows that the Athenian imperial project failed, but not that empire simply is doomed to fail. Rather, Thucydides teaches that empire, if presided over by leaders successful in presenting a public image of virtue, can indeed be compatible with the conditions of healthy political life, moderation and justice.[17]

Leo Strauss, like Riley, argues that Thucydides believed the Sicilian expedition was a perfectly feasible attempt to expand the Athenian empire. Thus, according to Strauss, the Athenian imperial project ultimately failed in Thucydides' eyes not because of its inherent injustice and immoderation, but rather, as Johnson suggests, due to a failure of political leadership in post-Periclean Athens. Yet, Strauss does not locate the failure of leadership that led to the Sicilian disaster and eventual downfall of Athens primarily in Alcibiades' public disrespect for the gods and conventional piety, as Palmer and Orwin do. Rather, like Riley, Strauss points to the opposite tendency expressed by Athenian commanders such as Nicias. Strauss claims that for Thucydides, "Alcibiades . . . might have brought the Sicilian expedition to a happy issue. But Alcibiades' proved or presumed impiety made it necessary for the Athenian *demos* to entrust the expedition to [Nicias] . . . whom they could perfectly trust because he surpassed every one of them in piety" (209).[18]

Although Thucydides, according to Strauss, presents Athens' desire for imperial expansion over other Greeks as a perfectly realistic goal provided that they had correct leadership, he also shows that Athens' desire for a universal *territorial* empire manifests a deeper desire for a universal *temporal* empire. The Athenian desire to expand themselves infinitely in space is a symptom of their desire to expand themselves infinitely in time; if the individual cannot achieve immortality, their city, through empire, can. As Strauss suggests, "there is something reminding of religion in Athenian imperialism" (229). It is the Athenian desire for collective eternal life through the imperialism of their regime, which Strauss calls the "universalism of the city," that is, according to Strauss, "doomed to failure" in Thucydides' eyes. Therefore, Thucydides guides his readers to another form of universalism, the "genuine universalism of understanding" or the "universalism of thought," manifested in Thucydides' work itself. Thucydides, Strauss argues, reveals his understanding of the universal nature of man as man as "the ground of the deeds, the speeches, and the thoughts" which he records, and thereby preserves and shares his understanding for all generations in all times to come (228). Thus, according to Strauss, the Athenian desire for immortality through empire "transcends the limits of moderation . . . on the political plane, [but] comes into its own . . . on the plane of thought, of the thinking individual . . . Not Periclean Athens but the understanding which is possible on the basis of Periclean Athens is the peak" (229).[19] Strauss therefore suggests that for Thucydides, the solution to the problem of the failure of empire to ensure immortality on the political level, is not a return to the conventional virtue and piety of Sparta, but a turn to the active intellectual life pursued by Thucydides.

While many modern political theorists have looked to Thucydides as the classical exponent of the possibilities and limits of the regime's pursuit of empire, few have turned to Herodotus. The neglect of the wisdom of Herodotus, which this book seeks to redress, is surprising given that one of the main themes of Herodotus' *Histories*, like that of Thucydides' *War of the Peloponnesians and Athenians*, is imperialism. The centerpiece of the broad political panorama of the *Histories* is Herodotus' account of the epoch-making clash between the Persian Empire and the Greek world, led by Athens. Yet Herodotus reveals, in his account of this great struggle between East and West two generations before the outbreak of the Peloponnesian war, that imperialism is a permanent temptation facing all strong and successful regimes, including the victorious Athenians who embark on their own imperial project at the end of the *Histories*.

The potentials and dangers of the empire pursued by Athens are illustrated by Herodotus in his account of what the Persians learned due to their own experience with imperialism. Herodotus tells us in book 3 that Persian king Darius, due to Persian conquests that brought him into contact with other cultures, was able to see and investigate foreign customs or conventions that differed from his own. Darius was thus able to discover the mere conventionality of all conventions, and thus to discover the distinction between nature and convention. Herodotus indicates that when one can identify a custom as merely a custom, which can only occur if one looks to, and compares, the particular customs of others with one's own, one can then identify the natural—or make the distinction between nature, which is universal, and convention, which applies to particular peoples. Only then can one have knowledge of nature and of self. Xerxes, in his wish to extend his father's empire into a universal one, or to make the world into one country governed by a single Persian king, seeks to destroy all foreign customs and conventions. By denying otherness in the world, he threatens to destroy the ability to identify the natural or to distinguish between nature and convention—and thus to destroy the privileged point of access to self-knowledge and the foundation for Herodotus' own activity as well.

Only Herodotus' *Histories* itself, I argue, can address the problem of Athens' desire for universal empire. What Xerxes and his father Darius come to possess and therefore destroy through conquest—other peoples and their foreign customs—Herodotus comes to possess and therefore preserve through writing. Building on Strauss' insight that the "universalism of thought" transcends the "universalism of the city," I argue that the *Histories* itself replaces the universal empire dreamed of by Xerxes, but is superior to it. Herodotus, in his writing, points beyond politics to satisfy the imperial desire to make the world one unified whole while also maintaining the diversity of the peoples and their conventions that exist within it.[20] Herodotus, in combining the universal with the particular, can moderate the desire of Athens, or other democratic regimes like Athens in the future, for a universal empire modeled on that desired by Xerxes, by providing them with a superior, intellectual empire in his *Histories*. He thus preserves the possibility of the discovery of nature and self-knowledge.

Rest and Motion in the *Histories*

Herodotus' political science, which points to the superiority of democratic Athens and the unique temptations and dangers of empire his best regime faces, itself comes to light within the much broader context of his reflections on the cosmological principles of rest and motion. In the *Histories*, the principles of rest and motion manifest themselves on four levels: nature, custom, regime, and speech.[21]

I explore the operation of rest and motion on the level of nature and custom in chapter two. I begin with the investigation of Egyptian geography, in which Herodotus represents Egypt's land as a reflection of the principle of rest or that which maintains limits or distinctions in nature. The Nile, on the other hand, is represented as a reflection of the principle of motion or that which seeks to overcome limits or distinctions in nature. This overcoming is related to its creative or life-giving powers. Herodotus also reveals that human beings, in both their bodies and their souls, share in the creative or life-giving powers of the Nile, as well as the limit or distinction-maintaining properties of the earth.

The principles of rest and motion are also manifest in the discussion of the customs of Egypt and Scythia. In his investigation of Egyptian customs, Herodotus reveals a people whose whole way of life is organized around the principle of rest. As such the Egyptians emphasize stability and the past, which means their almost total subsumption within religion and lack of poetry. When Herodotus looks to Egyptian history, however, he discovers that Egyptian customs mute the concern for justice, wisdom, and truthful speech. Next, I explore Herodotus' discussion of the Scythians. As Herodotus presents them, the Scythians are a nomadic people without a city, and thus in contrast to the Egyptians are a people whose whole way of life is organized around the principle of motion. As such the Scythians revere youth and the future rather than age and the past, which means, according to Herodotus, their almost total ignorance of nature and complete subsumption within images; the Scythians cannot distinguish between the real and the image of the real, fact and fiction, and hence are an almost completely poeticized people. Moreover, Herodotus illustrates that the perfection of the Scythian custom of nomadism, the extreme of motion, although allowing for external freedom, can precipitate a total loss of individual identity.

In chapter 3 I examine the Persians. Herodotus' discussion of their customs reveals that they are a people who combine the principles of rest and motion in their political, intellectual, and religious practices. The Persians, however, suffer from internal contradictions in their customs that causes instability in their regime. Herodotus' treatment of Persian king Cambyses reveals that the perfection of Persian customs leads to madness, and his treatment of Persian king Darius shows that the total dedication to truth telling leads to the collapse of the distinction between truth and falsehood. Also, in this chapter, I introduce my analysis of rest and motion on the level of the regime through an examination of the Persian debate on government in book 3 of the *Histories*. In this debate three Persians, Otanes, Megabyzus, and Darius—theorize or speak about the regime they believe would be best for Persia. However, the debate takes place after Persian customs, political succession, and religious authority have been overturned, and human nature seems to lie exposed. Thus, the debate between these three speakers concerning the best regime is also about which regime is most in accord with characteristics universal to all human beings. Addressing what are believed to be unchanging universals in persons and political structures, these Persian regimes in theory are therefore regimes at rest.

Herodotus indicates that the study of the best regime in theory is insufficient because regimes in theory abstract from the complex nature of reality by using words to universalize the particular, or to express aspects of human behavior as natural even though they are actually products of convention. Regimes in theory assume that human nature is static or unchanging, or, in Herodotus' "cosmological" analysis, analogous to the element of earth. Thus, regimes in theory abstract from the creative aspect of human nature, which is analogous to the creative or life-giving properties of the Nile. Herodotus indicates that human beings, by their nature, can create things that conceal or transform their nature. For instance, they can create conventions that distance themselves from their lower or bodily nature, as they allow their higher nature, located in the soul, to emerge, thereby making possible a life that may ironically point beyond conventions. By turning to the study of historical regimes in motion, Herodotus shows that thought can grasp and speech can express the particular *as* the particular as well as the universal. By revealing the particular *as* the particular or the conventionality of conventions, Herodotus' analysis of regimes in history allows for the discovery of what is truly universal or natural to human beings, thus providing the condition for the discovery of the best regime. A full understanding of politics requires that regimes in theory be corrected by a study of regimes in history.[22]

Regimes in history are the subject of chapter four. This chapter begins with an examination of Herodotus' reflections on the problem at the founding of political orders—the difficulty of combining political power with freedom and equality—revealed in book 1 of the *Histories*. Herodotus illustrates that this difficulty leads to a notion of divine support of the regime that obscures the human agency involved and leaves human beings susceptible to tyranny. I then examine the new founding, as it is described in book 5 of the *Histories*, of the Athenian democracy, a regime that, like Persia, combines the principles of rest and motion but in its own unique way. Herodotus' narrative of the coming into being of this new democracy shows a movement from divine to secular support of the regime, which allows Athens to resolve the difficulty of combining equality with government by instituting self-government. Athens also comes closest to integrating the whole of human nature therefore making possible a life according to the highest human potential. Part of this life includes having access to truth or reality, which requires an understanding of the complexity of speech such that speech is located between Persian "truth telling" and Egyptian "lying." Speech is the fourth level on which the themes of rest and motion appear. The Athenians, I argue, understand the complexity of speech, and thus Athens stands at the peak of the political possibilities that Herodotus explores. I also argue, however, that although Athens has a superior courage to Sparta's, Herodotus believes this to pose the danger that Athens will become as tyrannical as Persia or desire the universal empire that Xerxes did.

I conclude my discussion in chapter five by reflecting on Herodotus' own activity or project as embodied in the *Histories*. I argue that it is only the *Histories* itself, which represents a type of universal empire superior to the one that even Xerxes dreamed of, that can moderate Athenian imperial designs, which become manifest at the end of Herodotus' work. The *Histories* attempts to teach Athens, or other democratic regimes like it in the future, that one can know oneself and expand oneself beyond time without having to expand one's regime infinitely in space. Human beings, if they cannot achieve immortality, can at least acquire immortal fame through writing, without destroying the possibility of self-knowledge and the foundations of Herodotus' own activity at the same time. In the epilogue, I will explore the relevance of the *Histories* to our understanding of contemporary international relations. I contrast Herodotus' attempt to deal with the problem of empire through his own writing with the assumptions underlying contemporary reflections on the possibility of empire in our own time in the speeches and writings of Paul Wolfowitz, Colin L. Powell, Joseph S. Nye Jr., and Robert W. Merry.

Reading Herodotus

Before turning to my analysis of Herodotus' narrative of the customs and regimes of Egypt, Scythia, Persia, and Greece, I wish to pause and give an account of my methodological approach to the reading of the *Histories* and show how this methodology arises out of the text itself. Such an account seems necessary as it is no doubt strange to learn that the *Histories*, for so long regarded as simply an ancient travel guide or anthropological survey like *National Geographic*, has a political philosophy of better and worse regimes based on an understanding of universal principles of human nature. Commentators in the past have been inclined to read Herodotus unphilosophically because he chose the genre of history to articulate his ideas. History is often regarded as lacking in the philosophic qualities that poetry, for instance, possesses.

Poetry often appears more philosophic than history because, unlike history, which tells us who we were and what has happened, poetry reveals who we can be and what could happen.[23] Thus, poetry can make use of the stories of the past to predict the future, as it were, and show us both the worst and the best way to live. It forces the one who experiences it to ask: "What is the moral of the story?" Poetry has this philosophic quality because it embeds universal truths about human beings in its presentation of particular people in particular situations. But, how can the poet's audience discern these universal truths partially concealed by the particulars, or know that they have understood the larger meaning that the particulars are trying to express? In other words, although poetry may prod those who experience it to ask "What does this mean?," does poetry also provide the answer to this question? The key to this puzzle is the necessity of interpretation. The fullness of poetry requires the rational participation of its audience.

History, especially as practiced by Herodotus, like poetry, embeds universal truths in the particulars that it presents.[24] Rational interpretation of the text, therefore, is just as necessary for history as it is for poetry to render clear its relevance and helpfulness for present and future. The importance of interpreting the *Histories* in order to bring to light the values and lessons embedded within it means, I would suggest, that Herodotus should be understood as a poetic historian.[25] As poetic as the *Histories* is, it is also philosophic, prompting its readers to ask what it means and what it is trying to teach about the best way of life. The poetic qualities of Herodotus' writing can be illustrated by an analysis of the interpretation of oracles early on in the *Histories*. These examples suggest that Herodotus' work necessarily calls forth interpretation to be understood.

In book 1 of the *Histories*, Herodotus tells us that Croesus, tyrant of Lydia, fearing the growth of the Persian empire under Cyrus, consulted the oracle at Delphi concerning whether or not he should make war on the Persians (I.46, 53). The oracle responded to Croesus' inquiries by declaring that "if he made war on the Persians he would destroy a mighty empire" (I.53). Croesus, Herodotus tells us, was delighted with the prophecy, feeling certain that he would defeat Cyrus and destroy the power of Persia. The next question that Croesus put to the oracle was: "Would his monarchy last long?" The oracle answered that Croesus would rule until "a mule shall become sovereign king of the Medians" (I.55). Again, Croesus was delighted with the oracle, believing that he and his descendants would never cease to rule Lydia and its empire. Surely, Croesus thought, "a mule would never become king of the Medians instead of a man" (I.56). Croesus, "because he trusted in the oracle," crossed into the Persian territory of Cappadocia (I.73). There he engaged Cyrus in battle in the territory of Pteria, but the day ended in a draw. Certain that Cyrus would not follow him, Croesus withdrew back into Lydia, to his capitol in Sardis, intending to call on his allies and gather a greater force to attack Cyrus again the next spring. Croesus was mistaken in his judgment, however, as Cyrus immediately pursued the retreating Croesus and, contrary to what the latter believed was the plain language of the Delphic oracle, the city of Sardis and Croesus himself were soon captured by the Persians (I.84–86). Chafing at the betrayal by the god, Croesus, with Cyrus' permission, tried to insult the god by having messengers present on the altar at Delphi the Persian chains by which he had been bound. Furthermore, these messengers were instructed to ask Apollo if he was accustomed to lie to those who served him and honored him with gifts (I.90). In response to this challenge by Croesus, the oracle declared the following:

> Croesus does not rightly find fault. For the prophecy given by Loxias ran: if Croesus made war upon Persia, he would destroy a mighty empire. Now, in the face of that, if he was going to be well advised, he should have sent and inquired again, whether it was his own empire or that of Cyrus that was spoken of. But Croesus did not understand what was said, nor did he make question again, and so he has no one to blame but himself. (I.91)

The oracle defends the god against the charge of lying. Croesus did indeed destroy a mighty empire, his own. The problem with Croesus is that he did not step back and reflect upon the various meanings that the word "empire" could refer to, but rather unthinkingly assumed that it meant the Persian and not the Lydian empire. Both the oracle itself and Herodotus, who reports the words of the oracle in his *Histories*, point to the complexity of oracular or divine speech. It is complex because it both reveals and conceals the truth at the same time; it exists as a mean between veracity and deceptiveness. For instance, the oracle is truthful in the sense that it reveals Croesus' destructive powers, but it is deceptive in the sense that it conceals the fact that Croesus will destroy his own empire, contrary to the latter's obvious assumption.[26]

Yet, what of Croesus' second obvious assumption, that a "mule" rather than a man would never rule the Medes, and hence that neither he nor his descendants would ever be deposed? With respect to this second accusation of lying, the oracle responded in the following way:

> Furthermore, when he put his last question to the god, and Loxias spoke of the mule, not even that did Croesus comprehend. Truly, Cyrus was that mule. He was born of two parents of different races, whereof his mother was of the higher, his father of the lower, breed. For the mother was a Mede and Astyages daughter, who was king of Media; but the father was a Persian and a subject of the Medes, and, being in every way beneath her, he cohabited with her as his sovereign mistress. (I.91)

This response indicates that oracular or divine speech, as recorded in the *Histories*, is not only complex but sometimes metaphorical. It can use words as symbols or images of an underlying reality that it is trying to express. For example, it can use the image of a mule, a certain type of animal, as the symbol of Cyrus, a certain type of human being.

The story of Lichas and the return of Orestes' bones to Sparta, which Herodotus chooses to place in the middle of his narrative of Croesus' consultation with and misunderstanding of the oracle at Delphi, further illuminates both the complex and metaphorical character of divine speech in the *Histories*. The context of the Lichas story is the Spartan desire to conquer the Arcadian city of Tegea. Before starting out on this military venture, the Spartans, like Croesus, consulted the Delphic oracle concerning their chances of success. The oracle declared to the Spartans, "Tegea will I give you, to beat with your feet in dancing, and with a rope to measure, to your fill, her beautiful plainland" (I.66). The Spartans, Herodotus tells us, "trusting" in the oracle, set out against Tegea, but were beaten and taken prisoner by those same Tegeans whom they believed the oracle had promised to deliver into their hands (I.66).[27] As prisoners, the Spartans were organized into chain gangs and forced by the Tegeans to measure their land with a rope (I.66). Like Croesus, the Spartans did not take time to reflect on the various meanings which the oracle could have, because they did not grasp the complex character of divine speech. For instance, the oracle in this case did indeed reveal that the Spartans would be measuring Tegean territory with a rope, but it concealed the fact that the Spartans would be doing this as slaves rather than masters.

The Spartans, after this ignominious defeat, again consulted the Delphic oracle, this time asking what god they should propitiate in order to be victorious over the Tegeans. In response, the oracle declared:

> Somewhere there is Tegea, in Arcadia's level plainland, where two winds are a-blowing, under dire stress of compulsion; blow rings answer to blow, and evil is piled upon evil. There Agamemnon's son is held by the life-giving earth. And you, when once you bring him, shall then be Tegea's master. (I.67)

The Spartans understood well enough that they should bring Orestes' bones to Sparta, but, given the cryptic nature of the first part of the oracle, they were at a loss concerning where to find them. This confusion continued for some time until an elder Spartan named Lichas resolved the problem. During a temporary ceasefire between the two cities, Lichas happened to be in Tegea when he visited a blacksmith's shop. While there, Lichas "watched the welding of iron and was lost in wonder at what he saw being done" (I.68). Lichas then reflected back on the words of the oracle and realized he had found the resting place of Orestes' bones. Lichas made this discovery because, Herodotus tells us:

> [I]n [Lichas'] comparison he discovered that the bellows of the smith before his eyes must be the two blasts of wind, and the anvil and the hammer were the blow and counter blow, and the iron being welded on iron was evil laid upon evil, the image being that it was to man's mischief that iron was invented. (I.68)

Lichas then acted quickly, renting the shop from the blacksmith and proceeding to dig underneath it until hitting upon the bones of Orestes. Forthwith Lichas returned to Sparta, bones in tow, and from then on, Herodotus says, Sparta became exceedingly powerful, subjugating the Tegeans and nearly the rest of the Peloponnesus. Lichas could perform this service for his city because he, unlike Croesus, grasped the metaphorical character of divine speech. For example, the oracle used the phrase "where two winds are a-blowing" as a symbol for the bellows of a blacksmith, "blow rings answer to blow" as a symbol for the actions of the anvil and the hammer during the process of welding iron, and "evil is piled upon evil" as a symbol for iron being welded upon iron which is itself a symbol for the increased horrors of war that the invention of iron weapons brings.

In these examples of the misunderstanding of the Delphic oracle by Croesus and the Spartans, in contrast to the understanding of Lichas, Herodotus demonstrates the complex and metaphorical character of divine speech. That which links complexity and metaphor together is the need for interpretation if the meaning or truth of each is to become manifest. On this highest level complexity and metaphor are the same. The philosophic qualities of poetry are thus equally applicable to prophecy as Herodotus discusses it in the *Histories*. Yet, what I have set out to show is not that the words of the oracle call forth the rational reflection of their audience, but rather that the words of Herodotus himself require such interpretation to be understood. However, in book 2 of the *Histories*, Herodotus discusses different stories of the founding of the oracle at Dodona, the most ancient site of prophecy in Greece. As an account of human speech about divine speech, I believe it will show that Herodotus' *Histories*, like poetry and prophecy, calls forth the interpretive participation of its readers.[28]

The story of the founding of the oracle at Dodona begins in Egypt. Herodotus records that the priests of Zeus in the Egyptian city of Thebes say that two of their priestesses were abducted by the Phoenicians (II.54). One of these women was sold by the Phoenicians into Libya, where she founded an oracle of Zeus, and the other was sold into Greece in the area of Dodona, where she too founded an oracle of Zeus (I.54–55). The priestesses of Dodona themselves, however, have another version of how their oracle was founded. They say that two black doves took flight from Egyptian Thebes, one landing in Libya and one landing at Dodona in Greece (II.55). Like its counterpart in Libya, the black dove at Dodona, perched in an oak tree, spoke to the people there in a human voice, telling them that they should found an oracle of Zeus. Believing that they experienced a divine command, the people, according to the priestesses of Dodona, did what they were bidden to do (II.55). After recounting these two different versions of the story, Herodotus, comparing the words of the priests in Egypt with the words of the priestesses of Dodona, gives his own judgment as to the founding of this most ancient oracle in Greece. Herodotus says that if the Phoenicians sold the two priestesses they had abducted from Thebes, one into Libya and the other into Dodona in Greece, it is indeed likely that the women would have set up shrines to Zeus in their new homes (II.56). The one in Greece probably did so under an oak tree, and when she eventually learned the Greek language, she began to prophesy to the people there, as well as inform them that her sister priestess had been sold into Libya by the same Phoenicians who had sold her into Greece (II.56). As to the Dodonaean assertion that their oracle was founded on the command of a black dove, Herodotus says:

> I believe that the women were called by the Dodonaeans "doves" because they were barbarians, and so they seemed to the people of Dodona to talk like birds. After a time they said, "The bird spoke with a human voice," as soon as the woman talked comprehensibly. As long as she talked her own barbarian language, she seemed to them to speak like a bird. How, after all, could a dove speak with a human voice? That they said that the dove was black indicates that the woman was an Egyptian. (II.57)

Herodotus points to the fact that human speech, like divine speech, requires interpretation if the truth it contains is going to be revealed. It needs to be interpreted because it is both complex and metaphorical. In the Dodonaean version of events, the word "black" reveals that it was known that the women were of foreign extraction, but does not fully reveal, or partially conceals, the fact that they were from Egypt. The word "dove" is an image or symbol of the unintelligibility of the Egyptian language to the Greeks. Taken together, the two words become the phrase "black doves," a phrase containing both complexity and metaphor. Indeed it is this use of complexity and metaphor by the Dodonaeans of the founding generation which confuses the Dodonaean priestesses of Herodotus' time. Without the benefit of what the Egyptians say, they mistakenly trust in the truthfulness of the story of the supernatural origins of their oracle. Herodotus has the benefit of knowing what the Egyptians say, and hence does not have to place full trust in what the Dodonaeans say, but rather can interpret their words to make their true meaning manifest.[29] Yet, in a larger sense, what are the Dodonaeans talking about? They are speaking of significant events that occurred in the past; one would be tempted to say that they are speaking like historians. In other words, could one not say that the Dodonaeans, in a certain sense, are speaking like Herodotus?

One of the reasons Herodotus shows us how he interprets what the priestesses say about the history of the oracle at Dodona is to indicate how he wishes us to read what he says about the history of the war between the Persians and the Greeks. The reader must keep an eye open for complexity and metaphor and must be prepared to interpret the *Histories* in order to uncover the universal truths embedded in the particulars that Herodotus records. To understand Herodotus as writing something as straightforward as a travel guide or anthropological survey like *National Geographic* is to read the *Histories* in the same way that Croesus and the Spartans experience divine speech, and the Dodonaean priestesses' human speech. It fails to grasp its complexity and misunderstand its larger meaning. To argue that Herodotus' work contains a political philosophy of better and worse regimes based on universal principles of human nature, as I do, is to read the *Histories* in the same way that Lichas understands divine speech and Herodotus, human speech. Lichas and Herodotus discern its necessarily complex and metaphorical character, making it possible for them to discover its underlying truth. As my discussion of Herodotus' account of the content and founding of oracles suggests, I contend that the *Histories* is as philosophic as poetry because it requires interpretation to be understood.

My discussion thus far has sought to illustrate that the *Histories* has the same philosophic qualities that are attributed to poetry. However, to say that something is philosophic is not to say that it is a work of philosophy. What I mean to suggest is that the claim that both history and poetry are philosophic is really to subordinate both by making philosophy the standard. In other words, this claim points to the possibility that if one really wants to know truth and live the best way of life, then one should become the student of a great philosopher, rather than the student of a great historian like Herodotus or a great poet like Sophocles. The ultimate claim of the superiority of philosophy over both history and poetry puts my task in a new light. If we are to be persuaded that rational reflection on what the *Histories* has to offer is ultimately worthwhile, it is not enough to show that Herodotus is a poetic historian. Rather, it must be shown that Herodotus is a philosophic historian, or that history, at its best, is actually, as it were, philosophy.

The brevity and character of an introduction such as this one does not permit me to prove that Herodotus is a philosophic historian, but rather only to hint at it. Perhaps the best way to start is to note that, for Herodotus, his task as a historian is to discuss not only what was done, but also what was said; what people say is as important as what they do. Herodotus' discussion of the two different stories concerning the founding of the oracle at Dodona is an illustration of this principle of selection in the *Histories*. Yet, what people say, especially when they are responding to difficult but important questions, often reveals our most deeply held beliefs concerning such things as the good, the true, or the natural. Our opinions about these most important things in human life often contain much ambiguity and obscurity, and may even be contradictory, although we are often not fully aware of it. In other words, what is "at the tip of my tongue" often reveals what is "in the back of my mind," so to speak, but, paradoxically, what is at the back is often in direct opposition to what is on the tip. One could even say that it is the special task of the philosopher to bring to light this contradictory character of our thought concerning the most important things, in order to set us on the path to resolution. Certainly this appears to be the task that Socrates set for himself, as his devoted student Plato preserved for posterity in his dialogues.[30]

Herodotus, like Socrates, also examines what people say. He is especially interested in the *Histories* in what they say through their customs or laws, their *nomoi*. After all, a community's customs are an expression of their most deeply held collective beliefs concerning such things as the good, the true, and the natural. However, Herodotus does to a community's customs what Socrates does to the authoritative opinions of individuals within a community. He shows that, pushed to their logical extreme, they often contain ambiguity, and obscurity, but most especially contradiction. This Herodotean skepticism can be illustrated by a brief example taken from book 3 of the *Histories*. Here, Herodotus tells us that in Persia there is a select body of men known as the "royal judges" (III.31). These judges hold their offices during good behavior, and hence usually for life, and according to Herodotus, "they judge suits among the Persians and are the interpreters of the ancestral statutes, and everything is referred to them" (III.31). The institution and customs surrounding the royal judges, as Herodotus describes them, suggest the Persian belief that justice is law-abidingness. The underlying good it reveals is limited government. However, Herodotus then tells us that when Persian king Cambyses fell in love with his sister and wanted to marry her, he asked the royal judges, "Is there a law that orders any man who so wishes to live with his sister?" (III.31). Herodotus tells us that before this time it was not customary for the Persians to marry their sisters. Yet, the royal judges, according to Herodotus, responded to Cambyses' question in the following way:

> [T]hey gave him an answer that was both just and safe. They said that they could find no law that ordered brothers to live with sisters, but they *had* found another law, which said that he who was king of Persia could do anything he wished. So they did not break the law through fear of Cambyses, but, so as not to destroy themselves while protecting the law, they discovered another law, which would serve to help one who desired to live with his sister. (III.31; emphasis in original)

The royal judges, in order to defend justice as law-abidingness, must place the Persian king beyond the law by finding a law that actually undermines all law. In this example Herodotus brings to light the underlying contradiction in what the Persians say about justice and the good. For the Persians, the rule of law requires giving a powerful executive a discretion the extent of which ultimately undermines the rule of law entirely. Hence, in Persia the belief in government limited by law paradoxically leads to the acceptance of an unlimited or tyrannical power.

Herodotus and Socrates both explore what people say about such things as justice and the good, either collectively through their customs or individually through their opinions. Moreover, in these investigations both Herodotus and Socrates bring to light the often contradictory character of our beliefs, the result of which may be to set us on the path to a clearer understanding of these highest things. If Socrates differs from Herodotus, one of the reasons is that the former lightens the burden of the philosopher; Socrates shows that one does not have to leave one's city and travel the world to philosophize. However, one must keep in mind that Socrates' city is Athens, not Halicarnassus, Herodotus' city. Moreover, by committing his inquiries about the world to writing in the form of his *Histories*, one can say that Herodotus strives to make possible this kind of Socratic philosophic life.

Chapter 2

Egypt and Scythia

The Pious and the Poetic Regimes

Introduction

In Herodotus' narrative, Egypt and Scythia represent two opposing but parallel ways of life, the principles of which we will find combined in various ways by Herodotus' Persians, Athenians, and Spartans. It is important, therefore, to consider Herodotus' Egyptians and Scythians, as they are the two cultures whose complex syntheses are reflected in the ways of life of the Persians and the Greeks, the two great peoples whose war with another is recorded in the *Histories*.

The Egyptians are the most "holy" people in the *Histories*, and as such can be regarded as Herodotus' pious regime. Egypt, according to Herodotus, is the source for many of the religious practices of the Greeks and for important elements of Greek religious thought as well. From the Egyptians the Greeks learn how to serve their gods and to think about them as particular beings with individual identities. Herodotus gives content to the individuality grasped by the Egyptians and transmitted to the Greeks in his analysis of Egyptian customs. Here, Herodotus shows that to live a pious life means to be focused on the body and its purity, and therefore with the particular and private part of man. The Egyptians know the soul, but believe that human beings share this part of themselves with animals; thus, for the Egyptians what makes human beings unique in the world is not their soul but rather their particular bodily form. Yet, since the body comes to be and passes away, the Egyptian emphasis on the eternal means a feeling of shame for the human and the worship of animals rather than themselves. Although animal bodies are also perishable rather than imperishable, that they are not human seems to be enough.

Egyptian piety is concerned not simply with the body but also with the sexual duality of the body. For the Egyptians, women's bodies are unclean and therefore more human and closer to the families that they form. Through circumcision, men's bodies are made clean and share a closer proximity to the divine. Thus, for the Egyptians, gods are not only individual entities but masculine as well as feminine. Herodotus suggests that the Egyptians make a closer connection between the bodies of men and that which is divine, as opposed to the bodies of women, because they are a people who organize their whole way of life around the principle of rest. As such they tend to conceal and thus divinize the sexuality of men that, imitating the Nile, is feared as the source of all life. The sexuality of women, in contrast, is associated with the earth and rest and hence can be exposed and looked on directly.

The Egyptian emphasis on stability and rest is also manifested by their great reverence for age and the past. The Egyptians, according to Herodotus, are the greatest preservers of the past, both in memory and in written records. What belongs to the Egyptians, Herodotus suggests, is the ancestral. By looking only to the past and not the future, the Egyptians look only to what is determined and cannot change; the Egyptians regard themselves primarily as generated beings rather than as beings capable of generation themselves, and their identity as fundamentally given rather than open, a product of necessity rather than choice.

The concern for holiness in Egypt, Herodotus indicates, mutes the concern for justice and leads to skepticism toward human wisdom. Moreover, Egyptian customs also have a powerful affect on the Egyptian manner of speech; Herodotus suggests that the emphasis on the body tends to turn the Egyptians into "liars," as it were. On the level of speech, lying plays the same function as the body; both conceal the soul or the internal intentions of the speaker. For the Egyptians, words do not convey one unchanging meaning between speaker and listener but rather spawn an infinite variety of interpretations, the correct one only the speaker can know. To the Egyptians, the world presents itself as infinitely complex; the surface of things requires interpretation, but interpretation is impossible. Just as the true nature of their gods remains forever concealed at the beginning of time and behind animal form, the Egyptian soul remains concealed by their manner of speech; words do not reveal the truth.

The Scythians, on the other hand, are Herodotus' "poetic" regime because they confound the images of natural things with the natural things themselves. The distinction between the real and the artificial, fact and fiction, collapses; in Scythia, you are what you make yourself, and therefore what is made replaces what is given. The metaphor that Herodotus uses to express this abstract and self-creating individualism of the Scythians is his insistence on their nomadic way of life. As nomads without a city, the Scythians, in contrast to the Egyptians, organize their whole way of life around the principle of motion.

The motion of the Scythians reflects a love of freedom also shared by the Athenians. Following Francois Hartog's interpretation, it can be argued that Scythian nomadism, which allows them to defeat Persian king Darius' invasion, is itself a metaphor for the turn to the sea of the Athenians, which allows them to defeat Persian king Xerxes' invasion of Greece. However, Herodotus tries to moderate an otherwise admirable love of freedom on the part of the Athenians by linking this same love among the Scythians with an extreme ignorance and lack of thought.

The nomadic way of life is characterized not only by the extreme of ignorance but also, Herodotus indicates, the abstraction from the mother. In turning away from the mother and thus the sexual or bodily aspect of human reproduction that women represent, the Scythians suffer a cognitive separation from nature. Moreover, the Scythian abstraction from the mother does not mean a greater respect for the father, as the Scythians revere youth and the old show deference to the young. The Scythians, unlike the Egyptians, look to the future rather than the past, or regard themselves primarily as generators rather than as generated beings. Thus, their attempt to deny the mother is an attempt to deny everything that limits one to a given or predetermined identity—and hence that which cannot change and is at rest. This chapter concludes by arguing that although the nomadic way of life of the Scythians allows them to defeat Darius and his invading Persian army, Herodotus nevertheless believes that it is paradoxically informed by a near total materialism that actually precipitates a total loss of individual identity.

Egyptian Gods Becoming Greek

When we explore Herodotus' narrative of Egypt in book 2 of the *Histories*, it becomes clear that Herodotus regards the Egyptian way of life as the standard for what it means to be holy. One of the reasons Herodotus comes to this conclusion is that he believes that Greek religious thought and practice was derived from Egypt, a much older civilization than that of Greece.[1] Martin

Bernal, in *Black Athena: The Afroasiatic Roots of Classical Civilization*, makes a similar argument. According to Bernal, Greek culture originally arose from Egyptian and Phoenician colonizations around 1500 BCE and the continued Greek cultural borrowings from the ancient Near East. This model of Greek history—that Greek civilization was the product of colonizations and cultural borrowings from Africa to the south and Phoenice in the east—was, according to Bernal, held by the ancients themselves and manifested most clearly in the tragedies of Aeschylus and Euripides as well as the *Histories* of Herodotus.[2]

Bernal's thesis that Greek civilization was a transplantation of earlier Phoenician and especially Egyptian civilization has given rise to a debate among classical scholars concerning the true origins of what are commonly regarded as uniquely "Greek" cultural achievements in philosophy and science. Scholars such as Mary Lefkowitz deny that there is any evidence to support Bernal's claim of an invasion of Greece by Egyptians in the second millennium BCE, or that later Greek philosophy was taken from Egypt. For Lefkowitz, Greek philosophy is a fundamentally Greek invention, derived from the rationalism unique to Greek thought and the ability to express "impersonal abstractions" in the Greek language (124). Lefkowitz argues, therefore, that the relationship between Egypt and Greece is one of *influence* rather than *transplantation*, acknowledging that "it is true that the Greeks were influenced in various ways over a long period of time by their contact with the Egyptians" (161).[3]

Similarly, Robert Palter denies Bernal's dual claim that, first, there were scientific elements in Egyptian medicine, mathematics, and astronomy prior to any Greek science in these fields, and second, that Egyptian medicine, mathematics, and astronomy were the source of the corresponding Greek disciplines. Palter argues that the Greek disciplines influenced the Egyptian ones rather than the other way around and, with respect to medicine, it was the Greeks, not the Egyptians, who were the first to base their diagnoses on purely natural rather than supernatural foundations. Thus, in contrast to Bernal, Palter argues that we should continue to recognize "a revolutionary approach to the study of nature in classical Greece," made possible by two practices not present in Egypt: "public competitions between wise men, and open acknowledgement of uncertainty and error by wise men" (274).[4]

My discussion of Herodotus' Egyptians mediates between the claims of Bernal and the claims of scholars such as Lefkowitz and Palter. I agree with Lefkowitz and Palter that the development of philosophy and science can be considered a uniquely Greek achievement. Yet, like Bernal, I argue that for Herodotus significant elements of Greek culture, specifically Greek religious thought and practice, have their source in Egypt. Thus, like Lefkowitz, I believe that the relationship between Egyptian civilization and higher aspects of Greek civilization is one of *influence* rather than *transplantation*, but, as Herodotus suggests, such influence was crucial: Greek contact with Egypt established a spiritual framework through which the Greeks thought about their gods and served them. Also, Greek absorption of certain aspects of Egyptian religion, as we shall see in chapter four, manifests itself in their understanding of speech, especially divine speech.

In book 2 of the *Histories*, Herodotus maintains that the Greek gods, except for Poseidon, the Dioscuri, Hera, Themis, and the Graces and Nereids, are derived from Egypt (II.50). Moreover, Herodotus recounts that many Greek religious practices are derived from Egypt as well. For instance, according to Herodotus, Melampus, a wise man, learned of the phallic procession of Dionysus from Cadmus of Tyre from Phoenicea, who in turn learned it from the Egyptians. Melampus then introduced this form of worship into Greece (II.48). In teaching men that their sexuality belongs to the god and not themselves, the Dionysiac procession moderates them. Melampus also introduces a change. Whereas it is women who participate in this procession in Egypt, following puppets with phalluses, it is men who participate in it in Greece (II.48). Thus Melampus teaches moderation not only to men but to women as well, by excluding them from the procession. Moreover, Herodotus claims that the art of "divination" and "holy assemblies, processions, and services of the gods" came to Greece from Egypt (II.58). As proof of this claim Herodotus reasons that "the Egyptian practices are clearly very ancient indeed, and the Greek ones only lately established" (II.58). Most interesting with respect to religious practices, Herodotus argues that the oracle at Dodona, the most ancient site of prophecy in Greece, has its root in Egypt (II.54–57).

Not only are significant religious practices derived from Egypt, but significant elements of Greek religious thought as well. This is most strikingly illustrated in Herodotus' complex account of the Pelasgian adoption of the names of their gods from Egypt. The Pelasgians were the original natives of Attica and the Peloponnese from whom the Ionians and the Athenians spring, as opposed to the Dorians from whom the Spartans are derived.[5] Recounting the tale told to him at Dodona, Herodotus says that at first the Pelasgians did not have names for their gods, for they had not yet heard of such, although they called upon them in all their sacrifices (II.52). The Pelasgians called them gods (*theous*) because they "set" (*thentes*) "all things" (*panta pregmata*) "in order" (*kosmo*) and arranged all "roaming or wandering things" (*pasas nomas*) (II.52).[6] Then, after a long time had passed, they learned the names of their gods from Egypt, except for the name of Dionysus that came much later, and the Greeks learned these names from the Pelasgians.

Herodotus, however, in the next paragraph, appears to contradict himself when he says that not the Pelasgians, learning from the Egyptians and listening to the oracle at Dodona, but rather Hesiod and Homer "gave to the gods the special names for their descent" (II.53). Moreover, he claims that these two Greek poets distributed to the gods their particular "honors, their arts, and their shapes" (II.53). The latter refers to their human shape, or to the anthropomorphization of the Egyptian gods. This points to two significant differences rather than similarities between Egyptian and Greek religious beliefs. First, the Egyptians, unlike the Greeks, do not believe that a human being can be descended from a god, and hence have no heroes (II.50, 143). Thus, whereas the Egyptians believe in only one Heracles, who is a god, those Greeks whom Herodotus thinks are most correct have two Heracleses: "To one they sacrifice as to a god . . . to the other they worship as to a hero" (II.43–44). Herodotus indicates that the god Heracles is derived from Egypt, but that the hero Heracles is uniquely Greek.[7] The second and perhaps most striking difference is, as we shall see, the Egyptian belief that gods take on animal form, which is connected to the Egyptian worship of animals (II.38, 40–42, 65).

This still leaves us with Herodotus' claim in II.52 that the Greeks, through the Pelasgians, learned the names of their gods from Egypt, and his apparently contradictory claim in II.53 that it was Hesiod and Homer who gave the Greek gods their special names. Perhaps we can resolve this contradiction by looking to what it means that the Pelasgians can have gods without particular names. It suggests that they know the "class" of gods, but not the particular gods within the class. Because the Pelasgians know that there are gods, a class different from the human, they also know there is a class of humans. They know that humans, like gods, have universal characteristics in common. However, in teaching the Pelasgians that the gods have particular names, the Egyptians, Herodotus suggests, teach them about members of a class. Whereas Hesiod and Homer give the gods Greek names (II.53), the Egyptians establish the more fundamental truth that the gods should have names. The Egyptians show the Pelasgians and, therefore, the Greeks, the importance of the particular, or of the individual within the class. They teach the Greeks not so much a way of speaking about the gods, but a way of thinking about them.[8]

Egypt and the Humanity of the Feminine

The content of the individuality with which the Egyptians conceive of the gods becomes manifest in Herodotus' discussion of their customs. He begins by dividing his initial discussion of Egyptian customs into two parts. In chapters 35 and 36 he lists their secular customs, noting that they are opposite to those of all other human beings.[9] In chapter 37, Herodotus begins to list their religious customs, remarking that the Egyptians are the most pious of human beings. Thus, in discussing Egyptian customs, Herodotus discusses what it means to be holy. Herodotus lists seventeen secular customs:

1) The women buy and sell in the market; the men stay at home and weave.
2) When Egyptian men weave, they push the woof down, whereas all other people push the woof upward.
3) Men carry burdens on their heads; women carry burdens on their shoulders.
4) Women urinate standing up; men do sitting down.
5) They relieve themselves indoors, but eat outdoors in the street. They do this because they say things shameful (*aischra*) but necessary (*anagkaia*) should be done in secret, but things that are not shameful should be done openly (II.35).
6) No woman is dedicated to the service of any god, male or female; men are dedicated to all gods and goddesses.
7) Sons are not compelled to support their parents, but daughters must do so even if they are unwilling.
8) Egyptian priests shave their heads; everywhere else, priests wear their hair long.
9) Egyptians mourn for the dead by letting their hair and beard grow; all other people shave their hair.
10) Egyptians are the only people who keep their animals with them in the house; other people keep their daily life separate from animals.
11) Unlike all other people, Egyptians do not eat wheat and barley, but rather make food from coarse grain called smelt.
12) Egyptians knead dough with their feet, and they gather mud and dung with their hands.

13) Egyptians, save those who have learned from them, are the only men who practice circumcision. This, however, as Herodotus indicates, is a religious custom (II.37).

14) Every man has two garments; every woman only one.

15) They fasten their ropes on the inside of their boats, all other people do so on the outside.

16) The Greeks calculate and write from left to right, but the Egyptians do so from right to left, although they say they are moving from left to right.

17) The Egyptians use two types of writing, one called sacred and the other common.

The first thing to note about this list is that customs having to do with the religious, numbers six, eight, thirteen, and seventeen—appear in a list with secular customs. Herodotus cannot keep the secular and the religious separate in Egypt. Secondly, for the Egyptians who seek to live a pious life, the overwhelming concern is with the body. The body, although carrying force, is shameful and therefore should be hidden, as indicated in customs five, eight, and nine.[10] The Egyptian feeling of shame toward the body is also expressed in their focus on its cleanliness rather than beauty. Herodotus says that the Egyptians practice circumcision out of their concern for cleanliness, because they honor cleanliness of the body over the comeliness, or beauty, of the body (II.37).

The Egyptian lack of an appreciation for beauty, suggesting that love of beauty is in tension with piety, is in strong contrast to the Babylonians who are said to be similar to the Egyptians in many other ways (I.180, 182). For instance, in the Babylonian marriage auction, rich men pay high prices to take beautiful girls for their wives, and poor men agree to take ugly girls for their wives on payment of a dowry drawn from the money paid by rich men for beautiful girls (I.196). Thus, the Babylonian attraction to the beauty of the body leads beautiful girls to help ugly girls and rich men to redistribute their property to poor men. It forces individuals to help others, or to look, indirectly at least, to the common interest of the city. The Egyptians, without a love of beauty, are not directed toward the public sphere; they lack concern for the common interest. This selfish concern for their private interests is connected with their concern for cleanliness, which they also equate with the health of the body (II.77). It can be seen by the great proliferation of doctors in Egypt, each doctor dedicated to the healing of one disease (II.84).[11] Again, this is in strong contrast to the Babylonians, who have no doctors

(I.197). When Babylonians fall sick, they are carried into the marketplace. No one may pass by the sick without asking what their sickness is, providing comforting words, and giving advice about how to recover (I.197).[12] This second wisest of Babylonian customs, the marriage auction being their first, according to Herodotus, encourages common fellow feeling which the proliferation of doctors suggests is absent in Egypt.

Although emphasizing the cleanliness of the body, the Egyptians do know the soul. For instance, at II.123, Herodotus says:

> The Egyptians are the first to have told this story also, that the soul of man is immortal and that, when the body dies, the soul creeps into some other living thing then coming to birth; and when it has gone through all things, of land and sea and the air, it creeps again into a human body at its birth. The cycle for the soul is, they say, three thousand years.[13]

This Egyptian doctrine of transmigration, which Herodotus says some Greeks, whom he will not name, have adopted, effects a complete separation between the soul and the human body; the Egyptians cannot combine the two into a whole. Thus, although the Egyptians believe in a soul that is immortal, this soul, which can pass into all living animals as well as all other human beings, is particular neither to human beings nor to a particular human being. Thus, Egyptian belief in the soul offers no individual hope for a personal immortality and teaches that what makes human beings unique among the animals, as well as what is particular to a particular human being, are their bodies, not their souls.

If Egyptians believe they share their soul with the other animals, this would explain why Egyptians keep their animals in their homes with them. Also, if the body is the human, then contempt for the body, revealed in the other customs previously listed, means contempt for the human. This would explain why Egyptians calculate and write from the right to the left—but call it left to right. The Egyptians take the perspective of the inanimate page written on, not the perspective of the human writer. Furthermore, that no individual has a particular soul and therefore no personal immortality by means of it explains the Egyptian practice of mummification. The attempt to preserve the body from decay is a reflection of the tendency to transform what is in motion, coming to be and passing away, into what is eternal and at rest (II.86). In a surprising reversal, the body itself becomes deified (II.90).

The most striking aspect of Herodotus' account of religious worship is the Egyptian worship of animals. It seems that contempt for the human leads the Egyptians to worship the nonhuman. They hold all animals sacred, and, except during a religious sacrifice, no human may kill an animal. The penalty for doing so intentionally is death (II.41, 65). Especially sacred is Epaphus, called Apis in Greek, the bull-god of Memphis to whom the Egyptians believe all other bulls belong (II.38).[14] Although all Egyptians may sacrifice bulls judged unblemished by the priests, they cannot sacrifice cows, which they believe are sacred to Isis whom the Egyptians believe is the greatest of their gods (II.40, 41). Still, like the Greeks, the Egyptians can make a distinction between humans and the other animals. According to Herodotus:

> [N]early all the rest of mankind, except for the Egyptians and the Greeks, have intercourse in holy places and rise from intercourse with a woman and go into a shrine without washing, for they think that men are much as other beasts; they see the other beasts and the tribes of birds riding one another in the temples and sacred precincts of the gods. If this was not pleasing to the god, the beasts would not do it. But this kind of reasoning that they bring forward is one that for me, especially, is distasteful. (II.64)

The Egyptians worship animals and still believe in the distinction between humans and animals. They believe that animals, permitted to have intercourse in holy places, unlike humans, are higher and more beloved by the gods than human beings. This distinguishes them from the Greeks, who believe that animals are lower than human beings, as Herodotus makes clear in his discussion of the Greek poets' anthropomorphizing of Egyptian gods.[15] What Herodotus finds distasteful about men other than Egyptians and Greeks is not their refusal to regard animals as higher or lower than human beings, but rather their refusal to make a distinction.

Although they worship animals, Herodotus indicates the Egyptians know that animals are not actually gods but only the forms in which the gods choose to hide themselves.[16] Herodotus illustrates this by recounting a story from Egyptian Thebes. According to the Thebans, Heracles, whose name came to Greece from Egypt, desired to look on Zeus, but Zeus would not let himself be seen (II.42). Yet, Heracles was so persistent that "Zeus made a contrivance of flaying a ram, taking off the ram's head and using it as a mask, and entering the fleece of the sheep and so displaying himself to Heracles."[17] In addition to indicating that the Egyptians know that the gods are not animals but only adopt animal appearances, it also suggests that the Egyptians believe that one should not inquire directly into the nature of the gods, or try to see them with one's own eyes. The gods do not like inquiry into their true nature.

In their concern for piety, the Egyptians focus not only on the shamefulness of the body, leading to the separation of the soul and the worship of animals, but also on the sexual difference of the body. Thus, in Egypt, whereas women buy and sell in the market, men stay at home and weave (II.35). Also, Egyptian men practice circumcision, and every man has two garments, unlike women who have only one (II.36). These customs suggests that the male body is regarded as more shameful than the female body. However, Herodotus tells us that no woman is dedicated to the service of any god, masculine or feminine, whereas men are dedicated to all gods and goddesses (II.35). Pointing to the association of men with the pious and women with the impious, this custom is a surprising reversal considering that male sexuality appears more shameful than female sexuality. The explanation of this reversal is found in the practice of circumcision, which, Herodotus suggests, leads the Egyptians to believe that male sexuality can be given to their gods and thus that the male body, unlike the female body, can be made clean (II.36–37). Women's bodies remain unclean and therefore closer to the families that human beings form. In Egypt, sons are not compelled to support their parents, but daughters must do so even if they are unwilling (II.35). The family, rooted in the body, is more the domain of women than of men. Moreover, because men stay at home and weave unlike the women who buy and sell in the market, and because men's bodies remain hidden behind two pieces of clothing rather than the single one worn by women, it is men, more than women, who are associated with the invisible or unseen. The greater invisibility of men's bodies is coupled with men's greater proximity to the divine than women. In Egypt men, not women, are dedicated to the gods and goddesses.

Herodotus gives us some clues as to the source of the Egyptian predisposition to make a closer connection between the bodies of men and that which is divine, as opposed to the bodies of women which appear to remain unclean and closer to the human and the families that they form, at the beginning of book 2. Here, Herodotus recounts the story of Egyptian king Psammetichus' inquiry into the oldest human beings, before proceeding to an investigation of Egyptian geography. Herodotus records that before Psammetichus became king, the Egyptians believed themselves to be the first of all human beings to have come into being (II.2). Yet, Psammetichus, distrusting Egyptian belief, desired to know through rational inquiry who the first human beings actually were. To this end, he took two newborn children of common people and gave them to a shepherd to raise. Psammetichus ordered the shepherd to keep the children in isolation, allowing no one to speak in their presence, but at appropriate intervals to bring the goats to "give them their fill of milk." Psammetichus gave these orders because he wished to hear which language these children would speak first. After two years, the children rushed to the shepherd and, while clasping his knees, shouted "*bekos*." The shepherd brought the children to Psammetichus, and when he himself had heard them he inquired from which language this word *bekos* came, and discovered that the Phrygians called bread *bekos*. He therefore concluded, and the Egyptians "conceded," that the Phrygians were older than themselves, but that they, "the Egyptians, are older than anyone else" (II.2).[18]

Herodotus' account of the experiment of Psammetichus reveals two important things about the Egyptians. First, Psammetichus assumes that speech is natural to human beings, and even further, that a particular language is also natural to human beings.[19] Second, it reveals that the Egyptians believe the natural language will be the oldest. They unite origin (*arche*) with principle (*arche*), or the first things in time with what Aristole calls the universal first principles (*hai archai*).[20] They believe that one can learn what is universally true by looking to the beginning of history. Accordingly, the Egyptians dwelling in the cultivated country in Upper Egypt around Thebes are of all men the greatest preservers of the past, both in memory and in written records (II.77). By looking only to the past and not to the future, these Egyptians look only to that which is already determined and cannot change. By turning away from the future or what is indeterminate and in the hands of men and chance to decide, they try to make what is inherently in motion—and brings change and time—into something permanent and unchanging.[21] They seek to freeze time. Further manifestations of Egyptian reverence for the past is the great respect younger men show for older men, a custom alien to all Greeks except the Spartans, and the fact that they only follow the customs of their fathers, rejecting all foreign customs (II.79–80).[22] They reject the foreign because they fear the change or motion that it can bring. What belongs to the Egyptians, Herodotus indicates, is the ancestral.

After recounting King Psammetichus' story, Herodotus says he will turn away from a discussion of the gods, talking about them only when his narrative forces him to do so, toward a discussion of the human things (II.3–4).[23] He then promptly, yet oddly, begins to investigate the geography or character of Egypt's land and river. The land of Egypt, according to Herodotus, is of two parts; Upper Egypt is older, and Lower Egypt towards the Delta is newer (II.4, 10). Herodotus claims that the land in Upper Egypt, in the southern Thebaic province, has existed ever since human beings have existed. According to the Egyptian priests, before the time of Min, their first human king, but according to Herodotus, at least 10,000 years earlier, all of Egypt north of the Thebaic province was covered by water (II.4, 11). The land in Lower Egypt towards the Delta is thus black and crumbly as it has been produced by the constant silting action of the Nile (II.12).[24] As this land grew in size, many human beings spread down over it, but many stayed behind in Thebes (II.15). Thus in Egypt, although the land and the people of the Thebaic province are old, the land and people in the Delta region are the newest in the world.

The Nile, Herodotus tells us, flows through the middle of the country and empties into the sea through five mouths, one mouth of the Nile greater than any river in Ionia and Greece (II.10, 17). Also, in the Delta region, the Nile rises every summer for a hundred days from the summer solstice, floods and thereby fertilizes the land, then sinks back again to its original level (II.14).[25] Therefore, unlike the earth, at least in the Thebaic province, which never moves or leaves its place, the Nile is constantly moving or changing. It moves both vertically in its continual flow through the country and into the sea, and horizontally, when it rises, leaves its place, and moves over thereby fertilizing the land. The land therefore, which is at rest, represents that in nature which maintains limits or distinctions.[26] The Nile, on the other hand, in moving over and flooding the land, represents that in nature which seeks to overcome limits or distinctions, to transgress the boundaries that seek to keep things in their place. This transgressing is related to its creative or life-giving powers.[27]

Herodotus indicates in what way the natural elements of earth and water, stability and change, are reflected in the Egyptians themselves, in the story of the Deserters, a people whom he discovers by hearsay on his journey down the Nile (II.30). The Deserters were Egyptian soldiers who had been stationed in the southernmost Egyptian city of Elephantine. Having been unrelieved for three years they, by common deliberation, decided to revolt against their king, Psammetichus, and flee towards Ethiopia (II.30). Psammetichus, the "inquirer" king of chapter 2, upon hearing of the revolt, pursued and overtook the soldiers, and then pleaded with them not to abandon the gods of their fathers and their children and wives (II.30). In response, one of the soldiers exposed his genitals to the king and said that wherever they should be they would also have wives and children. He mentioned nothing about the gods of their fathers (II.30). Forthwith the soldiers gave themselves over to the Ethiopian king, who in return, allowed them to occupy the land of certain Ethiopians with whom he was feuding. These dispossessed Ethiopians, Herodotus tells us, learned Egyptian customs and became "more civilized" as a result.

The Deserters, looking back to their origins in time, discover that what makes it possible to have ancestors, to be a being created out of sexual generation, also makes it possible to have descendants, and thus to look to your future and become non-Egyptians. For the Deserters, the fathers are the gods. Psammetichus, however, in appealing to the gods of their fathers to try to stop the revolt, does not see, or does not want his subjects to see, their future and thus their own generative power. The Egyptians do not see their own ability to become ancestral gods, because they do not believe their sexuality—that which is reflective of the life-giving powers of the Nile—belongs to them for their use, but rather belongs to, or comes from, their gods—and thus is subject to control by them.[28] Perhaps Psammetichus and the Egyptians believe this is the only way to ensure loyalty to the regime and political stability. Thus, the Egyptians are in the midst of a contradiction. By putting the first principles at the beginning of time, reflecting their reverence for history and the ancestral, the Egyptians are trying to find something that is stable or permanent. They believe that the whole, or what is universally true, does not flow like water. However, if the first principles are first in time, they must create what comes after them, and thus are necessarily generative in nature. They either create motion or are in constant motion like the Nile. This, however, must remain hidden, or one will become a Deserter.[29]

Herodotus further indicates that the Egyptian gods are sexual in nature when he notes that the only gods which are worshipped by all Egyptians in common are Isis and Osiris, which in Greek are Demeter and Dionysus (II.42). If Plutarch can be believed, the public teaching in Egypt is that Isis is an allegory for the earth and that Osiris is an allegory for the Nile which fertilizes the earth.[30] However, the most learned and secretive of the Egyptian priests teach that Osiris is not just an allegory for the Nile, but is that faculty or principle in the world which can cause wetness or moisture. The same faculty causes "the emission of the genital humour," such moisture being the "spring and first original of all things."[31] Plutarch mentions no corresponding secret teaching about Isis, suggesting that her nature, in contradistinction to that of Osiris, can be taught publicly.

Herodotus confirms the view that for the Egyptians it is masculine sexuality, not feminine sexuality, that remains concealed when he discusses the Egyptian festival in honor of Artemis at Bubastis (II.60). Although Artemis is not Isis, or Demeter, it would appear that the various other goddesses in Egypt are just many particular manifestations of Isis, the only goddess that all Egyptians worship in common.[32] During this festival, men and women on their way to Bubastis sail together in boats shaking rattles, playing flutes, clapping, and singing. As they journey by river, whenever they come near a city they bring their boat close to the land, and some of the women set to deriding the local women, but some, according to Herodotus, stand up and "show their nakedness." However, in this female version of the Deserters story the women remain Egyptian; the exposure of feminine sexuality is not destabilizing.[33] Moreover, Herodotus says that in this festival in honor of Artemis men and women, up to 700,000 of them, congregate together in Bubastis, but he specifically points out that there are no children present (II.60). The Egyptians, Herodotus indicates, do not associate female sexuality in itself with generation and change. The Egyptians associate the feminine with rest, which therefore can be exposed, but associate the masculine with motion, which must remain hidden and hence seemingly more divine.

Returning to the subject of the Nile, Herodotus says that because it floods in the summer and not in the winter and never produces any wind, it is unlike all other rivers in the world (II.19). However, Herodotus says that he could not learn why the Nile has this peculiar character from the Egyptians, who could tell him nothing about its nature (II.19). Herodotus, however, puts forth his own opinion. He maintains that the irregular course of the sun in Libya during winter is the cause of the Nile flooding in summer (II.25-26).[34] Although his explanation is incorrect, it illustrates that for Herodotus the Egyptians do not know the nature of the Nile because they do not look up to the sun, but rather only care to look down. According to the Egyptians, Demeter and Dionysus are rulers of the underworld (II.123). Because they do not look up and therefore do not know the nature of the Nile, neither do the Egyptians know the effects of the Nile. For instance, they mock the Greeks, saying they will someday be struck with drought and all die of hunger because they rely on rain from Zeus to water their land, while they, the Egyptians, have no rain but rely on their river (II.13). However, Herodotus explains that if the land below Memphis, produced by the constant silting action of the Nile, should increase in height in the same proportion as it has in the past, the Nile will no longer be able to flood and the Egyptians themselves will die of hunger (II.14). Thus Herodotus' Egyptians turn away from the nature and effect of the Nile, that which is in motion and produces change, and look only to that which they believe to be at rest and unchanging, their land.[35] This is in accord with important tendencies we have already noted: the Egyptian reverence for age and preservation of history and their concealing of the sexuality of men in their gods while revealing the sexuality of women.

The representation of the Egyptians as associating the masculine with motion as opposed to the stability and rest associated with the feminine adds to our understanding of Herodotus' claim that the Pelasgians adopted the naming of their gods from Egypt. As discussed above, although the Pelasgians did not at first have names for their gods they nonetheless invoked them in all of their sacrifices (II.52). They were called gods because they "set all things in order" and arranged all "roaming or wandering things." It appears therefore that the Pelasgians associated the gods with that which maintains order or stability in nature and thus with the earth or that which is at rest. If we assume that the Pelasgians shared the same beliefs as the Egyptians about the earth and rest, this means that they associated the gods with feminine. The Pelasgians would have thus understood the human—that which is not divine or a class of beings distinct from the class of gods—as masculine and in motion like water. However, the two gods worshipped by all Egyptians in common are Isis and Osiris, and thus the Egyptians associate the divine not just with the feminine but also the masculine. Indeed, for the Egyptians, as their customs and stories reveal, it is the bodies of men that are more closely associated with the divine than those of women, and it is the true nature of Zeus and Osiris that must remain hidden as opposed to that of Artemis, perhaps a particular manifestation of Isis, which can be exposed for all to see. I would argue, therefore, that in teaching the Pelasgians to name their gods, the Egyptians, Herodotus implies, taught them not simply to particularize their gods but to give them a masculine character as well. In doing so the Egyptians would teach the Pelasgians, and through them the Greeks, that the human is not just masculine and always in motion, but also feminine and at rest. Therefore, in addition to an appreciation for the particularity or uniqueness of the individual, the Greeks, it appears, derive from the Egyptians an appreciation for the feminine qualities in human life as well.[36]

The Holy as Other than Justice, Wisdom, and Truth

Having discussed Egyptian beliefs, or what it means to be holy, Herodotus now seeks to understand the affect of the concern for piety and the body in the absence of beauty on the questions of justice, wisdom, and the nature of human speech. These three themes will continually reappear in Herodotus' discussion of the Persians and the Greeks, the two great peoples whose war with each other he records in his *Histories*. Herodotus reflects on Egyptian beliefs with regard to these themes by recounting what the Egyptians themselves say about two of the most prominent kings in their history, Proteus and Rhampsinitus.

Herodotus tells us that King Proteus has a beautiful precinct in Memphis that is located just south of the temple of Hephaestus (II.112). Inside this precinct a temple is dedicated to the "Foreign Aphrodite." Herodotus believes this temple is sacred to Helen the daughter of Tyndareus because he has heard the story of Helen's staying with Proteus in Egypt rather than with Alexander in Troy, and because the temple is named after the "Foreign Aphrodite." According to Herodotus, no other temple of Aphrodite has the appellation of "foreign" attached to it (II.112). Herodotus again suggests that beauty, and therefore a concern for the public that causes questions of justice and wisdom to arise, is foreign to Egypt as it is in tension with holiness that emphasizes cleanliness rather than comeliness.

The Egyptian priests, responding to Herodotus' inquiries about the story, say that after Alexander raped and abducted Helen from Sparta, he attempted to sail back to his own country—but a violent storm drove him to beach his ships at the Canobic mouth of the Nile (II.113). At this place the Egyptians have a temple to Heracles where the servant of any man, provided that he brand his body with certain marks and thereby give it to the god, can take refuge and be touched by no one. Alexander's servants, hearing of the law associated with this temple, took refuge there and told Thonis, warden of the Nile mouth, of the "injustice" (*adikien*) that Alexander had committed against Menelaus (II.113). Thonis then quickly sent a message to king Proteus in Memphis, saying that a stranger had arrived in Egypt after having committed an "unholy" (*anosion*) act in Greece, deceiving his host Menelaus, and stealing his wife (II.114). Proteus then responded by demanding that Alexander, having done an "unholy" (*anosia*) deed against his host, be brought before him (II.114). When Alexander gave an untruthful tale of what had happened, his servants refuted him and related the truth of his "injustice" (II.115). Proteus was outraged, and said that if he were not a good host, careful "not to kill any stranger" forced by winds to Egypt's coast, he would "have taken vengeance on [Alexander] on behalf of the Greek" (II.115). Calling Alexander the worst of men who had committed the most "unholy" deed against his host, he ordered him to depart from Egypt within three days leaving Helen behind whom Proteus said he would keep safe "for the Greek stranger" until Menelaus himself should come to take her back.

Herodotus indicates that he believes this story of Helen, in which both the Egyptians and the Greeks think that the rape of women understood as the violation of one's host or the husband is something to be concerned about. However, Proteus and the Egyptians are concerned with this deed because it is "unholy," whereas Alexander's servants, presumably Greek, are concerned with it because they think it is "unjust."[37] Because the Greeks think the deed is unjust, their vengeance is political, destroying the entire city of Troy. As an Egyptian, believing that the deed is unholy, if Proteus were to take vengeance, it would be private—wrought only on the individual Alexander and not his city. In book 2, holiness, or a concern for the gods, makes justice and injustice and hence the Greek concern with the political, unimportant. The Egyptians are concerned with the holy and therefore with the body in the absence of beauty and thus in the absence of politics. They separate the gods from questions of justice and injustice. Proteus' vengeance would be private not public, wrought against the individual Alexander and not the entire city of Troy. Herodotus suggests, however, that the holy and the just, the private and the public, are more closely connected to one another than either the Egyptians or the Greeks believe.[38] Herodotus says that Menelaus, having come to Egypt to reclaim Helen, was "unjust" toward the Egyptians because his sacrifice of two Egyptian children in the hopes of getting better weather for his return trip to Sparta was an "unholy" deed. Moreover, Herodotus indicates without fanfare that Menelaus and the Greeks may be just as prone to violate the hospitality of their host as Alexander and the Trojans.

Nonetheless, in the story of King Proteus in book 2, it appears that both the Greeks and the Egyptians are concerned with protecting the private family and thus what is one's own. What is surprising about Proteus, is that he will protect the private family "on behalf of the Greek" and "for the Greek stranger." Atypical of the Egyptians, Proteus has a universal attitude; he can think beyond what is necessary for the protection of his own. Herodotus implies that Proteus' ability to think universally, of the other beyond the self, is what allows him to self-consciously understand the importance of the particular and thus the preservation of the private family and what is one's own. His is a perspective that can combine universality with particularity or the unselfish concern for the other with the selfish concern for oneself.[39]

If Herodotus' discussion of King Proteus illustrates the tension in Egypt between holiness and justice, his discussion of the reign of King Rhampsinitus illustrates the tension between holiness and wisdom. According to the Egyptian priests, Rhampsinitus had a great wealth of silver. To store it safely, Rhampsinitus had a stone chamber added to the side of his palace (II.121). However, the builder of Rhampsinitus' treasure chamber was very crafty and deceitful. He, the builder, made sure that one of the stones in the wall of the chamber could easily be removed by his two sons. After their father's death, the two brothers quickly entered Rhampsinitus' treasure house in the dark of night through this secret passage and carried off much of the king's silver. The thieves had done this three times before Rhampsinitus, having noticed his loss but perplexed as to who could have done it, as the seals of the doors were unbroken and the chamber shut tight, ordered traps to be laid. When the thieves came again, the first to enter the chamber was caught in one of the traps. He called to his brother and told him to cut off his head so that he, his brother, would not be recognized and thus killed as well. The brother forthwith beheaded his entrapped brother and saved himself.

Rhampsinitus, perplexed at finding a headless corpse in his treasure chamber but no sign of entry, ordered the corpse to be hung on the outer wall and for his guards to arrest anyone seen mourning for it (II.121). The mother of the dead thief, valuing the body of her dead son more highly than the life of her surviving son, threatened her son that if he did not retrieve his brother's body, she would turn him in to the king. Desirous to avoid this fate, he, crafty and deceitful like his father, devised a plan whereby he beguiled the king's guards with wine and retrieved his brother's body without being detected. Rhampsinitus was furious but also had a great desire to discover who this crafty person was. In order to do so, Rhampsinitus ordered his daughter to prostitute herself to any man that wished to be with her; however, before performing the act, she was to compel each man to tell her the "wisest" and "most unholy" thing he had ever done, listening for the story of the thief (II.121). Rhampsinitus thus expresses the Egyptian belief in the tension between wisdom and piety. The thief, desirous to get the better of the king, cunningly used his "wisdom" and "impiously" cut an arm off the body of a newly dead man, and, with the arm under his cloak, went to the king's daughter. In response to her questions, he said that the most unholy thing he had done was to cut off his brother's head when trapped in the king's treasure chamber, and the wisest was to intoxicate the king's guards and retrieve his brother's body. The king's daughter tried to grab and restrain him, but "in the dark room," the thief gave her the arm of the dead man and thus escaped (II.121). When Rhampsinitus learned of this he was astonished at the thief's "great understanding" and "boldness," and proclaimed immunity and promised to reward him "if the thief would come into his sight" (II.121). The thief came before the king, and Rhampsinitus "admired him greatly" and gave him his daughter to marry as he was the "greatest of human beings in knowledge" (II.121). "The Egyptians excel all others," he said "and this man the rest of the Egyptians" (II.121). For Rhampsinitus, the wisest of men is the most unholy of men.

The story of Rhampsinitus also reveals the affect of the holy and thus the concern for the body on the Egyptian manner of speech. Rhampsinitus admires the thief due to the latter's superiority in deceiving other people, or his superior ability in hiding himself as the source of his actions. Wisdom is reduced to the selfish pursuit of one's own interests. This is related to the Egyptian emphasis on the body, or that which is external and visible and thus conceals that which is internal and invisible. On the level of speech, lying plays the same function as the body. Lies conceal the internal and thus invisible intentions of the speaker.[40] Herodotus indicates that the affect of

Egyptian customs on their form of speech, is to turn them, or the best of them, into "liars."[41]

That Egyptians are "liars" is related to the experiment of king Psammetichus. The underlying assumption of Psammetichus' experiment is that the first things as principles are the oldest things. As oldest, they will be at rest or unchanging. These oldest things resemble Plato's invisible "ideas"; as opposed to the many visible and particular things in the world that come to be and pass away, of which the ideas are the cause and the universal characteristic which they all share, the ideas never change.[42] Psammetichus and the Egyptians associate the oldest and hence supposedly unchanging things with speech, believing that they will somehow be revealed in the oldest language. Words for the Egyptians must represent that which does not change and is at rest, or something akin to an "idea," if they are to have meaning. However, for the Egyptians, words have meaning, representing something which is unchanging in the mind of the speaker, but, just as the "ideas" are the cause of the many particular things in the world, words spawn an infinite variety of interpretations—the correct one, from the Egyptian perspective, only the speaker can know. For the Egyptians, just as the many particular things in the world do not lead one back to the "ideas" which are believed to be their cause, words conceal the internal rather than reveal it; truth, or the "ideas," cannot be communicated from speaker to listener. This is perhaps why, in Egypt, the concern for holiness subsumes or suppresses the concern for wisdom understood as the independent human knowledge of universal and unchanging, and hence natural, truths.

Before leaving Egypt and moving on to Scythia, we will briefly speculate on whether or not Herodotus tries to possess the other. In a short digression in book 2, Herodotus says that the historian Hecataeus came to the Egyptian city of Thebes and contrary to the advice of the Thebaic priests, "traced his family tree and connected himself [to Zeus] in the sixteenth generation" (II.143). However, Herodotus tells us that the "priests of Zeus there did for him what they did for me, too . . ." (II.143). They brought Herodotus into a great hall where they showed him 345 huge wooden statues, each representing a priest in one generation, as the priesthood is hereditary in Egypt. The priests went through the whole line of statues, yet "failed to connect anyone of these with either a god or a hero," thus showing that a man could not be descended from a god. The priests did this for Herodotus, although he says "I was not tracing my family tree" (II.143).[43] Herodotus and Hecataeus are similar in that both understand that Egypt is the paradigm for the holy and is the source of the Greek gods. However, whereas Hecataeus tries to attach the holy or the divine to his family tree and thereby to himself, Herodotus does not. Herodotus, who looks on the other, does not try to make it his own.

The Return to Scythia

There are many indications that Herodotus wants the reader to understand his discussion of Scythia in book 4, chapters 1 to 144, as parallel to his discussion of Egypt in book 2.[44] Like the Nile, the Ister river has five mouths and its delta, which marks the southwest border of Scythia, is directly opposite the Nile's delta (II.34, IV.470). The Ister flows from west to east through Europe and then turns south into the Euxine Sea, running parallel to the Nile, which flows from west to east through Libya and turns north through Egypt to empty into the Mediterranean Sea (II.33–34). The eight rivers of Scythia provide Scythians their material needs, just as the flooding of the Nile means the Egyptians do not have to labor for their food (IV.59; II.14). Second, whereas Herodotus discusses the character of Egypt's land or soil in book 2, the only discussion of the nature of the land in his Scythian narrative occurs when he laughs at previous map-makers for incorrectly dividing and naming the continents of the earth (IV.36–45). This is a discussion of the land of the world, not of Scythia in particular, and it appears as if Herodotus wants to say that Scythia has no particular or peculiar land. In contrast to the Egyptians who neglect the nature and power of their river in their contempt for motion, the Scythians neglect the land, revealing their contempt for what they regard to be at rest. Finally, Herodotus says that the Scythians, like the Egyptians, shun the use of all foreign customs, especially those of the Greeks (IV.76, II.91).[45]

Herodotus first mentions the Scythians in book 1, where he says that it was during the reign of Lydian king Ardys, son of Gyges, that the Cimmerians were driven from their homes "by the nomad Scythians," and thus the Cimmerians came into Asia and captured Sardis, the capitol of Lydia (I.15). Unlike the Egyptians, the Scythians are nomads, and thus are a people in constant motion. Herodotus next tells us that during the reign of Median king Cyaxares, "a troop of nomad Scythians" wandered into Media (I.73). At first Cyaxares treated them well, entrusting to them some Median boys to learn their language and their "mastery of the bow." The Scythians were great hunters who never returned without something for king Cyaxares' table. When one day they brought nothing back from the hunt, Cyaxares, prone to anger, abused them shamefully. To take revenge on Cyaxares for this treatment, the Scythians cut up one of the boys under their care, dressed his flesh as they usually dressed the flesh of an animal, and after serving him up to Cyaxares and his guests, fled to Lydia for protection (I.73). In this story, Herodotus again refers to the Scythians as nomads. Furthermore, contrary to initial appearances, the Scythians are not cannibals. They know that cannibalism is an outrage; if they did not, they would not understand it as a punishment of Cyaxares.

Herodotus also tells another story of the relation between Cyaxares and the Scythians (I.103–6). The Scythians, in pursuit of the Cimmerians whom they had driven out of Europe, came into Median territory (I.103). They met the Medes in battle and were victorious. The Scythians thus won from the Medes the rule of all Asia east of the river Halys (I.103–4). They then marched against Egypt, but were bribed to turn back by Egyptian king Psammetichus (I.105). On their way back to Media, a few of the Scythians plundered the temple of Heavenly Aphrodite in the city of Ascalon in Syria, the oldest temple of this goddess (I.105). Thus the Scythians, unlike the Egyptians, seem to be very impious and adverse to the feminine. However, according to the Scythians themselves, those who plundered the temple and their descendants were struck with the "female sickness" (I.105). Their descendants, according to the Scythians, are a group of diviners called the "Enarees," which means androgynous or hermaphroditic (I.105; IV.67). Since these diviners say that Aphrodite gave them the art of divination, perhaps this pious art is what the Scythians regard as the female sickness (IV.67).

During Scythian rule all the land and wealth of Asia "was wasted by their violence and pride" (I.106). As well as being impious, the Scythians are thus hubristic and warlike. This may be related to their nomadism since war is the greatest motion.[46] The Scythians, who are always in motion, would seem to be always at or prepared for war; they imitate war in their way of life.

Herodotus begins book 4 with a story that will reveal certain things about the Scythians, the principles of which will govern the rest of Herodotus' account of them. Herodotus tells us that after putting down the Babylonian revolt, Persian king Darius himself led an invasion against the Scythians (IV.1). The pretext for this invasion was his desire to punish the Scythians for their previous invasion and subsequent rule of Asia (IV.1).[47] Herodotus, going back in time, then tells us that when the Scythians had tried to return to their country after twenty-eight years in Asia, they found a great army opposing them. During the long absence of their men, the Scythian women had "lived" with their slaves and thus produced many offspring (IV.1). When the offspring of the Scythian women and the slaves became men, they learned the circumstances of their origin and, not wishing to be enslaved as their fathers were, decided to fight the Scythians returning from Asia (IV.3).

In order to resist the Scythians' return, the offspring built a wide trench between the Tauric Mountains and the Maeetian Lake,[48] and from there they engaged the Scythians in many battles, preventing their entry into the country (IV.3). After failing numerous times to fight their way back into their territory, one of the Scythians said:

> What a thing we are doing, fellow countrymen! We are fighting with our own slaves . . . I think we should leave by our spears and bows. Let each one of us take up a horsewhip and go for them with that. As long as they are used to seeing us with arms, they think that they are our equals. Let them see us with whips instead of arms, and they will learn that they are our slaves; and once they have realized that, they will not stand their ground against us. (IV.3)

Having heard this speech by one of their compatriots, the Scythians carried out the plan outlined therein (IV.4). Seeing the Scythians charging them with horsewhips instead of weapons of war, the offspring were astonished and fled from the field of battle, thus allowing the Scythians to return. The success of the plan required that both the returning Scythians and the offspring understand this symbol of mastery, the horsewhip, as mastery itself. Herodotus indicates that the Scythians confound an image—the horsewhip—for that of which it is an image—mastery. As Benardete points out, the Scythians "confounded the sign with the object of that sign . . . An image would have replaced its original. What the Greeks keep separate, what is and what is made, the Scythians regard as one."[49] The Scythians confound the artificial with the real, the conventional with natural.

Origins and the Tribes of Europe

After the story of the Scythian return from Asia, Herodotus turns to stories about the origins of the Scythians. The Scythians themselves say that of all the nations or tribes theirs is the youngest in the world, there being only one thousand years between their first king Targitaus and the invasion of Darius (IV.5, 7). The Scythians pride themselves on being the youngest of peoples, unlike the Egyptians who prided themselves, until the time of Psammetichus, on being the oldest people in the world. The Scythians, but not Herodotus, believe they came into existence when a man named Targitaus, the son of Zeus and a daughter of the Borysthenes river,[50] first appeared in their country which was previously "desolate" (IV.5). Targitaus had three sons, the oldest named Lipoxais, the middle Arpoxais, and the youngest Colaxais. All three sons initially ruled together—who they ruled is mysterious—and during this time four gold implements, or *poiemata*, fell from heaven: a plough, a yoke, a sword, and a flask (IV.5). When first Lipoxais and then Arpoxais approached the implements with the intent to take them, they burst into flames. However, when Colaxais, the youngest brother approached, the flames were quenched "and he took the gold home." His two older brothers, as a result of this, turned over the whole kingly power to the youngest (IV.5). According to the Scythians, Lipoxais gave birth to the clan called Auchatae, Arpoxais to the clans called Catiari and Traspians, and Colaxais, who was then sole king, to the clan called Paralatae (IV.6). According to Herodotus, all clans together are called "Skoloti" by the Scythians, though "Scythian" is the name which the Greeks gave them (IV.6).

According to their self-understanding as revealed in their story, the Scythians associate their birth with the Borysthenes river. This association with water rather than earth is related to their nomadism or total motion. However, of the four implements that fell from heaven, two at least—the plough and the yoke—are related to agriculture. Thus, despite understanding themselves as being born from a river, the Scythians in some confused way also understand themselves as settled cultivators.[51] Moreover, the Scythians, believing that the plough, the yoke, the sword, and the flask fell from heaven, seem unaware of the human agency involved in their initial construction. They do not understand them as things made by man but rather as natural or unmade things. The Scythians, as in the story of their return from Asia, confound the conventional with the natural, the image of the real with the real itself. Unable to distinguish between the real and the image of the real, the Scythians live totally subsumed within images. The absorption of the Scythians within images is further indicated when they describe the land to the north of them: "The country of those that neighbor Scythia to the northward and above them—beyond this, none can see or penetrate, they say, by reason of the showers of feathers, the earth and the air are full of feathers, and these shut out the view" (IV.7). Herodotus, in a later chapter, then explains that the "feathers" the Scythians refer to is the snow that continuously falls due to the extreme cold in northern Europe, because, as he says "snow is like feathers" (IV.31).[52] What the Scythians do not understand is the likeness of the image—"feathers"—to that thing—snow—of which it is an image. The image becomes the thing, or "feathers" become snow. They therefore mistake the image for the real, and are thus divorced from the natural.

The cognitive separation from nature among the Scythians is illustrated in their inability to give a maternal line of descent from Targitaus as opposed to a paternal one. Although the Scythians claim to know that Targitaus is the father of Lipoxais, Arpoxais, and Colaxais, they make no mention of who their mother might be. Furthermore, although the Scythians say that the three brothers gave birth to four tribes, they do not mention that these brothers had any wives or what their names were, and neither do they mention the wife of Colaxais, although they say he had three sons (IV.7). In their story about their origins, the Scythians ignore the female in human reproduction and thus tend to deny its sexual or bodily nature. Herodotus implicitly contrasts them with the Egyptians, who expose the sexuality of women but keep that of men concealed, and whose customs show an overwhelming concern for the body rather than the soul.

The Scythian story of their own origins also reveals that among the Scythians the old show deference to the young. The two older brothers willingly turn complete political power over to their younger brother. Thus, the neglect of the mother in Scythian self-understanding does not necessarily lead to greater respect for the father. There is no patriarchy among the Scythians. Scythians look to the future, rather than the past, or see themselves as generators rather than as generated: perhaps the Scythians are the Deserters writ large (II.30). This is also unlike the Egyptians, who show great respect for age and the ancestral, which is related to their emphasis on what they believe is at rest. Their respect for the ancestral leads to their respect for fathers and the bodies from which they were derived. The Scythians, in showing disrespect for age, and hence a contempt for what they believe to be at rest and an emphasis on motion, also disrespect the body and necessity, the basis of the private family. This makes us wonder whether or not the Scythians, because they show contempt for the body, also show greater concern for the soul.

Herodotus next recounts the origins of the Scythians as told by the Greeks who live on the Pontus. According to the Pontine Greeks, whose story is just as fantastic as that told by the Scythians, Heracles came into the country, at the time "desolate," where the Scythians are now living, driving the cattle of Geryon before him (IV.8). When he entered the territory now called Scythia, meeting with cold and frosty weather he covered himself with his lion's skin and then lay down and slept. As he slept, his mares, which were yoked to his chariot, were miraculously spirited away (IV.8). Upon waking, Heracles searched for his mares all over the country, until he came to a place called Hylaea or "Woodland," and there in a cave he was astonished to find a creature who was a woman from the buttocks up and a snake below (IV.9). Heracles asked this snake woman if she had seen his mares. She responded that she had them, but would not return them, and therefore let him leave, until he had sex with her. Heracles performed his part of the bargain, but she only returned his mares after she bore three sons by him.

Before he left, the snake woman asked Heracles what she should do with their three sons when grown. "Shall I settle them here—I have lordship of this land—or send them to you?" (IV.9). In response, he gave her one of his bows and his belt with a golden flask on it, saying to her "That one of them you see stringing this bow, thus, and girdling himself with this belt, thus, him make to be a dweller in this country. But whichever of them fails in these tasks I have set, send him out of the land" (IV.9). When her sons had grown from boys to men, she put them through the test their father had ordered. Neither her oldest nor her middle son could bend Heracles' bow or wear his belt, but Scythes, the youngest, was able to do so. Thus, Scythes' mother expelled her two older sons from the country but kept her youngest with her, and therefore, according to the Greeks, all the Scythian kings are descended from Scythes (IV.10).

The Pontine Greek story has a number of similarities with the Scythian story. Both contain three sons, and in both the youngest son becomes sole king and gives his name to the Scythians. A crucial difference, however, is that the Greeks, unlike the Scythians, give a greater emphasis to the female (albeit she is half snake) in human generation, and thus emphasize the sexual or bodily nature of reproduction. Coupled with this greater emphasis on the mother is the fact that the test for overall kingship is based on physical strength. It is natural, not supernatural, as it is in the Scythian story.[53] The Greeks, it seems, due to their heightened awareness of the mother, can connect with nature or the real in a way the Scythians cannot.[54] This greater awareness of the mother, however, does not mean that the Greeks emphasize the power of the father or the ancestral. In their story of origins, just as in the Scythian one, the younger takes precedence over the older. Rather, the Greeks, having learned from the Egyptians to individualize and masculinize their gods, understand the human as feminine and not just masculine.[55]

Herodotus maintains that the Scythians are nomads, as seen from the story of origins toward which he inclines (IV.11). He does so despite the Scythian self-understanding that, although they are descended from a river and thus in motion, they may not be completely nomadic as illustrated from the first two implements that fell from the sky. This ambiguity about whether the Scythians are really nomadic, or what makes a Scythian a Scythian as distinct from other peoples, is further reinforced when Herodotus turns to describing the tribes of Europe, both Scythian and non-Scythian. Herodotus' discussion of the tribes of Europe occurs in two places. The first occurs between a digression on Aristeas and a discussion of mapmaking and world geography (IV.16–35). The second occurs between Herodotus' discussion of the tribal boundaries of Scythia, and the conference that the Scythians, realizing that they cannot repel Darius' invasion themselves, have with the kings of these neighboring tribes: the Taurians, Agathyrsians, Neurians, Cannibals, Black Cloaks, Gelonians, Budinians, and Sauromatae (IV.102–17). The following analysis of Herodotus' discussion of the tribes of Europe will combine these two "ethnographies."

Herodotus begins his account of both the Scythian and non-Scythian tribes of Europe by first describing those west and north of the Borysthenes river. This river runs straight through the middle of Scythia which is square (IV.17, 101). He then describes those east and north of the Borysthenes river. The first tribe west of the Borysthenes river and along the Hypanis river[56] are the Callippidae. They are, according to Herodotus, "Greek Scythians," who call themselves "the people of Olbiopolis" or the "city of good fortune" (IV.17–18). This adds to the confusion of what it means to be a Scythian, as now it appears that one can simultaneously be a Greek and a Scythian, even though the Scythians are said to be hostile to strangers and especially Greeks (IV.76). The next tribe further west of the Borysthenes and on the other side of the Hypanis are the Alazones. The Callipidae and the Alazones, according to Herodotus, have the same practices as the Scythians, except that they sow and eat corn, onions, garlic, lentils, and millet (IV.18). It seems that one can have the same practices as the Scythians but be a cultivator rather than a nomad. North of the Alazones are the Scythian ploughmen or husbandmen, who sow corn not to eat but to sell (IV.18). This is the first group of Scythians Herodotus mentions, and remarkably, they are not nomads but cultivators.

North of the Scythian ploughmen are the Neuri, who refuse to help the Scythians when Darius invades, and north of them the land is uninhabited (IV.17, 119). The Neuri, according to Herodotus, follow Scythian customs, but one generation before the invasion of Darius were driven from their land by snakes and came to live among the Budini (IV.105). The Greeks and Scythians think that the Neuri are wizards. They say that once every year each Neuri turns into a wolf for a few days and then returns to human form (IV.105). West of the Neuri across the Tyras river are the Agathyrsi, who also refuse to help the Scythians against Darius (IV.100). The Agathyrsi are the most luxurious of all the European tribes; they wear much gold and immoderately have intercourse with all their women in common. They do this in order that they will all be brothers and thus neither envy nor hate one another (IV.100). The rest of their customs, according to Herodotus, are very much like those of the Thracians.

The first tribe east of the Borysthenes and north of Hylaea are the Scythian farmers, the second group of Scythians Herodotus identifies

(IV.18). Again, it appears that there are Scythians who are cultivators, not nomads. North of the farming Scythians are the Man-Eaters, who, according to Herodotus, are by no means Scythian; the Scythians are not cannibals (IV.18). The land north of the Man-Eaters is uninhabited "as far as we know" (IV.18). According to Herodotus, the Man-Eaters, who also refuse to help the Scythians against Darius, are the most savage of all men, not just of the European tribes; they do not believe in justice nor obey any law (*nomo*) (IV.106). They are nomads (hence the Scythians are not the only nomads), and they wear clothing like that of the Scythians. However, the Man-Eaters have a language of their own, and, with the exception of the Issedones, they are the only European tribe who eat human flesh (IV.106).

East of the farming Scythians, across the river Panticapes, are the nomad Scythians, "who neither sow nor plough" (IV.19). These are the third group of Scythians Herodotus identifies, and they are the first and last he specifically names as nomads. Their country is, except for the Woodland, entirely barren of trees, and thus is suited to their nomadism. East of the nomad Scythians, across the river Gerrhus, is the area called "Royal," and, according to Herodotus, the best and most numerous of the Scythians live here (IV.20). They are the fourth group of Scythians Herodotus identifies; he does not say whether they are farmers or nomads, but just that they believe all other Scythians to be their slaves. Are these Scythians "royal" simply because they regard themselves as masters, and hence the best? North of the Royal Scythians are the Black Cloaks, and no other men are known to live north of them (IV.20). The Black Cloaks, according to Herodotus, are not of Scythian ethnicity or stock, but use Scythian customs, except for the fact that all of their clothing is black, hence their name (IV.107). They also refuse to help the Scythians against the Persians.

South of the Royal Scythians are the Tauri, who also refuse to help the Scythians against Darius. They live on what is called the "Rough Peninsula" which has its southern border on the Euxine Sea and its eastern border stretching to the Maeetian Lake. The Tauri, according to Herodotus, sacrifice all shipwrecked men and Greeks they capture in their sea raids to the Virgin Goddess, who they themselves say is Agamemnon's daughter Iphigenia (IV.103). Herodotus also says that the Tauri are headhunters who place the head of their enemy atop a pole high above their houses. They are therefore not nomads, even though they live by plundering and war, which makes them similar to the Scythians described in book 1.

East of the Royal Scythians across the Tanais river, where Scythian territory ends, live the Sauromatae, who do agree to help the Scythians when Darius and the Persians invade. The Sauromatae are descended from young

Scythian warriors and Amazon women, the latter's name in the Scythian tongue meaning "man-killer" (IV.110). The language of the Sauromatae is Scythian, but not in its purity since the Amazons never learned it properly according to Herodotus (IV.110). The women of the Sauromatae ride in the hunt with or without their men, go to war, and wear the same clothes as their men do (IV.116). The marriage custom among the Sauromatae is that no female virgin may wed until she has killed a male enemy, and many die unmarried as a result (IV.118). Herodotus' discussion of the Sauromatae is the only lengthy discussion of women in Scythia or Europe, yet it is a discussion of women who are almost identical to men, which is reflective of the Scythian repression of the female.

North of the Sauromatae live the Budini, whose territory is thickly wooded (IV.121). The Budini, according to Herodotus, are nomads (IV.109). They are different from the Scythians, however, because they are the only people in Europe to eat either "lice" or "fircones" (*phtheipotpageousi* has both meanings) (IV.109). Living among the Budini are the Geloni. Although the Greeks call the Budini the Geloni, they are wrong, according to Herodotus (IV.109). The Budini do not speak the same language as the Geloni, which is half Greek and half Scythian, and neither is the Budinian manner of life the same as the Geloni. The Geloni are tillers of the soil, eaters of grain, and possessors of gardens, whereas the Budini are nomads (IV.108–9). Furthermore, the Geloni have a city among the Budini, called Gelonus, built of wood (IV.108). Not only is the city wall wooden, but also the houses and all of the temples, which are dedicated to the Greek gods. The Geloni honor Dionysus by performing the Bacchic revels every three years. This is so, according to Herodotus, because the Geloni were originally Greeks who left their trading ports to live among the Budini (IV.108). Both the Budini and the Geloni agree to help the Scythians when the Persians and Darius invade.

Northeast of the Budini are the Thyssagetae, a large tribe of hunters who are "peculiar to themselves" (IV.22). Next to the Thyssagetae are the Iyrcae, who are also hunters (IV.22). However, their method of hunting is also very peculiar. Their land being thickly wooded, the hunter climbs a tree, and his horse and his dog, being so trained, crouch on their bellies lying in wait for their prey. When the hunter spots an animal, he shoots at it with his bow, drops from the tree onto his horse, and starts after the game with his dog following (IV.122). Northeast of the Iyrcae there are more Scythians, who are the fifth and last group of Scythians Herodotus identifies (IV.22). These are Scythians, according to Herodotus, who revolted from the Royal Scythians.

East of these Scythians, past stony and rough country, there are people called the Argippaei who live on the foothills of high mountains. Herodotus nicknames them the "Baldies" (IV.23, 24). They wear Scythian clothing but have a language of their own. According to Herodotus they are all, male and female alike, born bald, snub-nosed, and long-bearded (IV.23). Not only are the women like men, but all seem to be born adults. Thus, not only do the Baldies repress the feminine in the generative process, as the Scythians do, but seem to go even further, denying generation—children—and thus the family altogether. The Baldies are vegetarians, and they live under trees covered with white felt in the winter, but discard the felt in summer. No one does any injustice to the Baldies, according to Herodotus, because people believe they are holy. This is largely because they have no weapons of war (IV.23). As a result they are trusted to be just and allowed to act as judges to settle the disputes of their neighbors. They also show great hospitality and openness to foreigners, allowing no one to harm a person who has taken refuge with them. Furthermore, Herodotus says it is easy to "learn by asking questions" of them, and, although claiming that they have their own language, Herodotus implies that they can speak Greek as well as six other languages, but not Scythian (IV.24).

East of the Baldies live the Issedones, the furthest East of the European tribes (IV.26). The Issedones are cannibals. It is their custom, whenever a man's father dies, to cut up and mix the flesh of the deceased with the flesh of goats and sheep brought to the son by his neighbors, after which all feast on this stew (IV.26). The son then gilds the father's skull and sacrifices to it. The Issedones are also said to be a just people, whose women have equal power with the men (IV.26).

Herodotus' discussion of the tribes of Europe makes it very difficult to tell what makes a Scythian a Scythian. A Scythian cannot be defined by race or ethnicity that is rooted in the body, as it appears that some of the Greek race, the Callippidae, can also be considered Scythian, and the Sauromatae are also of half-Scythian stock. Furthermore, no particular language or set of customs define the Scythians, as many tribes, such as the Alazones, the Neuri, the Black Cloaks, the Baldies, and the Sauromatae are also said to have Scythian or Scythian-like language and customs while not being Scythian. Perhaps by looking to what distinguishes the Greeks from the Scythians, one can start to understand what it means to be a Scythian. Both Greek tribes mentioned in the two ethnographies, the Callippidae and the Geloni, have cities, Olbiopolis and Gelonus. They are the only tribes associated with cities, and thus it appears that the Scythians have no cities, or are those people who are outside the city. In the stories of origins, the

Greeks are also distinguished from the Scythians by their awareness of the importance of the female and so of what they believe to be at rest in human life. In this they have learned from and are like the Egyptians. Perhaps the acceptance of the female allows the Greeks in Scythia, who in other respects are like the Scythians, to have cities.[57] However, although outside the city, or civilization, the Scythians are not cannibals as the Man-Eaters and Issedones are. The Scythians are in between two boundaries or limits: one is the city, the other is cannibalism. Yet, being in between the city and cannibalism does not necessarily mean the Scythians are nomads. The first two groups of Scythians Herodotus identifies are not nomads, and the last two groups of Scythians, the Royal Scythians and those who revolted from them, are not specifically identified by Herodotus as nomads. Only the middle group of Scythians, the nomad Scythians, are identified as such. Yet, in the conclusion to his discussion of the tribes of Europe, in which he discusses the wisdom and ignorance of the Scythians, Herodotus again indicates, as he did in the opening story of book 4 and in the story of origins, that the Scythians, all of them, are nomads. According to Herodotus:

> The Euxine Pontus, against which Darius made his campaign, contains—except for the Scyhtians—the stupidest nations in the world. . . . [Yet] the Scythian nation has made the most clever discovery among all people we know, and of the one thing that is greatest in human affairs—though for the rest I do not admire them much. The greatest thing they have discovered is how no invader who comes against them can ever escape and how none can catch them if they do not wish to be caught. For this people has no cities or settled forts; they carry their houses with them and shoot with bows from horseback; they live off herds of cattle, not from tillage, and their dwellings are on their wagons. How can they fail to be invincible [*amachoi*] and inaccessible for others [*aporoi promisgein*]. (IV.46)

In the above passage, Herodotus indicates that the wisest discovery or invention of the Scythians is their nomadism. This cannot be understood literally, as Herodotus' enumeration of the tribes has shown. Is this wisdom their ignorance? Does being in total motion mean that they have no "ideas?" and is this why they fail to grasp that which is at rest and unchanging in nature? Perhaps this is related to their lack of cities.[58]

The adoption of the nomadic way of life is appropriate for the Scythians. Herodotus says it is "in a country that is very suitable for it, and their rivers are also their allies; for the land is level . . . and is well watered, and the rivers that flow through it are in number not much less than the canals in Egypt" (IV.47). The Scythians as nomads adopt a way of life that imitates war; they make their whole way of life a military strategy. When Darius crosses the

Ister, the Scythians, realizing that they cannot win an open pitched battle against the Persians themselves, attempt to enlist the help of their neighbors. The Geloni, the Budini, and the Sauromatians agree to join the Scythians, but the rest, the Taurians, Agathyrsi, Neuri, Man-Eaters, and Black Cloaks refuse. Upon this refusal, according to Herodotus, the Scythians "determined that they could not wage an open stand-up fight, seeing that their allies would not join them, but that they would withdraw and, withdrawing, fill the wells and springs as they passed and destroy the grass from the land, dividing their own army into two to do this" (IV.120). Not only does the Scythian army refuse to stand and fight, withdrawing either into the territory of those tribes who had refused to make an alliance with them or always one day's march ahead of the invading Persian army, but, of "their wagons, in which their women and children lived, and all of their flocks . . . of these they kept none back but sent them off with the wagons, telling the people to drive always northward" (IV.121).[59] They are always in motion.

After Darius had followed the retreating Scythians eastward all the way across Scythian territory and into the land of the Sauromatians, then northward into the land of the Budini where he burned the wooden city of Gelonus, and then back westwards through the land of the Black Cloaks, the Man-Eaters, and the Neuri, and then finally southeast back into Scythian territory, he sent a message to the Scythian king Idanthyrsus asking: "Why do you keep on flying from me when you might make a choice of courses? If you think yourself strong enough to oppose my power, stop this wandering to and fro and stand and fight. If [not] . . . stop running, give gifts—namely earth and water—to one who is your master, and come to words with me" (IV.126). Idanthyrsus, angered at the suggestion that he was cowardly and a slave, sent this message back to Darius: "Persian, matters are thus with me. I have never fled from a man in fear in days past nor now. I am not fleeing from you. What I am doing is no different from what I am wont to do in peacetime" (IV.127). Idanthyrsus' response indicates that the Scythians, in terms of their way of life, make no distinction between peace and war; as nomads they are always at or prepared for war. Herodotus indicates that this is due to their total dedication to freedom, understood as external freedom or freedom from foreign domination, for they were angered "when they heard the very name of slavery" (IV.128). Herodotus' discussion of Scythian history, therefore, is a complement to, or illustration of, their general custom of nomadism; nomadism, unlike Egyptian customs, emphasizes motion and thus imitates war.

Herodotus calls Scythian motion wise, because "no invader who comes against them can ever escape and . . . none can catch them if they do not wish to be caught." However, although the latter proves to be true according to Herodotus' account of the history of Darius' invasion of Scythia, the former does not. Darius does manage to escape after failing to catch and defeat the Scythians. Darius escapes due to the advice of a Greek named Coes, the general of the Mytileneans serving in the Persian army, and the advice of a prominent Persian named Gobryas. First, with respect to Coes, after Darius and his army had crossed the Ister, the latter ordered the Ionians who made up the Persian fleet to destroy the bridge over which they crossed (IV.97). Coes, however, advises Darius not to have the bridge destroyed, saying:

> My lord, you are about to march into a land where you will find no trace of ploughed ground or inhabited city. Do you let this bridge stand where it is, leaving as guards of it those who built it. If we find the Scythians and fare as we hope we will, there is a way for us to go home; if we cannot find the enemy, there is still a safe way home for us . . . we may come to some mischance as we wander about, being unable to find them. (IV.97)

Coes, aware of the implication of Scythian nomadism, realizes that the bridge is not a means to come into contact with [*prosmisgein*] the unbridgeable [*aporoi*] Scythians, but rather is only a means to escape them.[60]

With respect to the advice of Gobryas, the Scythians, after being angered by the name of slavery, decided to wage a pitched battle with the Persians, and, instead of earth and water, they sent to Darius a bird, a mouse, a frog, and five arrows (IV.131). Darius interpreted these gifts as images or signs of the Scythian surrender to him of earth and water and themselves: the mouse, living in the earth, symbolized earth; the frog, living in water symbolized water; the bird, being swift, symbolized a horse, and the arrows symbolized their fighting power, with the latter two together symbolizing the Scythians themselves, who are archers and horsemen. Gobryas, however, understands that the Scythians cannot distinguish between an image or symbol and that of which it is an image or symbol; he therefore interprets the gifts not symbolically, but literally as the Scythians would.[61]

> If you do not become birds and fly away into the sky or become mice and burrow into the earth or become frogs and leap into the lakes, there will be no homecoming for you, for we will shoot you down with our arrows. (IV.132)

Darius, accepting Gobryas' interpretation, decides to flee rather than fight the Scythians in a pitched battle. Again, Gobryas advises him wisely suggesting that Darius leave the weakest part of his army behind to light fires and to tie their mules to stakes, while they and the rest of the army quietly start to retreat in the middle of the night (IV.134).[62] As a result of hearing the mules and seeing the fires, "the Scythians . . . assumed that the Persians were in their usual encampment," which allowed the Persians to start their flight to the Ister without the Scythians knowing.[63] Once again they fail to distinguish image from reality.[64]

Thus, the problem still remains that Herodotus asserts that the Scythians as such are nomads, but, in his particular discussion of the tribes of Europe, he maintains that some Scythian groups are cultivators, others nomadic, and two are not identified as either. Francois Hartog argues that the nomadism of the Scythians, which allows them to defeat Persian king Darius' invasion, is a metaphor for the ships of the Athenians, which allows them to defeat Persian king Xerxes' invasion of Greece, tying book 4 of the *Histories* together with books 6–9.[65] If Hartog is correct in this, then Herodotus is trying to moderate an otherwise admirable Atheian love of external freedom, since he couples this same love among the Scythians with their extreme ignorance or stupidity. Furthermore, Hartog goes on to say that the Athenian navy, of which nomadism is a metaphor, is itself a metaphor for "insularity" or being like "an island-dweller."[66] As such, according to Hartog, not only is Scythian nomadism a model for the Athenian strategy in the Persian wars, it also prefigures the Periclean strategy during the Peloponnesian wars, as reported by Thucydides.[67] Advising the Athenians on how to reply to the Spartan ultimatum, Pericles says "sea-power is of enormous importance. Look at it this way. Suppose we were an island, would we not be absolutely secure from attack? As it is we must try to think of ourselves as islanders; we must abandon our land and our houses and safeguard the sea and the city."[68]

Although largely in agreement with Hartog's analysis, I believe it falls short in one respect. Hartog implies that Herodotus only attempted to understand the Scythians as the Greeks, and especially the Athenians, would understand them, not as the Scythians would understand themselves. Any particular feature of Scythian life for which a comparable analogy cannot be found in Greek life is in the narrative, Hartog maintains, simply to represent otherness from Greekness: the Scythians are the people other than the Greeks.[69] Although partly true, this is not the whole of Herodotus' analysis. Herodotus does try to understand the Scythians as they understood themselves, as shown in the opening story of book 4, the Scythian story of their own origins, as well as his discussion of the Royal Scythians.

Another explanation, therefore, for what Herodotus means by nomadism, and thus what makes a Scythian a Scythian, can be found by looking more closely at Herodotus' description of the Royal Scythians (IV.20). Herodotus says that the Royal Scythians, who are the best and most numerous, regard all the other Scythians as their slaves. This is reminiscent of the story at the beginning of book 4, in which the returning Scythians regarded themselves as masters and the army of offspring regarded themselves as slaves because both regarded the horsewhip, the sign of mastery and slavery, as the reality of mastery and slavery. Neither group could distinguish an image from that of which it was an image. Perhaps this "regarding" is at the heart of what it means to be a Scythian. Scythians are Scythians not because they belong to a specific territory, family, ethnicity, linguistic group, or even to a single community with a particular set of customs. Rather, they are Scythians because they regard themselves as such. The Scythian ploughmen, farmers, nomads, Royals, and rebels can all be called Scythian, not because of what they do, how they speak, or where they come from, but because of what they think—they think of themselves as Scythians.[70] Thus, being a Scythian is a state of mind, which can change and is therefore in motion, and is perhaps why the Scythians are invincible (*amachoi*) and inaccessible (*aporoi*), and why Darius, when he crosses the Ister, cannot see or come into contact (*prosmisgein*) with them.[71] What makes a Scythian a Scythian is radically subjective, relying on an individual act of will. This radical individualism means not only that the Scythians are trapped within images or "*poiemata*," as their story of origin reveals, but also that Scythians themselves are a "*poiemata*" or poetic construction.[72]

It is now possible to illuminate schematically the parallel opposition between the Scythians and the Egyptians. The Egyptians are a people who look to the earth but neglect the nature and power of the Nile. This is related to the greater publicity of the sexuality of women in Egypt in contrast to the attempt to conceal that of men. This in turn is linked to the Egyptian reverence for age and hence the bodies out of which they are derived. Their reverence for age and the past is coupled with their emphasis on stability and rest, believing that what is at rest, the first things, are first in time. Their emphasis on stability and rest is indicated by three things: one, their total subsumption within religion, in the Egyptian case meaning a contempt for the human; two, their great ability as builders, manifested in such things as pyramids (II.35); and three, their great wisdom in mathematics and history, the latter understood simply as memorizing and recording the past. However, the Egyptians lack both internal freedom and ultimately external freedom when they are conquered by Persian king Cambyses. The Scythians, on the other hand, neglect the earth and associate themselves with their rivers. This is linked to their neglect and even contempt for the sexual or reproductive role of women in human life and their celebration of male virility. This in turn is coupled with their reverence for youth and the future rather than age and the past, and thus by implication their neglect or denial of the limits of the body. Their reverence for youth and the future is related to their motion or nomadism, which can stand as a metaphor for their subjective individualism and willfulness. This leads to three things: one, their total subsumption within images, meaning that the Scythians, although closer to nature than the Egyptians—the Scythians are outside the city—are not aware of the distinction between nature and convention and thus are an almost totally conventionalized or poeticized people; two, their lack of ability to build physical structures such as stone houses or cities, because not being able to identify a made thing as a made thing as opposed to a natural thing, they cannot make anything of note themselves (IV.82), and, three, their almost total ignorance or stupidity. Paradoxically, their almost complete ignorance, a result of their motion, leads to their complete external freedom, illustrated in Darius' inability to defeat them.

This schematized understanding leads to two important questions. Although the Scythians, unlike the Egyptians, contemn the body, does this lead them to have a greater concern for or better understanding of the soul than the Egyptians do? Second, although the total motion of the Scythians, a metaphor for their subjective individualism, leads to their external freedom, can it also provide them with internal freedom? Or does it rather lead to internal subjection or slavery?

The Customs of Scythia

Herodotus first discusses the religious customs of the Scythians. The highest god whom they worship is Hestia, whose Scythian name is Tabiti, a god whom the Egyptians do not have (II.50). Next to Hestia in importance are Zeus, called Papaeus, and Earth, called Api, whom they believe is the wife of Zeus (IV.59). After these they worship Apollo, called Goetosyrus; Heavenly Aphrodite, called Argimpasa, and Heracles and Ares, for whom Herodotus does not give Scythian names. Perhaps the Scythians and Greeks share common names for these gods. These seven gods are common to all the Scythians, but in addition to these the Royal Scythians sacrifice to Poseidon, called Thagimasadas (IV.59). The strangest aspect of this list of the gods is that the Scythians worship as the highest divinity Hestia, whose name comes from the verb to stand or stay. She is a feminine goddess of the hearth (*histie*)[73] and therefore fixed abodes.[74] Yet, it has been argued that the Scythians show neglect for the feminine and praise the masculine, which is linked to the fact that they are nomads, or "carry their houses with them . . . on their wagons." Perhaps this paradox can be illuminated by what Herodotus says of the Pelasgians and their gods in book 2. The Pelasgians believed there was a type of being different from the human; gods exist, and human beings are not gods (II.52). The Pelasgians associated this type of divine being with the feminine and therefore with what they believed to be at rest. Accordingly they associated human being with the masculine and thus with what they believed to be in motion. The Scythians, in seeing the highest god as feminine and related to domesticity and fixity, would see the human being, that which is not divine, as masculine, undomesticated, and in motion.

Furthermore, Herodotus says that the Scythians make no images, altars or shrines to any of their gods except Ares, the god of war (IV.59). Thus, the only thing the Scythians try to visibly make stable and permanent is the greatest of instabilities and motions.[75] For the Scythians what never changes is the changing; only motion is permanent. The Scythian shrines to Ares are wooden pyramids which resemble the stone pyramids in Egypt. According to Herodotus, in every province there is a shrine to Ares, made out of bundles of sticks, three furlongs wide and long, but less so in height (IV.62). On this enormous pile of wood, which Herodotus says has to be replenished every year due to the wasting effects of winter, the Scythians build a square with three sheer sides and one with a slope that can be ascended (IV.62). On top of this square is placed an iron sword, "the image of Ares" (IV.62). This is the one image that the Scythians can identify as an image, and it is thus the one real or universal thing they can know.

The Scythians reveal their disrespect for the human body, in opposition to the Egyptians who deify the body, in their yearly sacrifices to this sword of Ares. According to Herodotus, in addition to sacrificing horses and cattle, they also sacrifice one out of every hundred of their enemy prisoners (IV.62). After pouring wine on the heads of these human victims and slitting their throats, they drain the blood into buckets and then pour it onto the sword atop the wooden pyramid (IV.62). Finally, the Scythians then mutilate the bodies of the dead men, cutting off their right arms and throwing them into the air, leaving these severed limbs and the rest of the corpses unburied (IV.62). Thus, whereas the Egyptians, in their practice of circumcision, offer their gods their sexuality, the Scythians offer Ares the blood of their human prisoners. The Egyptians associate their gods with birth and the generation of bodily life; the Scythians associate Ares with death and the taking of bodily life. Moreover, unlike the Scythians, the Egyptians refrain from both human and animal sacrifice, excepting the latter in certain special instances (II.41), because they believe that animals are higher or more beloved of the gods than humans. The Egyptians, with respect to their relation to the gods, distinguish between animals and humans. The Scythians, on the other hand, in sacrificing both animals and humans to Ares, fail to make a distinction between the two. Scythian contempt for the body does not lead them to believe that human beings have a closer relation to the gods than the animals do, but rather causes them to collapse humans with the other animals in this regard. For the Scythians, who are in constant motion, human beings are just another "herd."

Scythian contempt for the body also leads to their violation of the family. When two Scythians of the same family have differences they engage in a single combat to the death before the king (IV.65). The victor beheads his defeated family member, and, treating him as he treats his "deadliest enemies," saws off the top part of the skull above the eyebrows, cleans it out, gilds it and uses it as a drinking cup (IV.65). When visited by strangers, Scythians display these gilded heads, explaining that they belonged to family members who differed with them and thus whom they killed. They say that such family killing is manly virtue (IV.65). The Scythians regard themselves not primarily as members of families, but rather as isolated individuals at war, having differences with other isolated individuals who are their deadliest enemies. Herodotus suggests that the only thing that can maintain some control over the various differences among these isolated individuals, and which allows them to understand themselves as belonging to a larger group known as Scythians, is the king.

When turning from the religious customs of the Scythians to their customs that pertain to war, Herodotus more explicitly reveals that the Scythian contempt for the body does not lead to their greater emphasis on the soul. The first time a Scythian kills a man, he drinks his blood (IV.64). When Herodotus maintains that the Scythians are not cannibals, this seems to extend to a prohibition against eating human flesh, not against drinking human blood. Also, the Scythians present the heads of the men they have killed in battle to their king in order to obtain a share in the booty. Failure to show a head results in exclusion from booty. Most important, however, for the subject at hand, are the following Scythian customs of war that Herodotus relates. First, a Scythian, after presenting enemy heads to his king in return for booty, scalps these heads and kneads the scalp with his own hands making himself a kind of "napkin"; he then ties this scalp to the bridle of his horse (IV.64). The man with the most scalps, or "skins" (*dermata*), on his bridle is judged to be the best (IV.64). Second, many Scythians sew these "skins" together to make cloaks for themselves, and third, many Scythians make coverings for their arrow quivers out of the skin taken from the right hands of their dead enemies, "nails and all" (IV.64). Fourth, many Scythians remove the skin from the entire body of a man and stretch it on a wooden frame, carrying this framed skin around with them on their horses

(IV.64). As a result of these horrifying practices of war, the practices of motion, Herodotus comments that he was able to learn the true color and texture of human skin from the Scythians: "The skin of man, it would seem, is thick and bright—indeed, in point of whiteness, the brightest of all skins" (VI.64).

Scythia is covered in human skin, the visible and external part of human beings. Thus, the total contempt which the Scythians show for the body does not lead to their greater emphasis on the soul; it rather leads everything to become body. In Egypt, the overwhelming emphasis in their customs on the body, or the cleanliness of the body, produced a doctrine of the soul, albeit one which effected a complete separation between a universal soul and a particular human being and his or her particular human body. In Scythia, however, the complete neglect or contempt for the body produces not an alternative doctrine of the soul but the denial of the existence of anything but the body. Herodotus reveals this material monism when he describes the burial customs for ordinary Scythians—presumably those who have not already been beheaded by their family members in the presence of the king (IV.71, 73). Herodotus says that when a commoner dies, his body is carried in procession on a wagon by his closest relatives to all his former friends. When the procession reaches them, the friends prepare a feast and, most importantly, "offer a share of food to the dead man, the same as everyone else" (IV.73). After being carried around like this for forty days the body is buried. Herodotus indicates that the Scythians, in regarding the dead, at least for forty days, as equal to the living, make no distinction between this life and the next life, or between bodily life and the life of the soul. Although they do not put the body and the soul together, the Egyptians can distinguish between them. When the Scythians bury the body, it seems that they bury the entire human being: there is no immortality for the Scythians in any form, as there is no being or existence beyond the material. Although the Egyptian doctrine of the soul offers no particular immortality, it does support the notion that there is something that exists beyond the material or the particular bodies of human beings.

The customs that pertain to war reveal not only that in Scythia everything becomes surface or body, but they also illustrate the inability of the Scythians to make a distinction between nature and convention, or to identify an image as an image. This means that the Scythians, as Scythians, cannot make unnatural things or conventional imitations of nature themselves. As Benardete points out, this is connected to an extreme literalism among the Scythians.[76] For instance, they sew scalps or "skins" together to make cloaks (IV.64), skin being the natural covering of the body, indicating that they cannot make artificial or conventional coverings for their bodies. Also, as the hand is what holds arrows, the Scythians use skin from the right hand of their enemies to cover their arrow quivers. Furthermore, Scythians ride on horses, so they carry the stretched skin of an entire human body with them on their horses. In all of these customs, including their religious custom in which "the ox cooks itself," the Scythians, unable to distinguish between nature and artifice, turn the natural into the artificial (IV.61). This propensity is further revealed by their royal burial customs. According to Herodotus, a year after they have buried their dead king, the Scythians kill fifty horses and fifty of the dead king's most suitable servants.[77] The Scythians drive stakes through the bodies of the horses up to their necks and then mount these dead horses on half-wheels, one half-wheel supporting the front legs, the other half-wheel the hind (IV.72). They drive a stake along the spines of the dead servants up to their necks, and mount these impaled corpses onto the horses. These macabre constructions are then placed in a circle around the king's tomb, which is in the land of the Gerrhi, "who live furthest of all whom they rule." The Scythians, unable to see, and therefore imitate, nature, cannot build stone statues but rather, as Benardete points out, "Men themselves replace statues."[78]

In his discussion of Scythian King Ariantas' great bronze bowl, Herodotus turns to the question of whether the total motion of the Scythians, which leads to their near total materialism, can provide them with internal freedom as well. The story of the bronze bowl begins when Herodotus tells us that he could learn neither the exact number of Scythians nor whether their population was great or small, from the Scythians themselves (IV.81). However, they did show him an enormous bronze bowl, containing "easily 5400 gallons and in thickness is about 4 inches," in a place called Exampaeus between the Borysthenes and Hypanis rivers (IV.81). According to what "the natives say," who could be either Alazones or Farmer Scythians in this area (IV.52), this bronze bowl was made by Scythian king Ariantas out of arrowheads (IV.81). Ariantas, desiring to count the Scythian population, ordered each Scythian, on the pain of death, to bring him an arrowhead. An enormous mass of arrowheads was collected by Ariantas, but, forgetting to count them, he decided to leave a memorial to himself. He melted each individual arrowhead down from which he made this huge bronze bowl (IV.81). Thus, though Ariantas succeeds in leaving a memorial to himself, he fails to leave a memorial to the number of the Scythian population and thus to each individual Scythian.[79] Future generations, including Herodotus, cannot learn the number, because each individual arrowhead, representing each individual Scythian, has been melted into one. What was divided and separate has been mixed together by the Scythian king, making a one that destroys the parts.

Herodotus, in this loss of memory of "individual" Scythians, reveals that the consequence of Scythian contempt for the body that paradoxically reduces everything to body is actually a total loss of separate or individual identity. Although externally free, internally the Scythians suffer the greatest of subjections; they, except perhaps for their king, have no hope for individual immortality, or more specifically individual immortal fame.[80]

Herodotus, by looking to the customs and beliefs of the Egyptians and Scythians, discovers that each only recognizes a part of the whole in which human beings live. The Egyptians emphasize rest and the Scythians emphasize motion. From such partial perspectives, two opposing but parallel ways of life ensue. Furthermore, Herodotus discovers that Egyptian piety causes a devaluing of the concern for justice and wisdom and leads to the praise of "lying" rather than truth telling, and that Scythian nomadism, a metaphor for their completely isolated and abstract individualism, actually leads to a form of materialism that precipitates a total loss of individual identity. The Greeks and the Persians combine the principles of rest and motion, which the Egyptians and Scythians keep separate. Among the Greeks, the Spartans combine these two principles in one way, the Athenians in another. The Persians, however, whose civilization we will consider next, have their own unique way of combining the principles of rest and motion.

Chapter 3

Persia and Regimes in Theory

Introduction

Herodotus' Persians are both "rationalists" and imperialists; as such they combine rest and motion, the two principles that govern nature. The character of Persian rationalism, first revealed by the Persian chroniclers, is to grasp at the universal and that which is at rest while ignoring the particular and that which is in motion. The Persian intellect seeks to understand a nature that transcends the varying and changing customs of particular peoples. Persian kings, in their drive for empire, also grasp at a universal that denies the particular. This becomes especially apparent with Xerxes. In his desire to unify the world under a single Persian king, Xerxes seeks to destroy the different customs of the different peoples that exist in the world; he seeks a whole without parts. Persian imperialism is thus the political analogue of Persian rationalism, which forces the regime to be in constant motion. Continued imperial expansion toward universal empire means that if the Persian mind seeks rest, Persian politics requires motion.

The religious beliefs of the Persians as well as their manner of speaking also manifests the Persian emphasis on the universal and contempt for the particular. For instance, the Persians, Herodotus tells us, worship the universal objects of physical nature, such as the sky, sun, moon, stars, earth, air, fire, and water. Also, the Persians, unlike the Egyptians, insist on telling the truth, and lying is condemned as the worst thing a man can do. They therefore seek to make the internal intentions or mind of the speaker perfectly known to the listener. Persians desire that the soul be perfectly known and thus that the invisible become visible. Truthful speech is an attempt to universalize the soul, or to share it with others, which requires the abstraction from the body, that which is irreducibly private and particular to the individual. Yet, the attempt to "see" the soul by making it external is an attempt to make the soul act like the body and thus, paradoxically, everything becomes body in Persia; their attempt to get beneath the surface of things, as it were, turns everything into surface in Persia. Their view of the world becomes simple rather than complex. Herodotus further reveals the problem of this very important Persian custom in his discussion of Persian king Cambyses. There he shows that complete abstraction from the body and focus on the soul can lead to madness.

The Persian attempt to grasp at the universal in abstraction from the particular, reflected in their custom of truth telling, is also what allows Herodotus to place a debate about the best regime in theory in the mouths of three prominent Persians: Otanes, Megabyzus, and Darius. The theoretical regime that each man argues for is that which he believes to be best "in speech" rather than in practice or that which he considers the permanent nature of human beings without regard to local and changing conditions, such as religion, customs, or culture in general. Herodotus believes each of these theoretical regimes—democracy, oligarchy, and monarchy—are insufficient because they abstract from the complex nature of speech by using words to universalize particular aspects of human nature. This is related to the Persian belief that the meanings of the words they use are as unchanging and motionless as the human beings they describe. If speech is always going to reveal the truth, words must have one unchanging meaning between speaker and listener. In contrast to the Egyptians, the Persian view of speech is as simple as the world that they look at; interpretation is not necessary because the truth is immediately apparent.

Herodotus, by turning to a study of regimes in history rather than simply in theory as the Persians do, shows that thought can grasp, and speech can express, the particular *as* the particular—thereby providing the condition for the discovery of what is truly universal or natural to human beings. Moreover, in Herodotus' analysis words are shown to be complex; they reveal and conceal, lie and tell the truth, at the same time. Persian regimes in theory, therefore, must be corrected by Herodotus' study of actual regimes in history in order to lay the groundwork, as it were, for the discovery of what is truly the best regime.

Herodotus also shows, especially in the case of Persian king Darius, that the Persian insistence on always telling the truth can actually cause the collapse in the distinction between truth and falsehood. If truthful speech is an attempt not simply to express the reality of the world outside of the speaker but also to make visible or known the soul within the speaker, then it requires the abstraction from the body or the external part of human beings. Yet Herodotus illustrates in his Persian narrative, that the abstraction from visible exteriors in an attempt to "see," as it were, the invisible interior of things, means nothing visible or external to speech itself can verify its truth. Lacking the ability to be tested for its veracity, truthful speech becomes very difficult to distinguish from falsehood. Aware of this difficulty, Darius, Herodotus shows, threatens to transform all speech in Persia into merely "talk" without any substantive reality lying underneath.

Proem

The first introduction that Herodotus gives to the Persians is through the Persian chroniclers in the proem to the *Histories* and their account of the origin of the disagreement between the Greeks and the Asians (I.1-5). The Persian chroniclers say that the Phoenicians are at the origin of the dispute (I.1). They docked at Argos on one of their long trading voyages, and on the fifth or sixth day, after much of the Phoenician merchandise had been sold, the women of Argos, including Io the daughter of Argive king Inachus, came down to the coast to investigate the foreign wares. As the women stood at the stern of the ship and bought whatever their hearts (*thumos*) most desired, the Phoenician sailors rushed on them, raped Io and some of the other women, threw them onto their ship and forced them to sail away to Egypt with them (I.1).[1]

The Persian chroniclers characterize the Argive women as having *thumos* (I.1). In this passage *thumos*, or spiritedness, is connected with a love of the beautiful, and is presented as a desire to cross boundaries and to look on what is foreign to and other than oneself. It is also connected with the longing to possess this other and make it one's own; the Argive women buy the foreign wares displayed by the Phoenicians (I.1). In this sense something similar possesses the Phoenician men who rape and carry off, or make their own, the foreign women who come to their market.

This is how the Persian chroniclers tell it, but it is not, according to Herodotus, "how the Greeks tell it" (I.2). Herodotus thus points to the Greek version of how Io came to Egypt. This version is completely mythical. According to the Greeks, one day Hera saw her husband Zeus on the banks of a river with a beautiful cow, whose form she suspected concealed a beautiful woman. Hera was correct, as it was Io, the daughter of Inachus, whom

Zeus had fallen in love with but had changed into the form of a cow when he became aware of his wife's approach.[2] Hera joined Zeus on the banks of the river and asked for the cow as a gift from her husband. Zeus complied, but Hera, still not relieved of her suspicions, gave the cow to hundred-eyed Argus to keep a strict watch over it.[3] Zeus contrived to free Io from this prison by sending Hermes, who charmed all of Argus' eyes to sleep with sweet music and poetry and then cut off his head.[4] Undaunted, Hera sent a gadfly to torment Io, still in the form of a cow, and Io was driven in torment from land to land until she finally reached Egypt. Zeus then restored Io to her human form and bore a son with her in Egypt called Epaphus, worshipped by the Egyptians as the calf-god Apis, or Dionysus in animal form.[5] Compared to this Greek version of how Io came to Egypt, the Persian version is completely demythologized. There is nothing of the divine in how they tell it, but rather it is a completely rational and purely human story.[6] The Phoenicians also tell a purely rational and human version of the Io story, but it differs from that of the Persians. According to the Phoenicians, Io was not brought to Egypt against her will, but rather, having lain with and gotten pregnant by the ship's captain, was ashamed and sailed to Egypt voluntarily with the Phoenicians so as not to be discovered by her parents (I.5). The significance of this difference will be revealed in Herodotus' discussion of the Persian custom of truth telling.

There is a striking parallel, however, between the mythical story alluded to in the proem that the Greeks tell about Io and the story of Xerxes' love of Artaynte and her father Masistes' death that Herodotus tells right near the end of his *Histories* in book 9 (IX.108–13). According to Herodotus, Xerxes, on his way back to Susa from Greece after being defeated at the battle of Salamis, stopped in Sardis. While there he fell in love with his brother Masistes' wife, but despite his entreaties could not win her over (IX.108). In a final attempt to get his sister-in-law to capitulate to his desires, Xerxes arranged a marriage between his son Darius and Artaynte, the daughter of Masistes and his wife, and then set off for Susa. Upon arriving in Susa, he transferred his love from the mother to the daughter. Unlike her mother Artaynte responded to Xerxes' desires, and forthwith Xerxes began an affair with his son's wife (IX.108). Amestris, Xerxes' wife, suspecting the affair, wove a beautiful cloak for Xerxes, which he delighted in and wore proudly in front of Artaynte. Being delighted with Artaynte as well, Xerxes swore an oath to the girl, to give her whatever she wanted. According to Herodotus, "when he had sworn, she coolly asked for the cloak" (IX.109). Xerxes, not wanting to give her the cloak for fear that his wife Amestris would be confirmed in her suspicions, begged Artaynte to ask for cities, gold, or an army, which she could command herself, but not the cloak. Yet Artaynte would have nothing but the cloak, so Xerxes gave it to her, and she, "charmed with the gift, wore it exulting" (IX.109).[7]

Amestris, learning that Artaynte had the cloak, did not begrudge the daughter but turned her anger towards the mother, Masistes' wife, whom she believed was responsible. She waited until her husband's birthday, which, Herodotus tells us, is a festival in Persia during which the Persian king anoints himself and gives gifts to the Persians (IX.110). On that day, Amestris asked Xerxes for Masistes' wife. Xerxes did not want to grant his wife this request, as he knew his brother's wife was innocent of the whole affair and that Amestris intended her serious harm. Yet, feeling the compulsion of the law that stated that during this festival the king could not refuse what was asked for, he turned Masistes' wife over to Amestris (IX.111). Forthwith, Amestris had the woman's breasts, nose, ears, lips, and tongue cut off and thrown to the dogs. Xerxes attempted to get his brother Masistes to take his own daughter as a new wife, but Masistes refused and, upon seeing the savage mutilation, set off for Bactria with his sons intending to raise a revolt against the king. Xerxes however caught up with him and killed Masistes, his sons, and his supporters (IX.113).

In Herodotus' story of Xerxes' love and Masistes' death in book 9 and the mythical Greek story of how Io came to Egypt, there are many parallels between Xerxes and Zeus and Amestris and Hera. For instance, just as Zeus falls in love with Io and Hera guesses the truth of this, Xerxes falls in love with not one but two women who are not his wife, and Amestris guesses the truth in both these cases—albeit she is incorrect to see the first woman as responsible for Xerxes' affair with the second. Moreover, just as Hera asks for Io in the form of a cow and Zeus grants this request, Amestris asks for Masistes' wife and Xerxes, feeling compelled, turns the woman over. Also, when Xerxes makes promises and swears oaths to Artynte before he knows what is going to be asked of him, he imagines that he has total freedom. He assumes he is constrained by no prior commitments to his wife under law and that there is nothing private or particular about himself which he cannot give to others or make public. The Persians institutionalize this belief in their law which states that the king cannot refuse a gift which is requested on his birthday; it cannot be acknowledged that anything limits or constrains the king. Herodotus thus presents Xerxes imagining himself—and the Persians imagining their king—as godlike. The Persian chroniclers can tell the demythologized version of how Io came to Egypt because they tell it from the perspective of the divine looking down on the human, not from the human looking up to the divine, as the Greeks do.

Herodotus, however, shows that the Persians are not in fact gods. First, Herodotus tells us that Xerxes fell in love with his brother's wife after he was defeated in Greece (IX.108). Thus, although Xerxes, in explaining his desire to invade Greece, proposes to make the Persian empire universal and therefore like heaven and himself like Zeus (VII.8), he fails to do so. Second, whereas Zeus in the Greek mythical story of Io can conceal his mistress by hiding her human appearance in the form of a cow, Xerxes cannot help but reveal his mistress by giving Artaynte the cloak, which she wore "exulting" for all to see (IX.109). Moreover, unlike Zeus who can restore Io to her human form once she reaches Egypt, Xerxes is helpless to undo the savage mutilation wrought on Masistes' wife by Amestris (IX.111–12).

There are also significant differences between Hera and Amestris. Whereas Hera seems to be motivated by love for Zeus, as her efforts are directed toward putting distance between Io and Zeus thereby preventing the affair, Amestris seems to be motivated by vengeance. She shows a complete lack of jealousy toward Artaynte, being unconcerned with the actual physical affair itself, but rather directs her anger toward the girl's mother whom she thinks plotted to shame her publicly. Amestris is more prideful than Hera, a pride which is shown by Artaynte as well. Artaynte will not relent in her demand for the cloak, despite Xerxes' pleadings, and glories in it publicly regardless of the trouble this will cause for her lover and ultimately for her own parents and siblings. What is important for Artaynte is that Xerxes loves her—and not that she loves him. Amestris also shows a greater cruelty than Hera. The gadfly sent by Hera to torment her does not prevent Io from eventually regaining her human form and giving birth to a god, whereas Amestris' mutilation of Masistes' wife is irreversible.

The comparison between the story of Xerxes' love and Masistes' death and the Greek mythical story of how Io came to Egypt to which it has a striking similarity, reveals Xerxes to be more limited than Zeus and men weaker than the gods, and Amestris to be more vengeful than Hera and women more powerful than goddesses. Herodotus suggests that Xerxes cannot mitigate the tragedy that befalls Masistes, his wife, his sons, and supporters, because he, unlike Zeus (who frees Io from the eyes of Argus), cannot utilize the sweet music and poetry of Hermes. To completely demythologize the world as the Persian chroniclers do can be disastrous for human beings.

Herodotus further indicates the "rationality" and hence "divine" perspective of the Persian chroniclers in the proem when he has them separate wisdom and justice. After giving their account of how Io came to Egypt, the Persian chroniclers then maintain that certain Greeks, whom Herodotus assumes were Cretans, carried off Europa, daughter of the Phoenician king

(I.2).[8] Next, certain Greeks sail to Aea in Colchis and carry off the king's daughter Medea, refusing to restore her when her father requested it (I.2). Alexander of Troy, according to the Persian chroniclers, having heard the stories of these unpunished deeds, decided to take a wife out of Greece by rape—and so carried off Helen (I.3).

The Greeks, to avenge the rape of Helen, raised an army and destroyed the power of Priam and the city of Troy. For this, the Persian chroniclers maintain, the Greeks are greatly to blame, for they invaded Asia before the Persians ever invaded Europe (I.4). According to the Persian chroniclers, they believe rape to be unlawful, and therefore the deed of unjust men. The avenging of rape, since "the women would not have been carried off had they no mind to be," is, by contrast, the deed of foolish men (I.4). The Persians portray both Alexander and the Greeks as unjust, but the Greeks as more foolish and blameworthy in the affair because, whereas Alexander raped in return for rape—"it was only rape on both sides"—the Greeks sought to conquer an entire city in return for the conquest of a woman. Claiming to be wise rather than just, the Persian chroniclers maintain that they, unlike the Greeks, cared nothing for the rape of their women (I.4).

Herodotus, however, calls into question the distinction made by the Persian chroniclers between wisdom and justice in a number of ways. First, Herodotus presents the Persian chroniclers making this distinction in the context of blaming the Greeks and justifying themselves. Herodotus reveals that the Persians, despite their claims, are as concerned with justice as they claim the Greeks are.[9] Second, Herodotus, near the middle of book 4, tells the story of the fate of Sataspes, the son of Teaspes, and nephew of Persian king Darius. Sataspes raped the virgin daughter of a prominent Persian named Zopyrus, son of Megabyzus (IV.43). Xerxes, king of Persia at the time, was going to impale Sataspes for the rape, when his mother interceded for his life, proposing to subject her son to worse punishment than Xerxes had planned for him. She would force him to leave Persia and circumnavigate Libya (Africa) before he could return (IV.43). Xerxes agreed to these terms, but Sataspes, after having sailed through the Pillars of Heracles and halfway down the coast of Libya, turned round and returned to Persia before completing his task. Xerxes, upon his return, impaled Sataspes, not for having failed in his mission, but, according to Herodotus, on the first charge against him, that of having raped Zopyrus' daughter (IV.43). Moreover, Herodotus maintains in the story of Xerxes' love and Masistes' death that Xerxes, failing to persuade Masistes' wife to yield to his desire, would not, out of respect for his brother, use force against her (IX.108). Likewise, the woman herself, according to Herodotus, knew that Xerxes would not use force to bend her to his will (IX.108).[10] Herodotus indicates, contrary to their own self-understanding expressed in the proem, that the Persians clearly do care about the rape of their women and are concerned with justice. The Persian chroniclers, in their desire to blame the Greeks and exonerate themselves with respect to the cause of the Persian wars, make a separation between wisdom and justice which presents them as indifferent to rape and therefore to what men consider as their own, when in fact they are not.

Herodotus, turning from the Persian chroniclers's account of the origin of the dispute between Greeks and barbarians, says that he will not comment on whether these stories are true, but rather he will identify the man whom he knows to have committed the first unjust acts against the Greeks and then go on to give an account of both the small and great cities of mankind (I.5). Herodotus will do so because,

> For those [cities] that were great in earlier times most have now become small, and those that were great in my time were small in the time before. Since, then, I know that man's good fortune (*eudaimonien*) never abides in the same place, I will make mention of both alike. (I.5)

Herodotus, as the above passage indicates, turns from the issues of the proem to the issue of imperialism.[11] However, a moment's reflection will show that Persian imperialism is the political analogue to the Persian chroniclers' apparent contempt for justice and claim to wisdom.[12] The Persian chroniclers associate justice with the lawful, and therefore with convention. As conventional, justice varies with the particular customs of particular peoples in different places. Thus, the Persian chroniclers' apparent elevation of wisdom over justice indicates a preference for adherence to that which is believed to be universal and unchanging, rather than respect for that which is particular and changing. The Persian kings, in their desire for empire, destroy the particular customs of particular peoples. For instance, Herodotus says that after Cyrus conquered the Babylonians, they lost their most beautiful custom, the marriage auction, and, ever since then, Babylonian fathers, due to the economic ruin brought on by conquest, have made prostitutes of their daughters to get money for themselves (I.196). Herodotus also maintains that Persian imperialism not only destroys the particular customs of the peoples that it subsumes, but also that it assimilates them to oneness or universalizes them. According to one story, Cambyses invaded Egypt after a Persian woman had complimented Cassandane, Cambyses' mother, on the beauty of her children. Cassandane responded bitterly, however, that although she bore her husband Cyrus such worthy children, Cyrus dishonored her in favor of his new concubine Nitetis from Egypt (III.3). Cambyses, hearkening to his mother's complaints, said, "Mother mine, when I am a man, I will make the bottom of Egypt the top and the top the bottom" (III.3). In turning Egypt upside down, Cambyses will actually make it conformable to the rest of the world; Herodotus, when discussing the geography, climate, and customs of the Egyptians, had said that all were the exact opposite of those of other peoples (II.35).[13] Furthermore, Xerxes understands his imperialism to be above justice just as the Persian chroniclers believe that being wise is in contradiction with being just. Xerxes, as a result of conquering Greece and making the Persian empire universal, says that "those who are innocent in our sight and those who are guilty will alike bear the yoke of slavery" (VII.8).

Herodotus indicates that the drive for empire is an imitation in deed or on the spatial level of the drive for "wisdom" in speech or on the intellectual level. It is important to note that the Persian claim to wisdom does not cause Persian imperialism; Persian kings in their drive to expand their empire do not consciously imitate the Persian chroniclers in their drive for knowledge of universal or natural truths. Rather, the relationship is analogous, not causal. Xerxes' drive for universal empire threatens to collapse the distinction between nature, which is universal, and convention, which applies to particular peoples. According to Xerxes, "the sun will look down upon no country that has a border with ours, but I shall make them all *one* country, once I have passed in my progress through Europe" (VII.8). Xerxes threatens to make the world, or the universal, conform to the conventions of one particular people, the Persians.

The Persians, in their "rationality" and in their imperialism, combine rest and motion. Their concern for wisdom rather than justice reflects the Persian emphasis on that which is universal or unchanging and therefore at rest. However, the political analogue to Persian "wisdom" is empire, which means the Persian kings are or should be in constant motion. Xerxes, explaining his decision to invade Greece, says to a council of Persian noblemen:

> Men of Persia, it is no new law (*nomon*) that I initiate among you; it has come to me from the tradition. For as I learn from older men, we have never been at peace since we took over the supremacy from the Medes, when Cyrus deposed Astyages. It is the god that leads us on, and so, when we of ourselves set about our many enterprises, we prosper. (VII.8)[14]

Xerxes alludes to imperialism as a law or custom of the Persians, thus suggesting that what is particular to the Persians is the drive to conquest, the logical extension of such being universal conquest and thus the destruction of everything which is particular. The Persians, spatially or on the political level, emphasize motion over rest, and Persian imperialism, imitating Persian rationalism, turns rest into motion. An example of this can be seen when Xerxes, in preparation for his invasion of Greece, has a channel dug through the isthmus at Athos, which, for the sake of passage, converts land, representing rest, as it were, into water, representing motion (VII.22). Yet, since the drive to empire pushed to its extreme leads to universal empire, the logic of imperial expansion is to put an end to all future imperial conquest. Thus, Persian imperialism also turns motion into rest. For instance, Darius bridges the Bosporus in order to conquer the Scythians, and Xerxes bridges the Hellespont in order to conquer the Athenians and all of Greece. Both, again for the sake of passage, turn water into land, and motion into rest (IV.83–89; VII.33–36).

Having explicitly raised the theme of empire Herodotus says he will identify the first man to have done unjust acts of imperial aggression against the Greeks (I.5). This seems to be Croesus, a Lydian tyrant, who was the first barbarian Herodotus knows of to have subjected some of the Greeks—the Ionians, Aeolians, and Dorians of Asia Minor—to the payment of tribute and to make some of them—the Spartans—friends (I.6). Yet, Herodotus traces Croesus' lineage back to Gyges, a Mermnadae who took the tyranny from the Heraclidae. Gyges was the first barbarian to conquer a Greek city, Colophon (I.14). Thus, it appears that Gyges was actually the first man to have done an unjust act against the Greeks.[15] The issues raised in the story of Gyges (I.8–15) are at the heart of the issues of Persian "rationalism" and Persian imperialism.[16] Candaules, a despot, ordered Gyges to look on his wife naked. Candaules thus had the desire to make what was private, and beautiful to him because it was private, public (I.8). The Persian chroniclers, claiming to care nothing for the rape of their women because they are wise, show a desire similar to that of Candaules. To care nothing for the rape of one's women—a view which makes consent meaningless and therefore supports tyranny—logically implies the destruction of the private family, or the notion that a particular woman belongs to particular man. Therefore, Persian chroniclers also show a desire to make the private public, or to make what is one's own universal. The imperialism of the Persian kings, on the other hand, which ultimately leads to the desire for a universal empire or to make the world one country under one Persian king, is analogous to the actions of Gyges. Gyges, in killing Candaules and taking his wife, made what was not his, his own.

Customs

The first description of Persian customs, apart from their general custom of imperialism referred to in the proem, occurs in book 1 when a Lydian named Sandanis advises Croesus not to attack Cyrus and the Persians (I.71).

Sandanis, referring to the Persians before they became imperial or began to conquer other countries, lists three of their customs. The first is that the Persians wear leather clothing in their daily lives as well as into battle (I.71). Second, Sandanis says that the Persians "eat not what they want but what they have, for the country they live in is full of rocks" (I.71). Finally, Sandanis says that the Persians are water drinkers, as they have no wine, and neither do they have any "figs to nibble on, nor any other good thing" (I.71). The Persians have no luxury, or none of the bodily pleasures beyond the strictly necessary. Herodotus agrees when he says, "indeed, the Persians before they conquered the Lydians had nothing of delicate luxury nor any good thing at all" (I.71). Sandanis then gives his reasons for advising Croesus not to attack the Persians. The Persians are poor, so Croesus can gain nothing from them if he wins. However, if the Persians win, they will get a taste for the good things of Lydia. They will become accustomed to luxury and will never be cast off. Croesus, however, was not persuaded by Sandanis.

After the story of Cyrus' birth, education, ascension to the throne and then subjugation of Croesus, Herodotus gives a more general description of Persian customs, which includes both those which have continued since the time the Persians first were a people, as well as those adopted after they became imperial and conquered other countries (I.131–40). Herodotus first deals with their religious customs. The Persians, according to Herodotus, do not construct images, temples, or altars. This is because, unlike the Greeks, they do not believe the gods are "of human nature" (*anthropophueas*) (I.131). The gods are like men neither in visible form—they do not have a bodily shape—nor in invisible character—they do not have a creative power in their souls as humans do. The Persians build them no images, statues, or altars. Thus the Persians, unlike the Greeks, do not look up to heroes, or to standards of human excellence as determined by the poets Hesiod and Homer, but neither do they look up to animals as the Egyptians do. For instance, Herodotus says that far from worshipping animals, the Magi—priests of the Medes who became the priests of the Persians after Media was conquered—kill all living things, except humans and dogs, with their own hands, including ants, snakes, and "everything that creeps or flies" (I.140). Thus, although the Persians have a notion of the soul it is not the same as that held by the Egyptians. The Persians do not believe that humans share the same soul with animals, except for perhaps dogs.[17]

Persian religion, Herodotus indicates, is not poetic like that of the Greeks but "rational." Neither looking up to animals nor to themselves, they look up to nature and the cosmos. Persians from the beginning worshipped the sky as Zeus, and they also sacrifice to the sun, moon, and earth, as well as to fire, water and wind (I.131). The Persians, in their religious practices, are like pre-Socratic natural scientists such as Anaxagorus and Thales.[18] Their gods are the universal elements of nature and the visible bodies in the cosmos.[19]

Persian worship of the universal leads to their contempt for the particular or the private. The Magi, unlike the Egyptians, show contempt for the body and what is private or particular to a particular human being by refusing to bury the corpse of a Persian until it is mutilated and torn apart by birds and dogs (I.140).[20] Furthermore, the Persians are forbidden to vomit or urinate—particularly ugly manifestations of the bodily nature of human beings—in front of anyone (I.133). Contempt for the particular or what is private can also be seen in the collectivist or communal nature of praying in Persia. According to Herodotus, whenever a Persian sacrifices to their gods, it is unlawful for him to pray for his own good alone; he must pray for the good of all the Persians including the king, "for among all the Persians is himself also" (I.132). Another custom which points toward communism is the Persian manner of naming themselves. According to Herodotus, although "they have not noticed it themselves," their names "all end in the same letter, the one the Dorians call 'san' and the Ionians 'sigma'" (I.139). These names, all ending in the letter "s," tend to reduce the Persians to a certain sameness or oneness.[21]

The worship of the heavenly Aphrodite was introduced into Persia, according to Herodotus, after Persia became imperial, learning how to perform sacrifices to this goddess from the Assyrians and the Arabians (I.131). Aphrodite was the goddess of beauty and her son was Eros. Thus, as Sandanis predicted, attachment to the pleasures of the body beyond the strictly necessary, and thus to that which is private, came into Persia with foreign conquest. Yet Herodotus says that no Persian is allowed to sacrifice to any of their gods, including the heavenly Aphrodite, without a Magian present (I.132). Thus the Persians try to stamp out all secrecy with regard to religious worship. They try to make religion as public as possible. Furthermore, the Magi, when presiding over these religious sacrifices, sing a hymn to the "birth of the gods" (I.132). It seems that the Persians give a generated or bodily character to the universal natural objects they worship, and thus to particularize the universal. However, particularizing the universal can also mean its opposite, universalizing the particular, or making the private public, which is also consistent with the Persian imperialist drive. To make their empire universal means to reduce the changing customs in the world to one set of customs and to put an end to all further conquest and motion. Thus Herodotus indicates that the Persians, in their turn to imperialism, turn the universal into the particular and the particular into the universal.

There are, however, two other possible implications to the introduction of the worship of Aphrodite after the Persians become imperial. Aphrodite was in love with Ares, the god of war, and thus her worship perhaps symbolizes the Persian worship of war and conquest, and thus the worship of constant motion. This perhaps explains why Persians, according to Herodotus, of all the natural objects which they worship after having become imperial, "revere rivers most of all" (I.138). This second implication of the worship of Aphrodite is related to the first, in the sense that both pleasure and the honor achieved in war are goods beyond the strictly necessary. That the Persian concern for military conquest is tied to the Persian concern for honor can be seen in what Herodotus calls their "system of honor" in their empire. According to Herodotus, the Persians "Most of all . . . hold in honor themselves, then those who dwell next to themselves, and then those next to them, and so on, so that there is a progression in honor in relation to the distance" (I.134). Just as Persian imperialism is a spatial imitation of Persian "wisdom" or knowledge of the universal, Persians, in administering their empire, have a spatial understanding of honor, based on physical proximity to themselves. The Persian system of honor is also related to their universalism in that it attempts to reduce all peoples to one standard of virtue, the Persian one.

The third implication of the worship of Aphrodite, the goddess of beauty, is that the Persians, after they become imperial, worship or love the beautiful. Reflective of their desire to possess the beautiful, or that which is universal and not their own, the Persian worship of Aphrodite thus makes them like the Argive women and Phoenician men in the proem and like Candaules and Gyges. The Persians possess the type of spiritedness that is driven to transcend one's boundaries and to look on and possess what is foreign to, and other than, oneself. This is illustrated when Herodotus says that Persians, more than any other people, welcome foreign customs, and adopt the customs of the people they conquer. According to Herodotus, the Persians "decided that Median dress was more beautiful than their own, and so they wear it. They wear Egyptian breastplates for their wars" (I.135). Furthermore, adopting "enjoyments of all sorts," the Persians learned to sleep with boys from the Greeks (I.135). Also, ambiguous as to whether this was an adopted foreign enjoyment or not, Herodotus says that each Persian man, unlike the Greeks and Egyptians, marries many legal wives and has even more concubines (I.135).

At first glance, the above custom seems to reveal that the Persians lack sexual moderation and thus glory in the private or particular pleasures of the body. However, contrary to initial impressions, this can actually be interpreted as a Persian rejection of the private or particular. Persian men, it seems, do not love particular women, or particular boys for that matter, but rather all women or the whole class of women. Persian men, in this sense, seem similar to the lovers of wisdom, or philosophic rulers of Socrates' city in speech, described by Socrates to Glaucon in book 5 of Plato's *Republic* as a means into his discussion of the doctrine of ideas. According to Socrates, a lover of wisdom would not love one particular boy to the detriment of all the others, but would love all boys or the class of boys in general.[22] However, to love all members of a class is to love no particular member, or to love the class rather than its members.[23] Thus, the lover of wisdom, in loving the class rather than its members, loves the universal characteristic that all the particular members share in common, rather than the particular members themselves.[24]

The Persians, according to Herodotus, educate their sons from the ages of five to twenty "in three things only: horsemanship, archery, and truth telling" (I.136). Truth telling, however, is their most important secular custom for both children and adults alike, as the Persians, Herodotus claims, believe lying to be the worst of all things (I.138). They hold indebtedness, in the monetary sense, to be the foulest thing next to lying, because they believe "the debtor is bound to lie somewhat" (I.138). Thus the Persians believe lying stems from the individual's concern for their own material self-interest, indicating that their emphasis on truth telling is an emphasis on selfless dedication to the common good, rather than selfish concern for one's own good. Again, the Persians contemn the private in favor of the public. The Persian association of lying with indebtedness means that there are no marketplaces as there are in Greece (I.153). Persian king Cyrus regarded their lack of markets, and therefore their truth telling and suppression of private interest in favor of the public interest, as part of Persian military might. In response to the Spartan demand not to attack the Ionians, Cyrus claimed, "I never yet feared men [Greeks] who have a place set apart in the midst of their cities where they gather to cheat one another and exchange oaths, which they break" (I.153).

The Persian custom of truth telling shows their emphasis on speech, and therefore their emphasis on the soul from which speech proceeds rather than the body, and thus their concern with the internal rather than the external, the invisible rather than the visible. As Benardete points out, the Persians are not satisfied with the surface of things, but, unlike the Scythians for whom everything turns into skin, the Persians try to get beneath the surface of things or see what is beneath the skin.[25] Herodotus implies that the Persians universalize or idealize the soul, one part of the human being—the body being another but suppressed part of the human being. The Persian concern with the soul over the body can be seen in one of two secular customs Herodotus praises. A Persian boy, before he is five years old, lives with his mother and the other women of the household rather than his father so that, if he dies before reaching the age of five, his death will not distress his father's soul (I.136). The Persians suppress the private bodily attachments in favor of the health or tranquility of the soul.[26]

The contrast with Egyptian lying will help illuminate further the implications of Persian truth telling. As argued in chapter two, the Egyptians, in their praise of lying, believe that the highest form of speech conceals the soul or the internal intentions of the speaker rather than revealing it.[27] The Egyptians believe that words have meaning, representing that which does not change and is at rest, or something similar to a Platonic "idea," yet, as "liars," they believe that words are best used merely as the vehicle for the self-expression of the speaker and not as a means of communication to the listener. "Ideas," therefore, cannot be communicated because words, although representing something unchanging in the mind of the speaker, spawn an infinite variety of interpretations, the correct one only the speaker can know. Words are like the "ideas," which are the cause of the many particular things in the world, yet, for the Egyptians, just as the true nature of their gods remain concealed behind animal forms, the many particulars forever obscure the universals from which they proceed.[28] The Egyptians believe that words, or the surface of things, require interpretation, but that interpretation is impossible. Just as the particular things in the world do not lead one back to the "ideas," words do not reveal the truth.

The Persians, on the other hand, believe that speech reveals the soul or the internal intentions of the speaker rather than concealing it. Words have meaning or represent an "idea," but for the Persians, unlike the Egyptians, words always act as a vehicle for the communication of "ideas" between speaker and listener. This however relies on the spoken word having the same meaning for the listener as for the speaker, and thus words for the Persians do not just represent that which is at rest, but are at rest themselves; words, spoken correctly, are universal or have one unchanging meaning at all times for all individuals. For the Persians, unlike the Egyptians, words do not spawn an infinite variety of interpretations, and the many particular things in the world do not obscure the universal. The Persians believe that words require no interpretation, and thus it is always possible to get underneath the surface of things through speech. Just as the "ideas" are easily apprehended in spite of the many particulars, there is no reason why words cannot reveal the truth.

If the Persian custom of truth telling shows their emphasis on the soul over the body, they also go further, believing that the human soul has clear and distinct parts. This can be seen in the second of two secular customs Herodotus praises. Among the Persians, there is a custom that not even the king himself may execute anyone due to a single crime, nor may any other Persian do irreversible harm to any of their servants for a single deed (I.137).[29] According to Herodotus, "Only if, on consideration (*logisamenos*), he finds the wrongdoings more in number and greater than the good deeds may he use his pleasure (*thumo*)" (I.137). Thus the Persians believe that "*thumos*" or spiritedness should be ruled and directed by reason, and, given their attempt to suppress the body and its private pleasures, they believe that desires should be subordinate to spiritedness.[30]

The Persian belief in the internal stratification in the soul mimics the internal stratification within their own community. According to Herodotus,

> When [the Persians] meet one another in the street, there is a sign by which one may know if those who encounter are equals, and the sign is this: instead of greeting, they kiss one another on the mouth. If one of the two is a little humbler, they kiss on the cheek. If one of them is very much inferior in birth, he falls down and does obeisance to the other. (I.134)

This internal stratification among the Persians may be the most effective way to deal with envy under a regime of one man rule, in that it allows all classes except for the lowest, to look down on and contemn another. Unity is thus combined with hierarchy in Persia.[31] The internal stratification of classes among the Persians, which imitates the internal stratification they believe should exist among the parts of the human soul, turns into an external stratification of nations in their empire (I.134). However, as discussed above, when Persians look not within but without to imperialism and empire, the ruling principle explicitly changes from "wisdom," associated with reason, to honor, associated with spiritedness.

Related to their custom of truth telling, Herodotus says that the Persians are forbidden to say what they are forbidden to do (I.138). Thus, in Persia, truthful speech is lawful speech.[32] If the Persians cannot say what they cannot do, this also implies its opposite, that Persians cannot do what they cannot say. Thus, everything that can be done can be said; all deeds, or physical action, should be brought into speech, and therefore into the universal which speech, and the law, is supposed to represent for them. For the Persians everything should be externalized or made known through speech, and thus the Persians deny the need for internality or for some things to remain hidden. Herodotus indicates that the Persian belief that no deed done by them can be against the law—and therefore unspeakable—leads them to declare that no Persian has yet killed his or her parents (I.137). If it appears that patricide or matricide has taken place, the Persians claim that investigation necessarily reveals that the deed was done by a child who was either adopted or illegitimate (I.137).[33] Moreover, this is related to what the Persian chroniclers say in the proem. The women could not have been raped unless they wanted to be, and thus could not have actually been raped, because this would mean that the men did an unjust deed, and therefore an unlawful or unspeakable one. Might, in other words, makes right. Furthermore, the denial of internality, which is concomitant with the belief that all things can be universalized or brought into speech, involves the denial of the necessarily private, which is related to the Persian chroniclers' supposed indifference to the rape of their women. It also explains the difference in the Phoenician account of how Io came to Egypt. Io, according to the Phoenicians, was not forcibly carried off to Egypt by the Phoenician sailors; instead, having gotten pregnant, she left with them voluntarily because she was ashamed and feared discovery (I.5). That Io can feel shame indicates that the Phoenicians, in contrast to the Persians, believe that there is a necessary internality or privacy to human beings.

In addition to their concern with speech, the Persians are concerned that speech be true, and therefore that the internal and invisible become external and visible. Thus, Persian truth telling is actually an attempt to make the soul, in becoming external and visible, act like the body. This is illustrated in how the worth of a man is judged in Persia. According to Herodotus,

> After valor in fighting, the goodness of a man is most signified in this: that he can show a multitude of sons. To him who can show most, the King sends gifts every year. For multitude, they think, is strength. (I.136)

The above passage indicates that Persians move from valuing strength of soul, courage shown in battle, to the strength of body, a multitude of bodies means military power. The exclusive dedication to the soul and neglect of the body in Persia, paradoxically, it seems, leads everything to become body or "skin" as in Scythia.

History: Cambyses

In his discussion of the historical legacies of Persian kings Cambyses and Darius in the first half of book 3 of the *Histories*, Herodotus reveals that Persian customs contain certain internal contradictions which, when pushed to their extreme, cast their adherents out of the horizon these customs create. Herodotus' treatment of Cambyses reveals that the perfection of Persian customs leads to madness, and his treatment of Darius in the context of the Persian debate on the best regime shows that the total dedication to truth telling can actually lead to the collapse of the distinction between truth and falsehood. Before discussing the Persian debate and Darius' attack on the custom of truth telling, Herodotus recounts Cambyses' descent into madness after his invasion and conquest of Egypt.

Cambyses, according to the Persians, was propelled to invade Egypt by his anger at the deceit perpetrated against him by Egyptian king Amasis. The Persians say that Amasis, in response to Cambyses' request that he send his daughter to join the Persian royal harem, sent Nitetis, daughter of the former Egyptian king Apries whom he had overthrown, dressed as his daughter instead (III.1).[34] Cambyses, having been assured safe passage by the Arabian king, passed through the Syrian dessert and encamped his army near the Pelusian mouth of the Nile (III.4, 5). Opposite was the Egyptian army led by Egyptian king Psammenitus, son and heir of Amasis, the latter having died after a trouble-free reign of forty-four years before Cambyses could engage him in battle (III.10). The battle between the Persians and the Egyptians was hard fought, according to Herodotus, and many from both armies died, but in the end the Egyptians were defeated by the Persians (III.11). After their defeat, the Egyptians walled themselves in the city of Memphis (III.13). Cambyses then sent a Mytilenean ship with a Persian herald aboard upriver to Memphis to invite the Egyptians to come to an agreement. However, on seeing the ship approaching the city, the Egyptians rushed outside the walls, destroyed the ship, and then tore the crew to pieces (III.13).[35] Cambyses then laid seige to the Egyptians holed up in Memphis, and after a good while the Egyptians finally surrendered.

Ten days after his victory, Cambyses placed Psammenitus along with other prominent Egyptians in the outer part of the city, and devised a scheme whereby he could test Psammenitus' soul. This is in accordance with the Persian desire to make the internal external (III.14). First, Cambyses had the Egyptian king's daughter, along with the daughters of other prominent Egyptians, dressed in slave attire, and sent her and the others with jugs to fetch water. When the girls passed by their fathers screaming and in tears, their fathers, except for Psammenitus, screamed and cried in return. Psammenitus, according to Herodotus, made no sound, but rather "looked fixedly at them first, took it all in, and then he bowed himself to the ground" (III.14). The second thing Cambyses did was to take the son of Psammenitus, along with two thousand Egyptian boys of the same age, and place bits in their mouths and tie ropes around their necks. He then had them led out to their deaths. These boys were to die in return for the Mytileaneans killed by the Egyptians, as the Persian royal judges had determined that for every man killed on Cambyses' side, ten Egyptians should be killed (III.14). When these boys passed their fathers, the latter screamed and cried for them as in the case of their daughters. Psammenitus, however, did for his son the same as he had done for his daughter. Yet, when Psammenitus saw one of his former drinking companions, who had become poor due to the conquest, begging amidst the Persian army, he began to cry and to call out to his old friend by name (III.14). Cambyses, surprised, sent a herald to ask Psammenitus why he made no lament when he saw the degradation and plight of his children, but on seeing the plight of a friend, "you honor him thus" (III.14). Psammenitus responded by saying, "Son of Cyrus, my own griefs were too great to cry out about, but the sorrow of this friend is worth tears; he had much, and much happiness, and has lost all and become a beggar when he is upon the threshold of old age" (III.14).

Herodotus' discussion of Cambyses' trial of Psammenitus' soul can be interpreted in a variety of ways. The first interpretation, put forward by Benardete, is that Herodotus shows that although the body has powerful effects on the soul, these effects of the body cannot be expressed by words or external signs such as screams. The sorrow Psammenitus feels for his children, who have a special bodily connection to him, are sorrows of the body which cannot be shared with others. Thus, Benardete argues, Cambyses discovers the body, "the most private thing we have."[36] Contrary to the implications of the Persian custom of truth telling, not everything can be brought into speech, as the body, the foundation of the private family, cannot be universalized or made public. The Persian emphasis on the universal and contempt for the particular does not lead them to make the private public, but rather makes them unable to acknowledge the private although it exists.

Benardete's interpretation of Psammenitus' trial—indicating that for Herodotus the body cannot be expressed in speech or public signs—is generally sound. However, it cannot explain how the other prominent Egyptians sitting with Psammenitus and whose children suffer the same fate as his children can express their private or bodily sorrows in words of lamentation and external signs, such as tears. Therefore, perhaps Cambyses does not discover the importance of the body in this case but is satisfied that Psammenitus passes this testing of his soul, because he subordinates the sorrows of his body to the sorrow he feels for his friend. Herodotus, I believe, wishes the story to spawn both of these interpretations, the first revealing Herodotus' view of one of the problems with the Persian understanding of "truth telling," the second revealing Cambyses' adherence to the implications of that understanding.

After discussing the initial invasion and conquest of Egypt, Herodotus turns to detailing Cambyses' descent into madness. The first sign of Cambyses' madness, according to Herodotus, occurs on his campaign against the "long-lived Ethiopians," who lived far to the south of Egypt (III.17). Before setting out on this campaign, Cambyses sent spies to Ethiopia under the cover of wishing to establish a guest-friendship with the Ethiopian king by the exchange of gifts (III.17, 21). Not fooled however, but realizing Cambyses' messengers came as spies, the Ethiopian king gave the messengers a bow and charged them to tell Cambyses that when he could "draw so easily, as I do now, bows as big as this one"—the Ethiopians, according to Herodotus, are said to be the tallest men in the world—then he should march against the Ethiopians (III.19, 21). Until that time Cambyses, according to the Ethiopian king, should thank the gods that they have not encouraged the Ethiopians to attack the Persians (III.21).

When they returned to Egypt, the messengers reported to Cambyses everything that the Ethiopian king had said. Herodotus says that Cambyses was furious (III.25). He immediately set out against the Ethiopians, and because he was mad (*emanes*) and not of sound mind (*ou phreneres*), he did not take time to make provisions for food to feed his army while on the march (III.25). As a result, before they had finished a fifth of their journey, the army had eaten all of the provisions and began to eat the pack animals. Yet these were soon exhausted as well. According to Herodotus, if at this point Cambyses had come back to his wits and abandoned the campaign to lead his army back to Egypt, he could have been considered a wise man (*aner sophos*) (III.25). But Cambyses took no consideration for the situation and pushed forward. When they came to the desert, Cambyses' army, in their dire situation, turned to cannibalism to keep themselves alive; drawing lots they killed and ate one out of every ten men (III.25). Afraid of his men becoming cannibals, Cambyses finally abandoned his campaign and marched his army, much depleted, back to the Egyptian city of Thebes, and from there he sailed down to Memphis (III.25).[37]

The second sign of Cambyses' madness is his killing of the Egyptian calf-god Apis, whom the Greeks call Epaphus and believe is the son of Io and Zeus. According to Herodotus, when Cambyses arrived in Memphis after his failed Ethiopian campaign, the Egyptians believed that their god Apis, in the form of a calf, appeared among them (III.27). They immediately put on their finest clothes and began to celebrate their festival dedicated to this god. Cambyses, however, mistakenly believed they were celebrating his military defeat and summoned those Egyptians who were in charge of Memphis to demand answers (III.27). These men told Cambyses that the Egyptians were not making merry at his failure but were celebrating the appearance of their god Apis. Cambyses thought they were lying, and, as liars, he—consistent with the seriousness Persians place on truth telling—had them executed (III.27). Cambyses then summoned the Egyptian priests, and, on being told the same thing, ordered them to bring the calf-god Apis before him (III.28). When the priests did so, Herodotus says that Cambyses went almost insane (*hupomargoteros*) (III.29). He attempted to stab Apis in the stomach with his dagger but struck him in the thigh instead. Laughing madly, Cambyses mocked the priests, saying, "You miserable wretches, is that the kind of your gods, things of blood and flesh and susceptible to iron?" (III.29). He then ordered the priests to be flogged and to kill any Egyptian caught celebrating. The festival ended, and the priests, after Apis died of his wounds, buried him secretly without Cambyses' knowledge (III.29).

Cambyses' first full act of madness was the murder of his brother Smerdis. According to Herodotus, Cambyses had Smerdis sent back to Persia out of jealousy, as Smerdis was the only man among the Persians including Cambyses himself who could draw the bow sent by the Ethiopian king (III.30). When Smerdis had left Egypt and returned to Persia, Cambyses had a dream in which a messenger said to him that Smerdis sat on the Persian throne and touched heaven with his head (III.30). Fearing a coup, Cambyses sent Prexaspes, the Persian whom he trusted most, to kill his brother. Prexaspes went to Susa, the Persian capital, and carried out his orders (III.30).

The second full act of madness committed by Cambyses was the murder of his younger sister, who was his second wife and who had followed him into Egypt (III.31). Herodotus says there are two versions of her death, one Greek and one Egyptian. According to the Greek version, Cambyses organized a fight between a lion cub and a puppy, which both he and his younger sister, who was also his wife, had watched (III.32). When the puppy began to lose the fight, another puppy, its brother, broke its leash and came to the aid of the other puppy. The two of them together beat the lion cub (III.32). Cambyses' sister, seeing this, began to cry. When Cambyses asked her what was wrong, she said that the puppy who came to the rescue of his brother reminded her of Smerdis, and she realized that Cambyses, because his brother was dead, had no one who would rescue him (III.32). Cambyses, according to the Greeks, murdered her on account of this response. The Egyptian version maintains that as Cambyses and his sister sat down to dinner, she took a head of lettuce and tore off the leafs (III.32). She then asked

Cambyses which he thought was prettier, the lettuce with its leafs or without its leafs. Cambyses answered the former, and she retorted, "But you stripped the leafs of the house of Cyrus and made it like this bare lettuce!"—referring to his murder of Smerdis (III.32). Cambyses was furious. He jumped on her and, being pregnant at the time, she miscarried and died (III.32). It is important to notice that there is no Persian story of the sister's death. If, as we have seen, the Persians cannot say what they cannot do, therefore collapsing truth and law, it appears that it is against Persian law to murder one's sister.

If it appears that for the Persians Cambyses cannot, and therefore did not, murder his sister, it is clear that Cambyses can and therefore did marry his sister, although before his reign it had not been custumary, according to Herodotus, for the Persians to commit incest in this way (III.31). Cambyses managed to change this custom when he had first fallen in love with his older sister Atossa (III.31). He wanted to marry Atossa, but knowing that this was not customary, he summoned the royal judges, those men who judge suits among the Persians and interpret the ancestral statutes (III.31). Cambyses then put this question to the judges: "Is there a law that orders any man who so wishes to live with his sister?" (III.31). According to Herodotus, the judges gave a response that was both "just and safe" (III.31). They told Cambyses that no law could be found that ordered brothers to marry sisters, but that they had found another law that said that the king of Persia could do whatever he wished (III.31). Although it may seem that Cambyses violates the specific customary ban in Persia on incest by marrying his sister, in reality Cambyses is just practicing another form of Persian truth telling. Truth telling reflects the Persian wish that what is internal become completely external, or in other words, that the invisible become visible.[38] Waiting until it is codified in law, Cambyses' incestuous desire no longer remains illicit and secret, but licit and revealed for all to see.

After recounting the outrages Cambyses commited against his household, the Egyptians, and his army, Herodotus speculates that the cause of such madness in Cambyses was his "Sacred Sickness," or the epilepsy from which Cambyses suffered from birth (III.33). According to Herodotus, it is not unusual for a man who suffers a great sickness of body (*tou somatos nouson*), to be unsound of mind (*mede tas phrenas*) as well (III.33). Herodotus thus suggests that the body acts powerfully on the soul, and that this should not be forgotten.[39] Yet, as we have seen with Persian religious practices and their important custom of truth telling, the Persians tend to idealize the soul in separation from the body. The problem with Cambyses therefore, is that his mad acts are a reflection of the radicalization of Persian customs made manifest. Cambyses, gone mad, is a perfect Persian.

Many of the mad acts of Cambyses illustrate the perfection of Persian customs, or the complete contempt for the body and idealization of the soul. For instance, Cambyses enters incestuous marriages with two of his sisters, causing him to blur the distinction between sister and wife. To marry one's sister means to treat her as one would treat a stranger, or in other words to deny the importance of one's bodily connection to her through one's parents, and thus to deny the importance of the private family which is rooted in the body.[40] Although Persians may claim that no one among them has ever killed their parents (I.137), Herodotus shows in the story of Cambyses' incestuous marriages—patricide and matricide being the logical, if metaphorical, extension of incest—that the Persian denigration of the body and elevation of the soul, pushed to its extreme, would lead to just such a "crime." If marriage to one's siblings entails the denial of one's bodily connection to them through one's parents, the murder of one's siblings—as Cambyses murders his younger sister and his brother Smerdis—is a more radicalized version of such a denial. Cambyses not only shows his contempt for the body in his outrages against the family, but also in his killing of the Egyptian calf-god Apis. He scorns the Egyptians for believing in mortal gods, or gods of flesh and blood, which is also consistent with the Persian worship neither of animals nor of heroes but rather of the universal elements of nature and the visible bodies in the cosmos (I.131). It is also consistent with the Magian practice of killing all living things, except for humans and dogs, with their own hands (I.140). Finally, Cambyses' Ethiopian campaign ends in failure because he neglected to make provision for enough supplies of food to feed his army—a bodily concern—before he set out. Herodotus indicates that the abstraction from the body leads not only to the violation of the family but to cannibalism as well.

Truth telling, however, in its desire to make the internal external, is actually a desire to make the soul, which is concealed, act like the body, which is manifest—or vice versa, to make the body act like the soul. Thus, the abstraction from the body, which underlies the custom of truth telling, can actually reduce the person to the body in Persia. This can be seen in what Herodotus says are the other mad acts that Cambyses commited against the rest of the Persians (III.34). For instance, Cambyses asked Prexaspes, whom he trusted and held in high esteem—the Prexaspes who, obeying orders, had killed Cambyses' brother Smerdis—"what sort of man do the Persians think I am? What stories do they tell about me?" (III.34). Prexaspes replied that the Persians praised their king in everything except one; they said that Cambyses drank too much, or, in other words, was an alcoholic. Cambyses, interpreting this to mean that the Persians said that his addiction to wine led him to madness, was overcome with fury (*thumothenta*) and said to Prexaspes:

> Now, you yourself mark whether the Persians are speaking the truth or they themselves are out of their wits (*paraphroneousi*) when they say such things of me. Your son shall stand there in the doorway; if I shoot and hit him in the middle of the heart, the Persians are manifestly talking nonsense. If I miss him, you may say that the Persians are right and I am not in my senses (*me sophroneein*). (III.35)

Cambyses then strung his bow, took his shot, and hit Prexaspes' son right in the middle of the heart, killing the boy in the process. Overjoyed, Cambyses turned to the father and said, "Prexaspes, so I'm not mad (*ou mainomai*) and the Persians are . . . Now you tell me what man in the world do you know who could make a hit like that?" (III.35). Cambyses ignores the private bodily attachments of the family, in this case Prexaspes' special relationship to his son. In addition, Cambyses believes in this instance of madness that the sanity of his mind is reflected in the steadiness of his hand, that his soul acts like his body. The belief that the internal can become external, that soul can become like body, is consistent with the principles underlying the Persian custom of truth telling.[41]

Regimes in Theory

Herodotus concludes his discussion of Cambyses by claiming that his violation of the customs of both the Egyptians and the Persians are definite proofs that Cambyses was mad. Such madness, it has been shown, is actually the result of the perfection of Persian customs themselves, especially the custom of truth telling. However, Herodotus indicates that the Persian focus on speech and the desire that speech be truthful is also what allows a theoretical debate concerning the best regime to take place in Persia. The participants in the Persian debate on government each articulate a regime in speech that they believe is superior to all others. Yet Herodotus shows that regimes in speech are insufficient and must be supplemented by a study of actual regimes in history in order to discover the best regime. Moreover, Herodotus' narrative of the death of Cambyses and then the ascension of Darius to the Persian throne—between which the Persian debate takes place—illustrates that the total dedication to truth telling leads not only to madness, but paradoxically to the collapse of the distinction between truth and falsehood as well.

The death of Cambyses occurs in the context of the revolt of the Magi. Before leaving on his campaign against Egypt, Cambyses had appointed the

Magus Patizeithes to be steward of his household in Persia. Patizeithes had a brother, also a Magus, who had the same appearance as Cambyses' brother Smerdis, as well as the same name, "Smerdis" (III.61). After learning of the murder of Cambyses' brother and that this fact was known only by a few Persians, Patizeithes put his brother on the throne of Persia, "trading on the identity of his name and that of Cyrus' son Smerdis" (III.67). Patizeithes then sent heralds to all the subject kingdoms of the Persian empire, including Egypt, to declare to the Persian army that they now must obey Smerdis, the son of Cyrus—in actuality the false Magian Smerdis—rather than Cambyses (III.61). The herald sent out to Egypt found Cambyses and his army in the Syrian city of Ecbatana. Before a gathering of all concerned, this herald proclaimed the message given to him by Patizeithes (III.62). Cambyses immediately accused Prexaspes of having betrayed him and not killing his brother Smerdis when he was so ordered. Prexaspes, however, protested his innocence to Cambyses, assuring him that he had killed and buried his brother with his own hands. He suggested that the herald be examined as to who sent him, when he proclaimed Smerdis should be obeyed as king (III.62). Cambyses agreed, and Prexaspes, sending for the herald, asked him, "was it Smerdis, in visible form before you, that gave you these instructions, or did you hear it from one of his servants?" (III.63). The herald responded that since the day Cambyses began his march against Egypt, he had not seen Cambyses' brother Smerdis, the son of Cyrus, and that it was the Magus whom Cambyses had left as steward of his household who had given him his instructions, saying that they were the will of Smerdis, son of Cyrus. Cambyses, although convinced that Prexaspes had killed his brother Smerdis after hearing the response of the herald, was still perplexed. He asked Prexaspes, "which of the Persians can it be that trades upon the name of Smerdis and rebels against me?" (III.63). Prexaspes answered, "It is the Magians who have risen against you—the one whom you left behind as steward of your house, Patizeithes, and his brother, Smerdis" (III.63).

According to Herodotus, "When Cambyses heard the name Smerdis, the truth (*aletheie*) of both word (*logon*) and dream struck home" (III.64). Cambyses realized that he had misinterpreted his dream in which a messenger came and told him that Smerdis sat on the throne of Persia (III.30, 64). He now knew that the dream-messenger meant the Magian Smerdis, brother of Patizeithes, rather than his own brother Smerdis, son of Cyrus, and realized that he had killed his brother to no purpose. After weeping bitterly for his brother Smerdis, Cambyses, with the intent to return speedily to Susa and reclaim his throne from the Magus, leapt onto his horse. As he did so however, the scabbord of his sword fell off and the blade punctured his thigh, wounding him mortally (III.64). Suspecting this to be the case, Cambyses asked what city he was in. When told that he was in Ecbatana, Cambyses realized that not only had he misinterpreted his dream but also an oracle, which told him that he would die in Ecbatana. At the time he thought the oracle meant he would die an old man in the Median city of Ecbatana, where he carried on all of his administrative and imperial matters (III.64). He now knew, however, the oracle meant that he would die a young man in the Syrian city of Ecbatana.[42] Herodotus says that Cambyses, overwhelmed by his misinterpretations, what the Magi had done to him, and his wound, recovered his sanity (III.64). He said to himself, "Here is where Cambyses, son of Cyrus, is fated to die" (III.65). Thus the recovery of his sanity leads Cambyses to acknowledge his mortality, and therefore his bodily nature, and that his previous refusal to do so was the cause of his madness.

Cambyses, unable to right things himself, called the most notable Persians together and explained all to them. He told them of his dream and how, as a result of misinterpreting it, he had Prexaspes murder his brother Smerdis, and that now there was a false Smerdis, the brother of the Magus Patizeithes whom he had left in charge of his household, on the throne of Persia, claiming to be the true Smerdis, son of Cyrus (III.65). He then urged the Persians to reclaim the throne from these Median imposters, either by force or by craft, blessing them if they did, laying a curse on them if they did not (III.65). Soon afterwards, Herodotus says, Cambyses died completely childless and without an heir, having ruled for seven years and five months (III.66).[43] However, the Persians who had heard Cambyses' last words did not believe that the Smerdis on the throne was a Magus, but rather that it really was Smerdis, son of Cyrus. Herodotus gives two reasons for their incredulity. First, believing that he was still mad, the Persians thought Cambyses' claim that his brother Smerdis was dead was malicious, thereby hoping to plunge the Persians into civil war after his death. Second, Prexaspes strongly denied that he had killed Smerdis, son of Cyrus and brother to Cambyses, believing that it would have been unsafe for him to admit the truth now that Cambyses was dead (III.66). That Prexaspes, the most trustworthy of Persians, now lies, contrary to the most important Persian custom of truth telling, indicates the confusion and disorder into which Persia descends due to the madness and subsequent death of Cambyses.

The ascendancy of the Magi in Persia is short-lived, however, lasting only seven months, as seven noble Persians—Otanes, Aspathines, Gobryas, Intaphrenes, Megabyzus, Hydarnes, and Darius—soon discover that the Magian Smerdis, with the help of his brother Patizeithes, had indeed usurped the Persian throne. Conspiring together, under the leadership of Darius, the seven storm the royal palace and behead the two usurpers (III.78–79). Carrying their heads through the streets of Susa, the Persian capital, the conspirators incense the populace against the entire Magian priestly class, leading to what Herodotus and the Persians call "The Slaughter of the Magians" (III.79). Cambyses' childlessness and murder of his brother Smerdis, ensuring that Cyrus' royal line was defunct, leaves the conspirators with the task of debating Persia's political future among themselves without interference from traditional political authority or traditional religious authority.[44] Moreover, the question that the seven face is not simply *who* should be Persia's next king but *whether* Persia should have a king. What form of government would it be best for Persia to have? The circumstances surrounding Cambyses' death, therefore, provide the conspirators the opportunity not simply to be the saviors of the Persian regime but to be the founders of a new one.

Herodotus' narrative suggests that the Persian debate concerning the best regime—because it takes place after Persian customs, political succession, and religious authority have been overturned—is actually a debate about what regime is most in accord with universal standards of human nature unaffected by custom or law.[45] The regimes put forward by Otanes, Megabyzus, and Darius in this debate are—as Darius so insightfully points out—what they regard as "best in speech" (*to logo ariston*). These regimes reflect universal natural truths grasped by reason and expressed, so the Persians believe, by speech. According to Benardete, the speeches of Otanes, Megabyzus, and Darius, which "consider the nature of each regime as such [without any regard to local conditions], in light of the nature of man as man," are the most "theoretical speeches in Herodotus."[46]

Otanes, speaking first in the debate, argues in favor of democracy.[47] He begins by arguing against monarchy, and reminds the conspirators of the insolence (*hubris*) of Cambyses and the insolence (*hubris*) of the Magus. Otanes then asks, "[h]ow can monarchy be a suitable thing? The monarch may do what he pleases, with none to check him afterwards. Take the best man on earth and put him into monarchy, and you put him outside of the thoughts that have been wont to guide him. Outrageousness is bred in him by reason of the good things he has, and envy is basic in the nature of man" (III.80). Thus, Otanes begins with the assumption that all individuals are by nature characterized by a certain hubris or spiritedness in their souls, which, if unrestrained by law, leads them, even the best of them, to mad and violent behavior: absolute power corrupts.[48] As examples of such outrageous behavior Otanes says that the monarch kills good men but rewards bad men and that he is offended at those whose flattery is moderate but condemns those whose flattery is abject as obsequious toadies (III.80). For Otanes, it is impossible for his subjects to speak the truth or for the absolute monarch to know the truth.[49]

His greatest charge against the monarch, Otanes asserts, is that the monarch overturns or changes ancestral customs, rapes women, and kills men without trial (III.80).[50] The worst rulers are therefore monarchs unrestrained by law, whom Otanes calls tyrants (III.80). Tyrants, as seen from their overturning of ancestral custom and the raping of women, are characterized by a type of spiritedness that seeks to cross boundaries and make the other one's own. It is consistent with the Persian turn to imperialism and love of beauty that goes along with it (I.135). Is Otanes, in speaking for democracy, arguing against Persian imperial expansion begun by Cyrus?[51]

Otanes argues that rule should be turned over to the many for two reasons. First, "its title is the fairest (*kalliston*) of all—equality before the law (*isonomien*)" (III.80). Second, the universal curb of the law upon all men upheld in a democracy ensures that the multitude do not behave as tyrants do (III.80). Tyranny is prevented in this regime by three mechanisms according to Otanes. First, election to office is by lot, which assumes that all men are equal and that distinctions based on knowledge or character do not have to be made. Second, there is a trial when one finishes serving in office, (*hupeuthunon*), ensuring that one cannot simply do what one wishes as the tyrant does.[52] Finally, all deliberations must be brought before the community for judgment (III.80).[53] Otanes ends his speech by saying, "I vote therefore that we abolish monarchy and increase the power of the people; for in the Many lies All" (III.80).

Megabyzus, speaking after Otanes, argues for oligarchy (III.81). For Megabyzus, an oligarchy does not pursue wealth, nor does it mean the rule of the rich. Rather, he implies that the good or end towards which oligarchy aims is knowledge, achieved by the rule of the few best men by nature whose souls have been educated towards the beautiful and are thus capable of, and desire to perform, noble and courageous deeds of self-sacrifice for the common good.[54] He begins his defense of oligarchy by agreeing with Otanes concerning monarchy—which Megabyzus also calls tyranny—but disagreeing that the multitude should rule (III.81). According to Megabyzus, "[t]here is nothing stupider, nothing more given to outrage (*hubristeron*), than a useless mob (*demou*). Yet surely for men who are fleeing the outrage (*hubrin*) of a despot to fall into the clutches of the outrageous Many, on whom, too, there is no restraint, is in no way bearable" (III.81). Megabyzus claims that in Otanes' regime all will not be equal under the law, but the majority will make the law their instrument of oppression. Megabyzus speaks against the tyranny of the majority, rather than the tyranny of the one, because "[t]he despot, if he does something, does it of knowledge (*ginoskon*)" (III.81). Thus, even if the despot is insolent or hubristic, at least he has knowledge; the multitude only has insolence. The multitude cannot have or act with knowledge, according to Megabyzus, because "they have never been taught what is fine (*kalon*) nor have they any innate sense of it. They rush into things without intelligent purpose, like a river in winter spate" (III.81).[55] What Megabyzus considers beautiful can be seen by looking to the words and actions of Gobryas, who brought Megabyzus into the conspiracy. During the actual struggle with the Magi in the palace, one of the Magi ran into a dark room hoping to escape death, but Gobryas, followed by Darius, ran in after the Magus and threw himself on him (III.78). Gobryas saw that Darius did nothing, and asked him why he did not strike. Darius said "[f]or fear of hitting you," to which Gobryas responded "[d]rive the sword right through, even through the two of us" (III.78). Gobryas believes that achieving honor or glory, through death if necessary, is beautiful. Moreover, Herodotus tells us that in order to help Darius capture Babylon and achieve the honor of being named one of the "Doers of Good Deeds for Persia," Megabyzus' son Zopyrus mutilated his body, by having his nose and ears cut off, his hair shaved, and his body whipped (III.154, 160). He thereby deceived the Babylonians into thinking that he was deserting from the Persians for Darius' mistreatment of him, and thus aided Darius in recapturing the city (III.155, 158). As Benardete points out, the beautiful for Megabyzus and men like him has nothing to do with the body, or what is visible, but rather with the invisible actions of the soul.[56]

Megabyzus, anticipating Socrates, criticizes Otanes' democracy for giving, as it were, a "certain equality to equals and unequals alike."[57] Arguing that the conspirators "choose a society of the Best Men and entrust power to them" (III.81), Megabyzus appeals to what Aristotle will call "distributive justice" with its underlying principle of "geometric" or "proportional" equality, which awards individuals based on unequal natural merit or desert.[58] This is why Megabyzus cannot find beautiful the absolute equality imposed by *isonomien*, as Otanes describes it. In contrast to Otanes, Megabyzus' premise is the natural inequality of souls, based on knowledge and love of the beautiful. Megabyzus ends his speech by saying that among this select few, "we shall be ourselves" (III.81).

Darius, the last to speak in the debate, argues in favor of monarchy that he, unlike the other two speakers, does not call tyranny (III.82). Moreover, Darius structures his speech in defense of monarchy as a criticism of both Megabyzus' proposal for oligarchy and Otanes' proposal for democracy, the core of which is that neither speaker takes enough account of man's selfish regard for himself and his interests, or his private bodily concerns. For Darius, the prime motivator of all human beings is personal gain. He begins by critiquing Megabyzus' speech. Darius claims, "[n]othing is manifestly better than the one best man. He will have judgment (*gnome*) to match his excellence" (III.82). Darius thus implicitly refers to Megabyzus' claim that the despot always acts with knowledge, suggesting that, according to his own principles, Megabyzus should support the establishment of one-man rule rather than the rule of the few. Darius then explicitly addresses Megabyzus' argument for oligarchy. According to Darius, "[i]n an oligarchy, many try to practice virtue for the public good, but in doing so they engender bitter private enmities. Each of the oligarchs wants to be chief man and to win with his opinions, and so they come to great hatreds of one another . . . and from faction comes murder. From murder there is a relapse into (monarchy)" (III.82). That oligarchy degenerates into monarchy proves that the latter, according to Darius, is a superior regime. Darius suggests that Megabyzus' oligarchy cannot work, because the selfish desire among the few best men to be regarded as first in preeminence, or in service to the public good, will eventually lead to civil war and, if not checked by the rise of a monarch, bring the regime to ruin.

Next, Darius addresses Otanes' proposal for democracy. He says that "[w]hen the Many are rulers, it cannot but be that, again, knavery is bred in the state; but now the knaves do not grow to hate one another—they become fast friends. For they combine together to maladminister the public concerns" (III.82). Darius suggests that in a democracy, those few who would seek honor in an oligarchy as a means of satisfying their self-love, will in a democracy become base men who conspire together to use public offices to enrich themselves at the expense of the common good. In a democracy the love of honor turns into the love of money, and soon the entire regime is characterized by greed. Otanes' democracy cannot work therefore, because law, or convention, is too weak to curb the centripetal forces caused by the natural and universal desire for material gain.[59] The only thing that can do so, according to Darius, is the rise of one man who "puts a stop to the knaves," and in so doing is wondered at and revered by the people (III.82).[60] Democracy, like oligarchy, lapses into monarchy. That both these faulty regimes end in monarchy, according to Darius, proves that monarchy is the strongest (*kratiston*) regime (III.82). Thus Darius now refers to monarchy not only as the rule of the wisest, as he did at the beginning of his speech, but also as the rule of the one strongest man who, if he cannot inspire awe for his person, can force his subjects to obey him by inspiring fear of punishment or bodily harm.[61]

Darius concludes his speech by saying "from what source did we gain our freedom, and who gave it to us? The people, or the oligarchy, or the [monarch]? I give my vote that as we were freed by one man, so we should keep this freedom *through* one man . . ." (III.82; emphasis in original). Darius, in contrast to Otanes, praises Cyrus, who led the Persians in revolt against their subjugation to the Medes and began them on their road to imperial conquest (I.125–26).[62] The end or good towards which monarchy aims, according to Darius, is freedom from foreign domination and the pursuit of empire. Darius therefore believes that the requirements of external freedom make internal freedom—oligarchy, with its competition among the few for preeminence, but especially democracy, with its unchecked pursuit of material gain—impossible.[63] According to Herodotus, the other four conspirators, rather than taking the opportunity to establish a new regime, voted in favor of Darius' proposal to reestablish the monarchy (III.83).

When we examine the Persian debate on government in light of Herodotus' general reflections on the actual historical regimes in the *Histories*, it is apparent that he has important reservations about and criticisms of the Persians' abstract theoretical approach to politics.[64] Herodotus indicates that the theoretical study of the best regime is insufficient because regimes in theory make universal claims that cannot be supported when we look to actual regimes that come to be and exist in time.[65] Theoretical regimes rigidly assume that human beings are always the same by nature. They assume that the human is a static or unchanging being, or in Herodotus' "cosmological" analysis, analogous to the element of earth. For instance, Otanes says that human beings are always envious by nature, which leads monarchs unrestrained by law to hate good men, or to be glad at the death of the noble and survival of the base (III.80). Although this may be true of Persian kings some if not most of the time, Herodotus indicates that this is not always the case. For instance, before crossing the Hellespont in his invasion of Greece, Persian king Xerxes, from atop a hill near the town of Abydos, viewed his entire army gathered on the beach and his entire navy anchored along the shore. According to Herodotus, "When Xerxes saw all the Hellespont covered with his ships and all the shores and plains of Abydos full of men, then Xerxes declared himself a happy man; but after that he burst into tears" (VII.45). Artabanus, Xerxes' uncle, asked Xerxes why he wept. Xerxes responded, "pity stole over me as I made my meditation on the shortness of the life of man; here are all these thousands, and not one of them will be alive a hundred years from now" (VII.46). This response illustrates Xerxes' ability to see himself in his men and mourn the fact that although their noble deeds may allow them to conquer the world, human mortality means they cannot conquer time. Otanes is wrong; human beings are not always envious, and even monarchs unrestrained by law can sometimes show great sympathy and compassion.

Megabyzus also makes universal claims. He argues that monarchs, whom he also calls tyrants, always act with knowledge, whereas the many (the *demos*) always rush blindly forward without knowledge. Again, however, Herodotus shows that these two propositions may not always be true. Herodotus recounts that Polycrates, tyrant of Samos, would not listen to the wise counsel of his daughter but went off to negotiate with Oroetes, Persian viceroy of Sardis, despite her warnings. Polycrates was ignobly killed by him (III.124–25). Polycrates does not act with knowledge in this case. As for Megabyzus' second proposition—the inability of the demos to act with knowledge or to take counsel—Herodotus shows that this is not always the case either. After the mines at Laurium had produced a great wealth of silver for the Athenian treasury, the *demos* planned to divide this wealth among them evenly, each man receiving ten drachmas (VII.144). However, they allowed themselves to be persuaded by Themistocles not to redistribute the silver among themselves but rather to use it to build two-hundred ships for the war against Aegina (VII.144). According to Herodotus, "[t]hese ships were not used for the purpose for which they were built, but they were there for Greece at the moment of her need" in the war against the Persians (VII.144). Megabyzus further implies in his speech that oligarchs or the "few best men" always act nobly or without regard to their own selfish desires. Yet Herodotus gives many examples where the opposite is the case. For instance, both Ariston, one of the Spartan kings of the Spartan dual kingship, and his son, Demaratus, steal the wives of other men; in Ariston's case it is the wife of his friend (VI.62, 65). Another king, Leutychides, was caught taking a great bribe of silver not to subdue the country of Thessaly (VI.72).

Darius' main criticism of both Otanes' and Megabyzus' proposals is that neither takes enough account of the selfish nature of man. According to Darius, human beings always act with respect to their own self-interest or material gain, leading the few to be in a violent and bitter enmity with each other that can bring the regime to ruin. However, the example of Prexaspes, Herodotus indicates, proves that Darius' universal claim about human beings is incorrect in the case of some individuals.[66] While the conspirators were discussing how to proceed against the Magi (III.71–73), the Magi themselves attempted to take Prexaspes into a counter-conspiracy. Believing that Prexaspes alone knew that Smerdis, son of Cyrus, was dead, and that the death of Prexaspes' son at the hands of Cambyses (III.35) would bring him over to their cause, the Magi promised him great wealth if he swore not to reveal that the real Smerdis was dead and that the "false" or Magian Smerdis was actually on the throne (III.74). Prexaspes swore to this, and then the Magi made him a second proposition. They were going to call the Persians together and asked that he, Prexaspes, go to the top of the tower on the palace wall and proclaim to the crowd that Smerdis, the son of Cyrus, was on the throne and no one else (III.74). Prexaspes agreed to this as well, but when Prexaspes was on the tower, Herodotus says that he "chose to forget every word of what [the Magi] requested of him . . . [and] told the clear truth" (III.75). Prexaspes explained how he was compelled by Cambyses to murder Smerdis, son of Cyrus, and that the Magus Patizeithes and his brother Smerdis had usurped the throne. According to Herodotus, Prexaspes then "called down many curses on the Persians if they should not win back the power and punish the Magians. Then he threw himself headlong down from the tower. Such was Prexaspes, a notable man all his life and in his death also" (III.75). Prexaspes, in contradistinction to Darius' claim, does not act out of self-interest; having already lost his son, he gives up the wealth promised to him by the Magi as well as his own life for the good of Persia and for the truth.

Nor is Darius' universal claim about the selfishness and enmity of the few correct on the political level. For instance, at Thermopylae, three hundred Spartan hoplites under the command of Leonidas, together with a small group of Thespians, well aware of the end that awaited them, marched out against the Persians of their own free will, and died together in battle (VII.219-223). Furthermore, even when there is enmity between the few this does not always lead to the ruin of the regime or the tyrannical rule of one man. According to Herodotus, the two royal houses in Sparta had been feuding with each other ever since they were founded (VI.52). Yet Sparta had never been ruled by a tyrant (V.92), and it was one of the most powerful cities in Greece.[67] As for the *demos* acting for strictly selfish material reasons, Herodotus shows that this is not always true either. The Athenian refusal to give earth and water to Darius and their decision to fight at Marathon, (VI.103–16, VII.133), showing their willingness to confront the power of Persia, indicates that the Athenian *demos* is dedicated to something higher than mere physical security and pleasure, namely freedom.

The tendency to make universal claims, which assumes that human nature is one dimensional or unchanging, is related to the first problem of regimes in theory, that they unite in speech what is divided in history. For instance, Otanes says that a democracy is characterized by *isonomie* or equality before the law. However, the Athenian democracy that Herodotus describes in book 5 is characterized by *isegorie* or the equal right of speech (V.78). Yet,

Sparta, the regime in the *Histories* whose self-understanding most resembles Megabyzus' description of oligarchy, is ruled by law.[68] Demaratus, an exiled king of Sparta, speaking to Persian king Xerxes about the superior valor of the Spartan soldiers, says "[the Spartans] have as the despot over them Law (*nomos*), and they fear him much more than your men fear you" (VII.104). Thus, what Otanes puts together in speech, in practice becomes separated: equality characterizes Athens, but law characterizes Sparta.[69]

Another example of uniting in speech what is divided in history is Megabyzus' explicit, and Darius' implicit claim that the monarch always *acts* with *knowledge*; they put "wisdom" and action, the latter always performed by particular people in particular places and circumstances, together in speech. However, in book 4, Herodotus shows the particular Persian monarch or regime acting in history, and Darius does not act with knowledge in Scythia. Darius cannot find the Scythians because, as nomads, they are in constant motion. The Scythians, in constant motion, are the perfection of action. When the perfection of wisdom, as Darius presents himself, meets the perfection of action, as Herodotus presents the Scythians, wisdom experiences *aporia*, and therefore fails on the political plane. For Herodotus, the wise monarchs Darius describes in speech do not exist in deed. It is impossible to act with Persian "wisdom" in the human world. Herodotus shows that perfect knowledge is impossible, that no one person is completely knowledgeable. Darius, therefore, cannot justify the absolute rule of one man.

Given that the *Histories* as a whole refutes the universal claims made by the speakers in the Persian debate, Herodotus raises the question of why it is that regimes in theory assume that human beings are, as it were, always the same by nature. Herodotus indicates that this underlying premise of theoretical regimes reveals something about the nature of reason and speech. Thought, in the strict sense in which Socrates describes this phenomenon, tends toward what Socrates calls the "ideas" behind the many particulars in the world. Thought moves toward things that are unchanging or universal, that are always true and therefore can be known.[70] If everything is in flux or is changing, thought, and speech acting as thought's external manifestation becomes very difficult because the reality which words are meant to express keeps changing. The attempt to grasp and express an unchanging reality can be related to the Persian custom of truth telling. Truth telling relies on words spoken having the same unchanging meaning for the listener as for the speaker. Thus the words Persians use attempt to represent an unchanging or universal reality underneath. For Otanes, for example, human beings are always envious and monarchs always wish the death of the good and the survival of the base. For Megabyzus, the many always act in ignorance whereas the monarch always acts with knowledge and the few always act nobly. Darius also makes universal claims in speech, asserting that human beings always act in their own self-interest, whether they are the few who desire honor or the many who desire material gain.

Herodotus reveals the problem with this Persian assumption concerning their words in his treatment of the two "Smerdises"—the brother of Cambyses, and the Magian Smerdis brother of Patizeithes—the immediate historical context out of which the Persian debate arises.[71] The name Smerdis can have a double meaning: it can mean Cambyses' brother or it can mean the Magian Patizeithes' brother (III.61–64). Thus the name "Smerdis" itself can refer to two different realities although the word used to represent them remains the same. This double meaning or referent of the word "Smerdis," which causes confusion and error on the part of Cambyses, is one of the key factors in making the Persian debate on the best regime possible in the first place.[72] It causes Cambyses to kill his brother Smerdis (III.30, 61), and allows the Magian Patizeithes to put his brother Smerdis on the throne (III.61, 67), thus leading unintentionally to the conspiracy of the Seven. What Herodotus is pointing to is a fundamental defect in the Persian way of thinking and mode of speech. Persians such as Otanes, Megabyzus, and Darius grasp a particular aspect of human nature—for example, that they can be envious and greedy or that monarchs can act with knowledge—and use words—as Cambyses' does with the dream-messenger's use of the word "Smerdis," to universalize or idealize that particular. However, if reality is multifarious and changing, should not a real "truth teller" use words to express that variety or change? For example, although Herodotus may agree that human beings can be envious and greedy and that monarchs sometimes act with knowledge, he also shows in his *Histories* that the former can be noble and self-sacrificing and that the latter sometimes act in ignorance. In other words, Herodotus can use words to reveal the particular *as* the particular and therefore changing, and not mistakenly as the universal.[73] In doing so, Herodotus creates the conditions for discovering and therefore expressing what is truly universal about human beings.[74] Moreover, if words can express the particular and changing things in the world, and the universal and unchanging, and even make it seem as if a particular were the universal, then this means that words can conceal as well as reveal the "truth" at the same time.[75]

Another phenomenon making it difficult for speech to express the reality that the mind attempts to grasp is that words, in the attempt to act as thought's external manifestation of the "ideas," tend not simply to universalize the particular but also to make the complex things in the world appear as if they were simple or uniform beings without parts. For instance, the

Persians are aware that a human being is composed of body and soul, but in their debate on government each speaker proposes a separate regime based on either the assumed characteristics of the soul or those of the body. Otanes, who argues against monarchy on the assumption that the envious or hubristic nature of the human soul needs the restraint of law, and Megabyzus, who argues in favor of oligarchy in the belief that the few best men will have souls educated toward the beautiful, emphasize competing characteristics of the soul when proposing which regime will be best for Persia. Darius, on the other hand, especially when arguing against democracy and in favor of monarchy, looks to the characteristics of the body. In a democracy, according to Darius, the universal desire for material gain is too strong to be contained by law, whereas in a monarchy the ruler can force his subjects to obey him by inspiring fear of punishment through bodily harm. Otanes, Megabyzus, and Darius make it seem as if the essence of a human being is either the soul or the body, rather than portraying the human being as a complex combination of the two. Moreover, each speaker in the debate proposes a separate regime based on the incompatibility or antagonism between the rule of the many, the few, or the one. Yet, at Marathon, in book 6, when we see the Athenian regime pushed to its limit in war, all of its elements seem to be revealed. First, Miltiades, one man, is chosen by the many (*demou*) to be their general (VI.104). Then, in persuading the other Athenian generals to fight the Persians, it is Callimachus, the polemarch, a position still lingering from an older aristocratic order before Cleisthenes, who casts the deciding vote in favor of fighting (VI.109–10). Thus, Athens, at crucial moments in its history, seems able to combine the rule of the one, the few, and the many. Persian words, therefore, not only unite in speech what is separate in deed, but also do the opposite. They *separate* in speech what is *connected* in deed, or they take parts out of regimes or greater wholes in history by making the part appear as if it were the whole.

Darius: Truth and Falsehood

Herodotus' implication that words can deceive or both reveal and conceal the truth, points to another problem with the Persian dedication to truth telling: the Persian attempt to tell the truth absolutely and at all times can actually lead to the collapse in the distinction between truth and falsehood. That lying and truth telling become blurred in Persia is illustrated by the fact that although the Persians are exceptionally committed to telling the truth, Herodotus shows that in practice they lie. Perhaps the most memorable example of this is Darius' deception of his coconspirators in having himself chosen as Persia's next king. After the majority of the co-conspirators voted in favor of Darius' proposal for monarchy, they, excepting Otanes, decided to choose a king from among themselves (III.83–84).[76] The peculiar method they settled on to select Persia's next king required "that all of them should mount their horses in the outskirts of the city and, as the sun rose, whichever horse neighed first, his rider should possess the throne" (III.84). Not satisfied as his fellow conspirators were to leave the selection of king to chance, Darius secretly approached his groom Oebares with the plan and instructed him as follows: "if you have any trick to deal with this, contrive that we win the prize and not someone else" (III.85). Duly cooperating in his master's plan of deceit, Oebares, in the middle of the night, led the stallion that Darius would ride in the contest along with the mare that this horse loved most to the outskirts of the city. After restraining him for some time, Oebares finally let the stallion mate with his favored mare. At dawn the next day, as the contestants for the kingship rode through the outskirts of Susa, when Darius' horse reached the spot where he had been allowed to mate with the mare, he "plunged forward and neighed," thus clinching the throne for Darius (III.86). According to Herodotus, immediately upon the neighing of his horse, "[t]he other riders jumped down from their horses and did obeisance to Darius" (III.86).

By illuminating the fact that the second royal line in Persia after Cyrus' line had become extinct was founded on a deception perpetrated by Darius, it would seem, as Thompson suggests, that "Persian truth telling is . . . [Herodotus'] broadest subject of attack."[77] Herodotus, according to Thompson, shows that Persian claims to be truth tellers are simply belied by deeds.[78] To understand how the custom of truth telling can lead to deceit, we must understand that the Persian insistence on telling the truth is not simply an attempt to express or name correctly the reality of the world that exists outside of the speaker. It is also an attempt to express the reality or truth of the soul that is within the speaker. The Persian insistence on truth telling seeks to make the internal intentions or mind of the speaker perfectly known to the listener, and therefore to make the invisible visible or to make the soul perfectly known. Truthful speech is an attempt by the Persians to universalize the soul or to share it with, and let it be known by, others. However, knowing or "seeing" the soul, as it were, requires the disappearance of the body and hence the material and visible part of the human being. The Persians idealize the soul or attempt to get beneath the surface of things to see what is under the skin.[79] Yet setting aside the visible exteriors in an attempt to reach into the invisible interior of things means that in Persia nothing visible or external to speech itself can verify its truth. This makes it very difficult to distinguish truthful speech from speech that lies. If "seeing is *not* believing," as it were, how can we come to know what is real, or distinguish fact from fiction?

The difficulty in distinguishing truthful from untruthful speech, leading to the collapse in the distinction itself, is illustrated by Herodotus in his account of Otanes' exchange with his daughter Phaedyme before the revolt of the Seven against the Magi, followed by Darius' speeches to his coconspirators after having joined the conspiracy himself. Otanes, after the death of Cambyses, was the first to suspect that the Smerdis on the throne was actually the Magian Smerdis and not Smerdis, the son of Cyrus (III.68). He suspected this because the Magus never appeared before the Persian nobles but kept himself hidden within the palace. To confirm his suspicions, Otanes inquired of his daughter Phaedyme with whom he was sleeping. After having been married to Cambyses, Phaedyme was now married to the Magus who had taken all of Cambyses' wives when he usurped the throne. Phaedyme sent back to her father that, since she had never seen Smerdis, the son of Cyrus, she had no idea with whom she slept (III.68). Otanes then sent Phaedyme a second message, saying, "[i]f you yourself do not know Smerdis, the son of Cyrus, find out from Atossa with whom she and you are sleeping. Certainly she knows her own brother" (III.68). Phaedyme then sent word to her father again, telling him that she could not speak with Atossa or any of the other wives, as the man with whom she now slept had secluded all of them in separate apartments in the palace. Otanes, according to Herodotus, was now almost certain that the Magian Smerdis had usurped the throne. But, not trusting fully in the words of his daughter, Otanes wanted one last proof. He sent again to his daughter and said, "[d]o this now: when he is sleeping with you and you know that he is deeply asleep, feel for his ears. If you find that he has ears, you may be sure that you are sleeping with Smerdis, the son of Cyrus. If not, you are with Smerdis the Magian" (III.69). Herodotus says that Cyrus, during his reign, had cut off the Magus' ears for some serious offense that Herodotus does not identify. Phaedyme courageously carried out her father's orders, and found that the man with whom she was sleeping had no ears. At dawn, she sent her father Otanes the news.

Upon receiving the news, Otanes decided to conspire against the Magian Smerdis. Otanes gives his reason for wishing to revolt against the Magus in his third message to his daughter: "[i]f this is not Smerdis, son of Cyrus, but the man I suspect he is, he should not get off scot free with sleeping with you and ruling Persia; he must pay for both crimes" (III.69). The Magus can commit what Otanes considers these crimes because, "trading on the identity of his name and that of Smerdis, son of Cyrus," he can pretend to be the person he is not. Otanes is outraged at the Magus because he is not who he says he is, and thus practices deceit; he lies or conceals the truth. The Magus is therefore in violation of the Persian custom of truth telling, which seeks to make "what is," or the true nature of something, manifest. Otanes' motive in conspiring against the Magian Smerdis and his brother Patizeithes is to restore adherence to law and the customary—and therefore to restore what he regards as adherence to truth. Otanes wants to bring "what is" and "what ought to be" back together again. In order to effect such a restoration, Otanes initiates a revolt against the usurper.

In the exchange between Otanes and his daughter Phaedyme, particularly when Otanes has his daughter feel for the Magus' ears to confirm his suspicions, Herodotus indicates that in the absence of sight—the Magus never appears before the Persians and Phaedyme had never seen Smerdis, son of Cyrus—the truthfulness of words, in this case the name "Smerdis" and those of Phaedyme to her father, need the confirmation of touch.[80] Yet, given the Persian emphasis on truth telling that elevates the soul over the body or the invisible over the visible, it seems that in a sense this is always the case in Persia—and not just with respect to the discovery of the Magus. In Persia nothing visible or external to speech, aside from actual touch, can verify the truth of speech itself. This makes the determination of whether speech is true or false very difficult. For example, although we cannot touch the sun, as Phaedyme can touch the man with whom she is sleeping, must not we speak as if it is there, both during the day when we can see it and even at night when we cannot?

Herodotus reveals the collapse in the distinction between truth and falsehood in a series of exchanges between Darius and Otanes on how the conspiracy should proceed. Darius both implicitly and explicitly advocates lying. The last to enter the conspiracy, Darius counseled haste, arguing that they should move to kill the usurper without delay (III.71). Otanes, a more moderate and cautious man than Darius, says to him, "do not be foolish about this plan, but do so at a more prudent pace. It would be better to make the attempt when there are more in the plot" (III.71).[81] In response to Otanes' appeal for prudence and caution, Darius says to the conspirators:

> You men who are here: if you follow the way described by Otanes, you will find that you will die, and die most horribly. For someone will give information to the Magian; this someone's aim will be personal gain. You would have done best to run the risk on your own. Since you decided to enlarge the conspiracy and take me in, we must either act today or, I would have you know, if a single day goes by beyond this, no informer

> will outstrip me myself: I will go and tell the whole matter to the Magian. (III.71)

Otanes, exasperated with Darius' rashness and selfish threats, again tries to restrain him by asking, "Come, tell us how we are to get into the palace and attack these men . . . the guards are set all around . . . [h]ow shall we get past the guards?" (III.72). Darius responds, "Otanes, there are many things which cannot be described in word (*logo*) and yet they may be done (*ergo*), again there are many that are capable of being planned in word (*logo*), and yet no great action (*ergon*) has ever resulted" (III.72). In proposing the separation of speech and deed, Darius denies the Persian claim that they cannot do what they cannot say and thus that everything done can be said. As we learn from Herodotus in book 1, "whatsoever things it is not permitted to [the Persians] to do, of these they must not even speak" (I.138). By severing the truth which words are supposed to express from the actual deeds or bodily movements of men, Darius implicitly undermines the Persian custom of truth telling by transforming all speech in Persia into simply meaningless "talk" or "chatter." Persian words become images that do not represent an underlying reality to ground them or prevent their manipulation. However, Herodotus, as we have seen, shows in his account of the exchange between Otanes and his daughter Phaedyme (III.68–69), that this transformation is actually the result of the principle underlying the Persian custom of truth telling pushed to its extreme. Truth telling wishes to suppress the body and thus nothing visible or external to speech can verify the truth of speech itself, making it almost impossible to distinguish between truth and falsehood. Darius, in separating speech and deed—and thus implicitly undermining the distinction between true and false speech—is actually speaking perfect Persian, as it were.

Darius explicitly undermines the Persian dedication to truth telling when he says, in an attempt to calm the queries of Otanes, if the palace guards do not give the conspirators entry simply from respect and fear for their high rank, he will lie and tell the guards that he has "just come from Persia" with an important message from his father to the king (III.72). Darius justifies this very un-Persian plan by saying:

> Where a lie must be told let it be told. Those of us who lie and those of us who tell the truth are bent upon the same object. The liars lie when they would win profit by convincing others of their lies, the truth-tellers tell the truth so that by their truth they may draw gain to themselves and be the more trusted. Our practices are different, but our aim is the same. If it were not for the hope of gain therefrom, the man who tells the truth might equally lie, and the liar tell the truth. (III.72)[82]

Darius thus collapses the distinction between the one who lies and the one who tells the truth by maintaining that either form of speech is motivated by personal gain. The motivator of human beings for Darius is selfish interest. Thus, just as Darius turns the Persian custom of truth telling upside down by advocating lying, so he turns the Persian elevation of soul over body upside down by elevating the body, out of which our private or selfish interests are derived. Moreover, like Cambyses' confusion over the meaning of the name "Smerdis," Darius' blurring of the distinction between lying and truth telling is crucial in making the Persian debate on government possible. It convinces the other conspirators to take swift and immediate action against the Magi, rushing on the palace and killing the usurpers (III.78–79).

In his narrative of the Persian debate on government and the death of Cambyses and conspiracy of the seven leading up to it, Herodotus indicates that words can conceal as well as reveal the truth. They can represent the particular not simply as the particular but also incorrectly as the universal—and make what is complex seem simple. It is this truth about words that is related to the fact that regimes in theory not only unite in speech what is separate in deed, but also that they, as we have seen, separate in speech what is connected in deed—or take parts out of wholes by universalizing the particular.

Herodotus illustrates the tendency of words to separate in speech what is united in deed in many places in the *Histories*. For instance, Herodotus explains in book 1 that the Athenians and the Ionians of Asia Minor are in fact all of one Ionian stock, who in turn are descended from the ancient Pelasgian race (I.143). Yet the Athenians, according to Herodotus, were ashamed of the name "Ionian," meaning something disgraceful to them, and thus refused to identify themselves by that name (I.143). The Ionians of the "Twelve Cities" or "Panionium" in Asia Minor however, were proud of the name "Ionian," meaning something glorious to them, and thus openly identified themselves as such (I.143). It seems that just as democracy, oligarchy, and monarchy—as well as body and soul—can be divided in speech by the Persian debaters, so the one common Pelasgian race, due to the double meaning of the word "Ionian," can be divided into "Athenian" and "Ionian," two different names or words themselves.[83] Perhaps words separate what is united or take parts out of wholes to make intelligible the unchanging things that exist within wholes—human beings, cities, nations, or races—that are in motion or act in history. Yet Herodotus believes that words also distort the truth or make things unintelligible. He suggests that it is impossible to speak without lying and telling the truth at the same time, or to occupy a middle position between Darius' proposal for dissimulation and Otanes' insistence on truthfulness.

Herodotus indicates that a true understanding of speech would regard the use of words as a mean between lying and truth telling. If words, in contrast to Persian assumptions, can both reveal and conceal, lie and tell the truth at the same time, they are complex and thus require interpretation because words like "Smerdis" and "Ionian" can incorporate a variety of meanings. Yet there is a correct interpretation; they do not mean whatever Cambyses, the Ionians, or the Athenians want them to mean. There is a reality lying underneath. Words incorporate permanence and change, the complex and the simple, the universal as well as the particular. Regimes that have this understanding of the complex character of speech, and therefore have access to the truth, would have a Herodotean rather than a Persian perspective and, in Herodotus' eyes, would be best. It is to this best regime that we turn next.

Chapter 4

Athens and Regimes in History

Introduction

In Herodotus' survey of actual historical regimes, Athens stands at the peak of the political possibilities that he explores.[1] It is Athens, not Sparta, which is responsible for preserving Greek freedom against Persian attempts to incorporate Greece into a Persian empire ruled by a single Persian king. Crucial for Athens' service to Greek freedom is the Athenian mind's inclination, like that of the Persians, toward universal truths, such as the nature of human beings unclothed by custom or regime. Herodotus demonstrates the Athenian grasp of the universal in his account of the battle of Marathon. The Athenians are victorious over the Persians because they approach the latter not as divine conquerors destined to rule but as human beings like themselves who share the same nature.

The Athenian access to universal or natural truth leads them to possess a form of courage that differs from that possessed by the Spartans. As demonstrated in the battle of Thermopylae, Spartan courage is defensive and characterized by a self-regarding spiritedness that seeks to defend its boundaries and what is its own. Spartans on the battlefield "stand firm" or are at rest. The Athenians, on the other hand—as demonstrated in their actions at the battles of Marathon and Salamis—possess an aggressive form of courage that is characterized by a spiritedness directed outwards. It leads to the attempt to transcend boundaries, to look on and possibly acquire what is foreign to oneself. Athenians on the battlefield and at sea are in motion. Their grasp, in mind, of the universal or that which is at rest leads the Athenians, like the Persians, to be on the move politically. Although Herodotus indicates that the Athenians possess a higher type of courage than the Spartans, he also implies that this in itself creates the danger that Athens will become as imperial as Persia. Herodotus points to the prospect that Athens, like Persia, may attempt to imitate in the political world the universalism that they grasp in the natural world.

The Athenian mind's access to universal truth, with the particular form of courage and the danger of empire that it spawns, is derived from Athens' democratic regime. The Athenian democracy, characterized by *isegorie*, or the equality and freedom of speech, moves the Athenians from a belief in the divine foundation of their regime to a human one, and thus allows the Athenians to internalize their regime. For the Athenians, the regime is something within themselves and not a product of something, such as the gods, outside themselves. Because the human rather than the divine is brought to light as the source of politics, Athens is able to solve the difficulty of combining equality with government by instituting self-government. Moreover, unlike the Egyptians, Scythians, and Persians, the Athenians are more successful in integrating the whole of human nature, both body and soul, in a way that makes possible a life according to the highest human potential—or seeing things in the way that Herodotus does. This includes an appreciation for the complex character of speech. Athenians, guided by Themistocles, understand that words can have more than one meaning, incorporating permanence and change, the universal as well as the particular, and thus require interpretation for the truth to be revealed. Speech, especially divine speech, can both reveal and conceal the truth at the same time.

Herodotean scholarship has been divided over the question of whether or not the *Histories* reveals a systematic analysis of politics. Sara Forsdyke argues that it is only in the last two decades that scholars have begun to view Herodotus as a thinker with deep political understanding rather than simply as a storyteller of the wondrous with no interest in politics. Specifically, Forsdyke points to recent trends that recognize Herodotus' narrative of Spartan and Athenian history in the pre-Persian Wars, archaic period as an important reflection of the values, beliefs, and ideologies of his later fifth-century BCE Greek audience.[2] Also, Forsdyke argues that in his explanation of Persian expansion and in his portrait of Persian king Xerxes, Herodotus intends to draw a tacit parallel between the imperialism of Persia—the perceived injustice of which was confronted by the Greeks, led by Athens, during the Persian Wars—and the imperialism of Periclean Athens at the root of the Peloponnesian War.[3]

Scholars have been divided not only over whether Herodotus thinks politically. Among those scholars who view the *Histories* as a work of political theory there is considerable debate over which regime Herodotus thinks is best. For example, Stanley Rosen and Stewart Flory focus on the theoretical regimes of the Persian debate on government in book 3 of the *Histories*. They argue that Herodotus, thinking like a Persian, favors monarchy. Darius' portrait of the monarch in his speech in the Persian debate comes closest to representing Herodotus' own views because, for Rosen, he resembles Machiavelli's prince; for Flory, he resembles Plato's philosopher king.[4] On the other hand, Charles W. Fornara argues that Herodotus expressed high regard for the political freedom of Greece as opposed to the despotism of Persia. However, Fornara claims that this should not be understood as an endorsement of Athenian democracy on the part of Herodotus, as his admiration for Spartan government was greater than any positive feeling he expressed for Athens.[5] Christopher Pelling agrees, arguing that *isonomia* as used by Otanes in the Persian debate on government does not signify a democratic regime but rather reflects the absence of tyranny. *Insonomia* can thus embrace nondemocratic Greek states such as aristocratic Sparta.[6] Carl Page and E. N. Tigerstedt also think that aristocratic Sparta, largely due to its manifestation of courage displayed at the battle of Thermopylae, stands at the peak of Herodotus' classification of regimes.[7]

Others argue, as I do, that Herodotus preferred Athenian democracy to Spartan aristocracy and Persian monarchy. For instance, Sara Forsdyke and Kurt Raaflaub, unlike Fornara and Pelling, closely link Herodotus' positive attitude toward political freedom with his praise of Athenian democracy and its most important institution, *isegorie*, the equality of speech. Moreover, Forsdyke and Raaflaub argue that for both Herodotus and the democratic ideology of his fifth-century Athenian audience, it was *isegorie* that gave rise to Athenian military strength and their decisive victory at Salamis under the leadership of Themistocles.[8] Similarly, Binyamin Shimron concludes that the *Histories* reveals Herodotus' appreciation for the superiority of Athenian naval power during the Persian Wars.[9] Peter Euben and Arlene Saxonhouse go further than Forsdyke, Raaflaub, and Shimron. Euben maintains that Herodotus recognized Athenian political freedom not only as the foundation of their victory at Salamis but also of his own activity of writing the *Histories*.[10] Saxonhouse argues that Herodotus believed that *isegorie*, understood as the freedom of speech, made the Athenians "better" and that this belief was also adopted by Plato's Socrates and his interlocutors in their philosophic conversations. For Saxonhouse, there is an "association of both freedom of speech and democracy with the practice of philosophy as understood in the world of

Socratic dialogue."[11] Moreover, Saxonhouse claims that Herodotus' "ethnographic" or cultural studies in the first four books of the *Histories* reveal his commitment to a human equality that is at the core of democratic institutions. Thus, Saxonhouse argues, like Donald Lateiner, that the principle of equality and the opposition to tyranny that underlies Otanes' speech in favor of democracy makes him the speaker in the Persian debate on government closest to Herodotus' own political perspective.[12]

Building on those who view Athens as Herodotus' best regime, I argue that the *Histories* reveals Athenian democracy at the peak of Herodotean political science. However, I also claim in this chapter and the next that Herodotus' portrait of Athens as the best regime must be understood in light of his simultaneous critique of Athens' potential for imperialism. Moreover, I argue that Herodotus' praise of Athenian democracy comes to light against his narrative of its founding in book 1 of the *Histories* and then its refounding in book 5. In book 1 of the *Histories* Herodotus investigates the founding of the Athenian democracy within the context of his larger investigation into the origins of the regimes that existed in Sparta, Media, and Persia. Herodotus' analysis sheds light on the problems of founding political regimes in a way that helps us to better understand them. The difficulty of combining government with freedom and equality, and the subsequent appeal to the divine as a source of legitimacy, appears as a persistent problem at the origin of the Athenian, Spartan, and Median political orders. Herodotus, however, indicates the essentially provisional character of such an appeal in the story of Cyrus and the founding of the Persian Empire. It is to the founding and then refounding of the democratic regime in Athens that we shall now turn.

The Origins of Political Power

Herodotus recounts that the Athenian democracy was first founded by Solon, a "wise" man who made laws for the Athenians at their request (I.29).[13] Yet, Herodotus says that in order to remove the people's temptation to petition him for changes to the new laws that he had made, Solon bound the Athenians by oath to obedience to his measures and then left Athens himself for ten years (I.29). During this time abroad Solon came to Sardis and the court of Croesus, tyrant of Lydia (I.29). Thus, Herodotus indicates that in order to obey the laws, the Athenians cannot see the man behind the law; he must withdraw or become invisible. The Athenians must come to believe that the power behind the laws, especially new laws, is not simply human but rather, in its invisibility and distance, god-like or even divine. This is true, according to Herodotus, of the Spartans as well.

Herodotus maintains that before Lycurgus the Spartans, of all the Greeks, had the worst laws (I.65). Yet, they dispensed with their bad laws in favor of good ones at the behest of Lycurgus (I.65). Unlike this positive judgment on the laws of Lycurgus, Herodotus is silent on whether Solon's laws were good or bad. Furthermore, although not giving an account of any of the laws that Solon gave, Herodotus is slightly more specific with regard to Lycurgus' laws. According to Herodotus, the good laws of Lycurgus had two components: those which related to war and those which related to the structure of government. With respect to war, Lycurgus instituted the "sworn companies," the "regiments of thirty," and the "communal meals" (I.65). Lycurgus' military institutions therefore emphasized friendship and the public, as opposed to the private, enjoyment of pleasure. Thus the common good was emphasized over the individual good. With respect to the structure of government, Lycurgus imposed the institution of the ephors and the "council of elders" (*gerousia*) onto the dual kingship. The latter, Herodotus indicates, predating Lycurgus' reforms.[14] The Council of Elders was composed of a small group of twenty-eight Spartans over sixty years of age who held their positions for life, as well as the two kings (VI.57).[15] The ephors were five in number and held their position for a year.[16] They were elected by the entire citizen body, but full citizenship itself was quite small. Many people in Sparta and the surrounding area of Laconia were reduced to the very cruel slavery of "helotry" under the reforms of Lycurgus (VI.58).[17] Thus, although in form a type of mixed regime, Lycurgus' structures lean more towards "oligarchy," the rule of the few.[18] From both his laws having to do with war and those having to do with governmental structures, Herodotus indicates that the regime founded by Lycurgus aimed to combine political hierarchy with the suppression of the private in favor of the public; it attempted to fuse inequality with community.

Herodotus maintains that before his founding activity Lycurgus left Sparta and traveled to Delphi (I.65). There the Pythia suggested that Lycurgus was more divine than human, saying,

> Is it you Lycurgus that comes to my rich temple? Lycurgus, dear to Zeus and to all that hold the halls of Olympus? I ask myself whether, in prophecy, as a god or a man I shall hail you. Nay, but tis rather a god that I see in you, Lycurgus. (I.65)

According to Herodotus, many Greeks believe that the Pythia declared to Lycurgus all of the laws that he established in Sparta (I.65). The Spartans themselves, however, believe that Lycurgus then traveled to Crete and brought his laws back from there (I.65).[19] Yet, after his death, the Spartans erected a shrine in Lycurgus' honor, and they still, according to Herodotus, worship him as a hero (I.66). Thus, the Spartans—like the Athenians—in order to obey the law must believe that the power behind the law, or the lawgiver, is divine or god-like.

In the stories of Solon and Lycurgus, Herodotus indicates that at the same time laws or regimes are founded, a notion of divinity behind the laws arises, and that such a notion obscures the rational human agency involved. This leads to the discrepancy between what people say of the regime—that it is divinely inspired—and what actually operated in its creation—human reason or will. Herodotus shows the political dangers of such divine founding myths in the story of Pisistratus and his establishment of tyranny in Athens.

Pisistratus, Herodotus indicates, first established his tyranny in Athens approximately two years after Solon's visit to the court of Croesus (I.34, 46). Solon's attempt to have his laws take root by leaving Athens for ten years—thereby making the power behind the law invisible or god-like—did not work. Rather, a civil war broke out among the Athenians between the "Men of the Coast," led by Megacles, son of Alcmaeon, and the "Men of the Plain," led by Lycurgus, son of Aristolaides (I.59). Pisistratus, having an eye on tyranny according to Herodotus, contrived his own faction, the "Men of the Hill."[20] Forthwith he injured himself and his mules and drove his carriage into the marketplace, claiming that he had just escaped his enemies' attempt to kill him (I.59). Pisistratus then asked the common people (*demou*), among whom he was held in high regard, for a bodyguard to protect his person and their interests (I.59).[21] Deceived, the people, according to Herodotus, granted Pisistratus' request (I.59). With this new body of troops Pisistratus seized the Acropolis and established his rule over the Athenians. Yet, Herodotus maintains that Pisistratus "in no way deranged the existing magistries or the ordinances (*thesmia*) but governed the city well and nobly according to [Solon's] laws that were established" (I.59).[22]

Not regarded as divine or supported by the divine, however, the all-too-human Pisistratus was soon driven out of Athens by the factions of Megacles and Lycurgus, having reconciled their differences for this purpose (I.60). Yet, as soon as the common threat of Pisistratus was removed, the two factions fell into feuding with one another again. According to Herodotus, when Megacles began to lose to the faction of Lycurgus, he made overtures to the exiled Pisistratus, proposing that if he agreed to marry his daughter, the latter would help Pisistratus regain the tyranny of Athens (I.60). Pisistratus agreed to the terms, and the two men contrived what Herodotus calls the "most simple-minded" deceit against the Athenians. According to Herodotus, the Athenians were supposed to be the "first in intelligence" among the Greeks who in turn were reputed to be distinguished from the barbarians for their "cleverness" (I.60). Megacles and Pisistratus took a very tall and beautiful Athenian woman named Phya, dressed her in full armor, and put her into a chariot. As they drove her into the city, they sent heralds ahead shouting, "Men of Athens, receive with good will Pisistratus, whom Athena herself, having honored him above all mankind, is bringing back from exile to her own Acropolis" (I.60). The rumor immediately spread throughout the city that Pisistratus was being escorted back by Athena, and the people, according to Herodotus, were convinced "that this woman was the goddess herself and offered prayers to her, for all that she was only human, and they welcomed Pisistratus" (I.60).[23]

The story of Pisistratus' second establishment of his tyranny illustrates the dangers of divine founding myths. Because the Athenians believed that their regime was a product of divine rather than human agency, Pisistratus was able to convince them that divine will had changed, thus enabling him to overturn the democracy and establish himself as tyrant. Athenian belief in divine support of their law left them susceptible to tyranny.[24]

Pisistratus, however, loses his tyranny over Athens for a second time because, although marrying Megacles' daughter as per his agreement, he refused to have sex with her "after the customary manner" (I.61). According to Herodotus, Pisistratus did not want to have children with his new wife because he already had grown sons whom he wanted to succeed him and because he believed the Alcmaeonidae were under a curse (I.61).[25] Megacles was furious when he learned of the situation and once again reconciled with the party of Lycurgus. In response Pisistratus removed himself from Athens and fled to Eretria. Yet, after ten years of exile, on the advice of his son Hippias, Pisistratus decided to return to Athens. According to Herodotus, Pisistratus and his party marched to Marathon, and, while encamped, "there came to them factionaries from the city, and there was influx, too, from the country villages, of people to whom the rule of one man (*turannis*) was more welcome than freedom" (I.62).[26] With these reinforcements Pisistratus took over Athens for a third time and, according to Herodotus, he now "rooted his power securely" (I.64). First, he brought in mercenary soldiers loyal to him (I.63–64). Second, he collected revenues from "both the people on the spot and from the districts about the river Strymon," and, third, he took the sons of prominent Athenians as hostages and removed them to Naxos (I.64). Herodotus shows that in the absence of divine support, a man who wishes to rule other men can do so through fear, the seizure of property, cruelty, and forced depopulation.

Herodotus' story of Pisistratus shows not only the dangers of divine founding myths, but also allows us to consider why Athens succumbs to tyranny while Sparta does not. Herodotus presents one difference between the founding or law-giving activity of Lycurgus and that of Solon that may be relevant. Whereas Lycurgus leaves Sparta and travels to Delphi and Crete before he returns to give his laws, Solon gives his laws to the Athenians first and then leaves the city. As far as we know from Herodotus, Solon never returns, but simply disappears from the narrative.[27] In the case of Lycurgus, who leaves but then returns to the city, the divine or god-like founder is visible and present. Thus it would seem that although the divine has to be invisible to be thought of as divine, it also has to be visible or present to be feared and obeyed. For instance, Xerxes, who tried to make himself and was believed by his subjects to be like Zeus (VII.8, 56), had a notion of the divine similar to that of Lycurgus. Xerxes believed that his navy had not fought well at the battle of Artemisium due to his absence; when Xerxes decided to engage the Athenians at sea in the battle of Salamis, he was determined to be present. He watched his men from a distance on a raised throne on a hillside in Phalerum (VIII.69). Although he lost the battle, Xerxes' men did fight better at Salamis than they did at Artemisium because, according to Herodotus, "everyone fought with zest and in fear of Xerxes, and every man of them thought that the King was watching him" (VIII.86). Xerxes, representative of Zeus on earth for his subjects, was distant enough to give his sailors room to fight—he did not partake in the battle himself—but was also close enough to touch them with his eyes and thus make them fight well.

For Solon, on the other hand, the god-like founder who leaves the city and never returns in the narrative, the divine is more invisible than visible. The gods are understood as divine, but they are not feared by the Athenians as they are by the Spartans. For instance, the Athenians, who bound themselves to obedience for ten years, break their oaths and fall into civil war only two years after Solon had left. Solon leaves the gods too distant to be concerned directly in political affairs or to punish violations of their laws—they are not as public-spirited as the gods of Lycurgus. Solon's laws, therefore, need to be maintained and enforced by a human being. It is in this sense that Solon's understanding of the divine as mostly invisible or absent leaves Athens susceptible to tyranny and opens the way for Pisistratus. As Herodotus remarks of Pisistratus' first tenure as tyrant, "[he] governed the city well and nobly according to the laws that were established" (I.59).[28] Yet, Herodotus also shows in the story of Pisistratus that human enforcement relies on external compulsion, as opposed to divine enforcement which relies on internal compulsion produced by belief in punishing gods.

Solon, however, despite having left the city himself, did leave laws in Athens. He is thus a mix of staying and going away, of visibility and invisibility. Yet, in disappearing after his founding activity is complete, Solon, in contrast to Lycurgus, places more stress on the invisible and absent character of the gods. He thus places stress on only one half of the whole of their dual identity. This distant and antinomian aspect of the divine, emphasized by Solon, can also be seen in his exchange with Croesus about the question of happiness. Herodotus says that, when Solon arrived in Sardis, Croesus had his servants take Solon on a tour of all his treasure houses (I.30). Croesus then asked Solon to name the happiest human being he had ever seen, sure that he would win the prize for his great wealth (I.30). However, Solon answered that the happiest man he knew of was Tellus of Athens. Tellus had sons who were both beautiful and good when his city was in a good condition, and he died bravely in battle fighting for his city, for which the Athenians honored him with a public funeral (I.30). The understanding of happiness that Solon expresses in his story of Tellus is clearly from the point of view of the city and its laws, as it suggests that the good life can only be found in the enjoyments of the family, which depends on the good condition of the city, as well as activity within, and sacrifice for, the public sphere.

Croesus, however, was surprised at Solon's answer and prodded him further, asking him to name the second happiest human being he knew of, thinking that he would surely be named this time (I.31). Once again Solon disappointed Croesus and named Cleobis and Biton, two Argive brothers who were strong and who both won Olympic prizes (I.31). Cleobis and Biton were extremely dutiful to their mother and, when the oxen failed to come in from the fields, harnessed themselves to their mother's wagon and pulled her forty stades to Hera's temple, so that she could celebrate the festival in honor of the goddess (I.31). Overjoyed with this deed of her sons, their mother prayed to the goddess to give her sons what it was best for men to have. Forthwith Cleobis and Biton, after sacrificing and feasting, died in the temple (I.31). This second understanding of happiness that Solon expresses shows that death is good because life is bad. It is clearly from the point of view of the divine rather than that of the city. Herodotus indicates that Solon believes that a notion of divinity behind the laws must be propagated when laws are founded. He also believes, as his story of Cleobis and Biton suggests, that the divine is a being so superior and distant to human beings that it makes human life worthless and thus political life meaningless.

Solon further manifests this apolitical perspective of the divine underlying his second answer, when he explains to Croesus why he did not choose him as an example of happiness. According to Solon, "man is entirely [chance]. To me it is clear that you [Croesus] are very rich, and clear that you are the king of many men; but the thing that you ask me I cannot say of you yet, until I hear that you have brought your life to an end well" (I.32).[29] To say that the whole of human life is chance, thus leaving no room for human beings to improve either their individual or collective prospects by adopting and obeying good laws for their benefit, is to adopt the perspective of the divine in the story of Cleobis and Biton. Solon's emphasis on this antinomian perspective of the gods links them with the tyrant, who also seeks to be "antinomian" or above the laws that govern all other citizens and human beings.[30] Herodotus shows how Solon's antinomian inclinations may have gotten the better of his public-spirited activity as lawgiver; it may have caused him to foster an all-too-distant notion of the divine transcending the law, which prepared for the rise of Pisistratus.[31]

Herodotus turns to the question of why a notion of divine support needs to arise when the regime is founded in his discussion of Deioces' establishment of tyranny in Media. According to Herodotus, after five hundred and twenty years of Assyrian rule, first the Medes and then the rest of the Asians revolted, casting off their slavery and winning their freedom. Yet, Herodotus tells us that they soon relapsed into being ruled by tyrants again (I.95–96). This occurred because lawlessness (*anomies*) and therefore injustice (*adikon*) broke out in Media after Assyrian rule was cast off (I.96). Herodotus links such lawlessness and injustice with rape and plunder, the forceful violation of women and, by extension, the subjection of the men related to them, such as fathers, husbands, brothers, and sons (I.97).[32] Injustice involves a dialectic of mastery and slavery in which the weak are subjected to the strong.

Among the Medes, however, a wise man named Deioces fell in love with tyranny (I.96). Due to his desire for tyranny, Deioces, according to Herodotus, began to practice justice (*dikaiosune*) (I.96). As a result the Medes in his village chose him as their judge, and he, desiring rule, was honest and just (*dikaios*) (I.96).[33] As Deioces' reputation for justice grew, men from all over Media came to submit their disputes to his judgment (I.96). When Deioces realized that none would entrust their cases to anyone but him, he refused to sit as judge any longer, arguing that looking to the interests of others caused him to neglect his own affairs (I.97). Justice was not profitable to himself. As a result of this withdrawal, rape, plunder, and lawlessness increased. The Medes, sorely pressed by their plight, gathered together and persuaded each other to be ruled by a king (*basileuesthai*). They unanimously chose Deioces to assume the throne (I.98).[34] The legitimacy of Deioces' rule is initially grounded in consent and the deliberation and speech that this implies.

Not satisfied with being a king and wishing to become a tyrant, Deioces turns himself into a god. Having secured rule, Deioces had the Medes build him a fortress on a hill, a fortress which came to be known as Ecbatana (I.98). This fortress was composed of seven encircling walls rising up to the sky, with his palace sitting at the top (I.98). Furthermore, Deioces allowed himself to be seen by no one, stipulating that all business was to be transacted through messengers. Herodotus says that Deioces made himself god-like, "so that those who were his equals and of the same age, brought up with him, and of descent as good, and as brave as he, might not, seeing him, be vexed and take to plotting against him but would judge him to be someone grown quite different—all because they did not see him" (I.99). Herodotus suggests that human beings are hard to govern, because they are jealous for their equality. They quickly conspire against any other human being seen trying to rule them.[35] The divine seems a necessary supplement to consent to legitimate rule. Consent among equals may establish government, but the continuation of government, and the inequality of power that it implies, is often at odds with the notion of equality that is at its origins. What enables human beings to create or consent to government is precisely what makes them hostile to it. Herodotus suggests, therefore, that at the same time the regime is founded, a notion of divine support arises to make its continuation legitimate.[36]

Herodotus relates that, after Deioces secured his tyranny by making himself into a god, he "was very exact in his observance of justice" (I.100). As divine, Deioces is not only invisible but also visible. He is both absent and present—and thus feared, at the same time. Herodotus indicates the character of Deioces' justice by claiming that whenever any of his spies and eavesdroppers reported someone "as a man of insolent violence," Deioces would have him apprehended and punished accordingly (I.100). In keeping these proud and insolent men in their place, Deioces prevented the weak from being subjected to the strong as happened in the time just prior to his rule. Deioces' justice therefore consisted in enforcing equality. Yet, Deioces himself, a tyrant, claimed to be radically superior, and therefore unequal, to all other men. Deioces thus appears as the unequal, but necessary, source of equality. The Medes, in order to secure equality among themselves, had to give up their internal freedom to be ruled by Deioces, who hid the tyrannical source of his justice under the cloak of the divine.[37]

Herodotus' view of the relation of the divine to politics is a much discussed question in the literature. Binyamin Shimron argues that Herodotus approaches human affairs from a rational perspective and that he distinguishes the divine realm from the human realm. The latter is characterized by free will and choice, and it is skeptical toward the notion of divine guidance in human affairs. However, Shimron claims that this leaves Herodotus facing a dilemma that all believing historians and political thinkers face: how can one believe in God or gods at the same time believing that he or they play no role in human or political affairs? Herodotus, according to Shimron, could not solve this contradiction within his framework because he did not have the aid of the philosophical and theological reflections of such monotheistic religions as Islam, Christianity, and Judaism.[38] We have seen, however, that through the stories he tells, Herodotus consciously identifies and explores the problem of the role of the divine in human affairs. Contrary to Shimron, Herodotus' treatment of the divine and human realms is not a contradiction in his understanding. For Herodotus, one of the key problems at the founding of the political order involves the difficulty of combining equality and freedom with the need for political power. The inability of human beings to reconcile their desire for equality with the need for political power leads to the belief that the regime is a product of divine will—a belief that alienates human beings from themselves and leaves them susceptible to tyranny. Thus, in book 1, political power arises when some men become like "gods" and others become like "beasts." A radical inequality emerges that alienates both "gods" and "beasts" from their nature as human beings.

In the story of Cyrus' birth and recognition, Herodotus indicates the "childish" or primitive character of Deioces' attempt to resolve the conflict between equality and power. According to Herodotus, Cyrus' grandfather Astyages, a descendant of Deioces and tyrant of Media, feared his daughter, because of a dream. So he married her off to a Persian much her social and political inferior (I.107). After she became pregnant, Astyages had another dream, which made him terrified of his daughter's progeny, so he kept her under close guard, intending to kill her child, Cyrus (I.108). Yet, due to the machinations and pity of Astyages' servants, Cyrus was switched at birth with the infant of a cowherd's wife, so he escaped and was raised by the cowherd's wife (I.109–13). At age ten, however, Cyrus' true identity was revealed. Cyrus was chosen by his playfellows, thinking that he was the cowherd's son, as their imaginary king (I.114). As a child-king, Cyrus beat the son of Artembares, a noble Mede, for refusing to obey his orders. For this, Cyrus was brought before Astyages, who demanded to know how he, the son of a cowherd, would dare to beat the son of a noble Mede. Cyrus responded that he did so with justice, as "the children of the village, of whom I was one, in their play made me their king . . . but [he] was deaf to my orders and would [have] none of them, until finally he was punished for it" (I.115). Impressed with Cyrus' forthright answer, together with his looks and age, Astyages recognized Cyrus as his grandson.

For Herodotus, the child-kingship of Cyrus has important parallels to the Deiocesan regime. For instance, the first ground of legitimacy for both Deioces and Cyrus is in consent among equals. Just as Deioces was chosen by the Medes to be their actual king, Cyrus was chosen by his playfellows to be their imaginary king. Moreover, both the justice of Deioces and the justice of Cyrus consisted in enforcing equality. Similar to Deioces' punishment of proud and insolent men who seek domination, Cyrus beats a noble boy who refuses to obey his orders like all of the other boys.

The crucial difference between the two regimes, however, is that Deioces establishes his rule and practices justice when he is an adult, yet Cyrus, in this story, assumes the kingship and dispenses justice when he is only ten years old. Furthermore, Herodotus indicates the "childish" character of the Deiocesan regime's attempt to subordinate the desire for equality and freedom to the need for government by appealing to the divine. Instead of trying to turn himself into a god to continue his rule, Cyrus is simply sent away to his parents in Persia after he is discovered by his grandfather Astyages (I.122). Moreover, the mature Cyrus, to reestablish his authority over both the Persians as well as the Medes, does not appeal to their awe for the divine, as Deioces did to continue his rule over the Medes, but rather promises the Persians imperial success if they will obey him as their leader (I.126–27). Cyrus' appeal to empire, which replaces Deioces' appeal to the divine, is a purely secular justification for his rule or source of legitimacy for his regime. By way of contrast with Deioces, the story of Cyrus reveals that, for Herodotus, although an appeal to the divine may be adequate to combine equality with the need for government at the founding of the regime, it is insufficient to maintain the legitimacy of political power as the regime exists, and perhaps changes, through time. Herodotus thus raises the question of how authority is re-established in the other regimes, particularly Athens, discussed in book 1. Herodotus turns to this question in book 5, where he discusses the refounding of the Athenian democracy.

The Refounding of the Athenian Democracy

In book 5 of the *Histories*, there is a new founding of the Athenian democracy. I have argued that Solon's founding was defective in comparison to that of Lycurgus inasmuch as it left Athens susceptible to tyranny. This very defectiveness at the beginning, however, at a later time allows Athens to refound its democratic regime, so that it represents what Herodotus believes is the best regime. The very "goodness" of Lycurgus' founding imposed a "childishness" or unchanging stability on the Spartan regime that at once makes it noble but not the best. Solon's unstable founding, in contrast, allowed Athens to make a remarkable push forward, culturally and politically.

According to Herodotus, during the reign of Darius in Persia, Athens was freed from her tyrants by the Alcmaeonidae, who had been exiled by the Pisistrads (V.62). The Alcmaeonidae, now under the leadership of Cleisthenes, bribed the Pythian priestess to order any Spartan who came to Delphi, either on private or public business, to free Athens (V.63, 66). The Spartans, in obedience to the Pythia, raised an army under king Cleomenes to drive Hippias—Pisistratus' son who now held the tyranny—out of Athens (V.63). Cleomenes, "accompanied by such Athenians as stood on the side of freedom," entered the city of Athens and besieged Hippias and his family who had barricaded themselves in the Acropolis (V.64).[39] Herodotus asserts that the Spartans would never have driven the Pisistrads out of Athens—they had no intention of executing a long siege—except for a "chance" event that occurred (V.65). The children of the Pisistrads were captured as they were being secretly conveyed out of the country and thus "everything on the Pisistrad side was brought to confusion, and they were reduced to making any terms the Athenians wanted in return for their children; the terms were that the Pisistrads should get out of Attica in five days" (V.65). The Pisistrads, after ruling Athens for thirty-six years, retreated to Sigeum on the Scamander river. So Athens was freed of her tyrants (V.63). For the Pisistrads, their private family concerns, especially the desire to perpetuate their family, was their undoing. Tyranny, as revealed in this story, is characterized by an antinomian or apolitical concern for private interests.[40]

Herodotus' account of the expulsion of the Pisistrads shows the piety of the Spartans in contrast to the impiety of the Alcmaeonidae who, understanding the piety of the Spartans, corrupt the Pythia in a successful attempt to rid Athens of her tyrants. Cleisthenes' father Megacles also showed impiety by manipulating the Athenian belief in the goddess Athena, though in that case he does so to institute the tyranny of Pisistratus rather than rid Athens of her tyrants (I.60). The Alcmaeonidae, in their history, have no intrinsic hatred for tyranny as such, but rather are a family, much like the Pisistrad family, who primarily aim at personal power and prestige. If tyranny furthered that aim, they aided its establishment, when it did not, they did everything in their power to overturn it.[41] That Cleisthenes' corruption of the Pythia aimed at the end of Athenian tyranny is thus accidental. If an Athenian democracy had stood in the way of his rise to power, he would most likely have tried to corrupt the Pythia in order to overturn the democracy rather than the Pisistrad tyranny. By this means, along with the capture of the Pisistrad children, Herodotus reveals the role of accident in history. The expulsion of the tyrants from Athens, which was a preliminary for the refounding of the democratic regime, was not a necessary stage in Athens' history. It was an incidental result of the Alcmaeonidae's desire for power and prestige. Although Solon's defective founding makes this refounding possible, it does not make it inevitable; it is the necessary but not the sufficient condition.[42]

Herodotus recounts that, after the Pisistrads under Hippias were expelled from Athens, factious war broke out between "two men who held the power," Cleisthenes of the Alcmaeonidae and Isagoras, also of notable family but for whom, Herodotus says, he "cannot declare what their antecedents were" (V.66). When losing to Isagoras in the struggle for supreme power, Cleisthenes, according to Herodotus, took the common people (*demou*), previously "deprived of all rights," into partnership (V.66, 69). The rights Herodotus refers to here are most likely those of citizenship that would include *isegorie*, or the equal right of speech, which Herodotus says characterized the Athenian regime after the expulsion of the tyrants (V.78). This added power of the people allowed Cleisthenes to defeat Isagoras, resulting in the emergence of the democratic regime.[43]

In order to win the people to his side and perhaps to make his victory over Isagoras permanent, Herodotus says that Cleisthenes did two things. First, he redivided the tribes of Athens into ten (from four), and he renamed all the tribes except one after native heroes, expelling the old Ionian tribal names of Gelon, Aegicores, Argades, and Hoples (V.66). Second, Cleisthenes established the demes, assigning ten demes to each of the ten tribes (V.69). In establishing the demes, Cleisthenes effected a shift in the basis of citizenship from membership in a family or kinship group to residence in a given locality. As a result, individuals of low origin as well as foreign extraction were admitted into citizenship.[44] The redivision and renaming of the tribes after native heroes, along with the establishment of the demes, is a paradoxical combination of patriotism with openness to others. For the Athenians, after the democratic reforms of Cleisthenes, what is theirs is the other. One of the things that attaches them to the regime and makes them patriotic is the regime's acceptance of difference and diversity.

In his reforms in Athens Cleisthenes, according to Herodotus, imitated his maternal grandfather, Cleisthenes tyrant of Sicyon, after whom he was named (V.67). Cleisthenes of Sicyon despised the Argives, a Dorian people. To prevent the Sicyonians and the Argives from having the same tribes he expelled the heroic Dorian names and gave the Sicyonian tribes new names such as "Hogites," "Assites," and "Porkites." He called his own tribe the Archelaioi, or "Rulers of the People" (V.68). Cleisthenes of Athens took from his grandfather, Cleisthenes of Sicyon, this expulsion of foreign names. Yet, whereas the renaming of the tribes in Sicyon debased and alienated the people from themselves, the renaming of the tribes in Athens after native heroes increased the power of the people and gave them a greater sense of ownership in the regime.[45]

Cleisthenes, the democratic reformer in Athens, imitated his maternal grandfather because he, according to Herodotus, "had the same contempt for the Ionians" as Cleisthenes of Sicyon had for the Dorians (V.69). Yet, in book 1, Herodotus says that the Athenians and the Ionians are from the same Ionian stock, descended from the ancient Pelasgian race (I.143). Thus Herodotus shows in book 5 that changes in names—from Ionian to Athenian—changes the Athenian people's belief about their origins. Athenian identity after Cleisthenes is more determined by names, or what the Athenians call themselves, than by ethnicity or any particular set of customs. The democratic regime instituted by Cleisthenes therefore has two foundings. The first founding is by force—the physical strength derived from the body. This occurs with the expulsion of the Pisistrads and the defeat of Isagoras. The second founding is in speech. It occurs with the renaming of the tribes from Ionian names to the names of native heroes.[46] After this second founding an Athenian will be an Athenian more by what he or she thinks, or his or her state of mind, rather than ethnic origin or any particular set of customs. In this sense the Athenians resemble the Scythians.

With Cleisthenes' renaming of the tribes, Herodotus shows a movement from support for the regime because it is believed to be divine in book 1, to support for the regime because it is believed to be Athenian, or native, in book 5. It is a movement from divine support to patriotic support, from a divine foundation to a secular foundation of the regime. In showing a movement from divine to patriotic or secular support for the democracy, Herodotus reveals that the Athenians support the democracy because they believe the regime is "theirs." Athenians believe it is theirs, Herodotus indicates, in two ways. First, because the regime is Athenian, or native. Second, characterized by *isegorie* or the equality of speech, all share equally in deliberation. Thus all, it is thought, participate equally in its decisions (V.78).[47] The Athenians themselves are the regime. Herodotus indicates that, by instituting self-government, Athens managed to combine equality with political power. Athens ameliorates the felt contradiction between consent and rule. That patriotism replaces divine support for the regime means that what people say of the regime—that "it is ours"—and what it actually is—a product of human agency—come closer together. The ability to capture what the regime is in speech allows the Athenians to internalize their regime. They believe it to be something within themselves and not a product of something outside of themselves, and thus they also possess a sense of wholeness rather than alienation. In Athens, no one is either a "beast" or a "god," but all are human. This internalization leads to their willingness at both the battle of Marathon in book 6 and the battle of Salamis in book 8 to forsake their city walls and Athens' physical location. Athenians become characterized by motion, like the Scythians, but, unlike the Scythians, the Athenians do have a city. It is in themselves or their mind—Athens becomes an "idea." The Athenians have external motion but internal rest; they have an "idea" of the city within themselves.[48]

Athens resolves the difficulty of combining equality with government in a secular way. The Athenians are also more successful in taking account of the whole of human nature. Herodotus, in his investigation of Egyptian customs, shows that the Egyptians emphasize the cleanliness of the body as opposed to the beauty of the body—and thus the purely physical part of man (II.35–37). The Egyptians know the soul, but do not believe it is particular to human beings. What is particular to a human being is his or her body (II.123). In emphasizing the body, the Egyptians deemphasize the public and enlarge the private. They lack concern for the common interest in their pursuit of their own private good (II.84). The Persians, on the other hand, have customs that denigrate the body and emphasize the soul (I.131–33, 139–40). In emphasizing the soul rather than the body, the Persians contemn the private in favor of the public. They elevate selfless dedication to the common good over concern for one's own individual good (I.138). However, the Persian emphasis on the soul, as reflected in their most important custom of truth telling (I.136), is an attempt to make the invisible visible. It is a paradoxical attempt to make the soul act like the body. Herodotus thus indicates that to preserve life according to the higher part of human nature—the life of the soul or mind—one must also look to the concerns of the lower part of that nature. To ignore the body paradoxically reduces everything to body.

In contrast to Egypt and Persia, the Athenian regime, as refounded by Cleisthenes, emphasizes both the soul of human beings and their private bodily concerns. Herodotus reveals this in the context of recounting Spartan king Cleomenes' attempt to reinstate the party of Isagoras in Athens, along with his attempt, with the Boeotians and Chalcidians, to punish the Athenian *demos* after his failure to do so. After having been defeated by Cleisthenes and marginalized by the democratic regime which Cleisthenes founded, Isagoras sought the aid of Spartan king Cleomenes to expel his rival, overturn the democracy, and place the government of Athens into his own hands and those of his party (V.70). Cleomenes responded positively to the appeals of Isagoras. Herodotus implies that he did so because he had become the guest-friend of Isagoras during the siege of the Pisistrads. Herodotus also reports the "ill-rumor" that Cleomenes "was the lover of Isagoras' wife"—and so wants to do the husband a favor (V.70). In any event, Herodotus says that the first thing Cleomenes did, under the instruction of Isagoras, was to send a herald to Athens demanding that Cleisthenes be expelled because the Alcmaeonidae family was "under a curse" (V.70). Upon learning of the herald sent by Cleomenes and his demand for the expulsion of the "Accursed," Cleisthenes voluntarily removed himself from Athens (V.72). Cleomenes then entered Athens "with no great military power," according to Herodotus, and proceeded to banish seven hundred Athenian families identified by Isagoras (V.72). Next, Cleomenes "tried to do away with the Council and entrusted the government to three hundred partisans of Isagoras," thereby dissolving the democracy (V.72).[49] However, the Council, according to Herodotus, "resisted and refused to obey," forcing Cleomenes and Isagoras with his faction to retreat to the Acropolis, as the Pisistrads had done (V.72). Herodotus then says that the rest of the Athenians, agreeing with the Council, against the attempted usurpation of Isagoras, surrounded and besieged the Acropolis for two days (V.72).[50] On the third day Isagoras and the Spartans under Cleomenes made terms with the Athenians and marched out of the city (V.72). The Athenians, however, took the faction of Isagoras into custody and executed them. Having done so, they recalled Cleisthenes and the seven hundred families expelled by Cleomenes (V.72–73, 74). They then sent messengers to Sardis, according to Herodotus, seeking to form an alliance with the Persians against the Spartans (V.73). However, when the messengers took the risk of promising earth and water to king Darius, they were severely blamed by the Athenians (V.73). Herodotus indicates that the Athenians wanted to enter an alliance with the Persians on terms of equality, not as a subject city, and so the alliance was never made.

Cleomenes, according to Herodotus, "recognized that he had been extremely insulted both in word and deed by the Athenians." So he raised a great army of Spartans and their allies to avenge himself on the "popular party" in Athens and establish Isagoras as tyrant (V.74). Cleomenes then invaded Eleusis with his army, and the Boeotians, acting in concord with Cleomenes, seized the Attic demes of Oenoe and Hyspiae. The Chalcidians invaded and plundered other parts of Attica (V.74). Herodotus says that the

Athenians, "caught between two fires," delayed fighting the Boeotians and Chalcidians in order to confront the Spartans immediately (V.74). Among the Peloponnesian allies in Eleusis, the Corinthians, Herodotus says, began to regard the Spartan mission to impose the tyranny of Isagoras as unjust. So they abandoned the army and went home (V.75). The other Spartan king at the time, Demaratus the son of Ariston, also abandoned Cleomenes' mission and returned to Sparta—the reason for which Herodotus is silent (V.75).[51] As a result of these two blows, Cleomenes abandoned his attempt to impose the tyranny of Isagoras on Athens. The rest of the Peloponnesian allies disbanded and returned to their cities (V.76–77). The Athenians, however, desiring revenge, attacked the Boeotians at the Euripus and won a great victory, killing many Boeotians and taking seven hundred more prisoner (V.77). The Athenians then crossed into Euboea and attacked the Chalcidians. The Athenians defeated them also, taking many prisoners and leaving four thousand settlers on land formerly belonging to the Chalcidians (V.77). The Athenians eventually ransomed the Boeotian and Chalcidian prisoners of war for "two minas apiece." As a memorial to these first military victories of the democracy, the Athenians hung the chains with which they bound the prisoners on the walls of the Acropolis, and they built a bronze, four-horse chariot with a tenth of the ransoms. They placed this chariot in the Acropolis as well (V.77).

Herodotus, reflecting on Cleomenes' attempt to dissolve the democracy refounded by Cleisthenes, the Athenians' single-mindedness in resisting this attempt, Cleomenes' attempt to punish them for this resistance, and the resulting victory of Athens over the Boeotians and Chalcidians, remarks:

> So Athens had increased in greatness. It is not only in respect of one thing but of everything that equality and free speech [*isegorie*] are clearly a good [*spoudaion*]; take the case of Athens, which under the rule of [tyrants] proved no better in war than any of her neighbors but, once rid of those [tyrants], was far the first of all. What this makes clear is that when held in subjection they would not do their best, for they were working for a taskmaster, but, when freed [*eleutherothenton*], they sought to win, because each was trying to achieve for his very self. (V.78)[52]

Herodotus indicates in this passage that the internal freedom reflected by *isegorie*, or the equality of speech, proceeds from the soul, and is better than tyranny because it supported the Athenian superiority in war, a superiority which proceeds from the strength of the body. It did so, according to Herodotus, because the expulsion of the tyrants meant that now in war, each person, when fighting for the city, fought for himself or his own individual good rather than the good of the tyrant. Each felt a sense of ownership in the regime and believed that the city served their interests. This identification of the city with the self drastically improved the fighting spirit, and hence the military effectiveness, of the Athenians. The democratic reforms of Cleisthenes, therefore, solved the problem of the tyranny of one person by making every person in the city a "tyrant," as it were. It allowed individuals to pursue their own interests rather than forcing them to pursue the interests of others or the "common" good—in abstraction from their individual good. Herodotus indicates that the community of speech—or the regime—shared by all and reflecting the soul, allowed each and was used by each to pursue his own private advantage, rooted in the body.[53] Moreover, not only did Athens combine the Persian emphasis on the soul with the Egyptian emphasis on the body in this way, it also combined the Egyptian emphasis on the private with the Persian emphasis on the public. This is apparent from the inscription on the bronze four-horse chariot placed in the Acropolis to memorialize the Athenian soldiers who defeated the Boeotians and Chalcidians (V.77). The inscription, according to Herodotus, reads as follows:

> Boeotians and Chalcidians, both nations have been conquered, by sons of the Athenians [*paides Athenaion*], in deeds of warlike valor. In murk and iron bondage they quenched the flame of their insolence, and from the tenth of their ransom gave these horses to Pallas. (V.77)

On this inscription no name of any single individual appears, but the fighters are memorialized as "sons of the Athenians," the implication being that they were generated by their city or political community. They become completely politicized or collectivized in speech. This inclusion in the inscription as "sons of the Athenians" rather than as particular, named individuals, gives to the city a unified identity. Democratic individualism in deed becomes consistent with universalism in speech or thought. Considering this inscription together with Herodotus' judgment that the equality of speech led to Athenian superiority in war, it seems that, for Herodotus, the pursuit of private material gain in Athens coincided with the public good only when conquering other cities. The presence of an external threat was needed to successfully combine private interest with public interest, and body with soul.[54] Thus, when Herodotus suggests that Athens takes account of the whole or both parts of human nature, therefore making possible a life according to the highest human potential or the life of the mind, he suggests a potentiality or pinnacle of the regime, not its condition at all times.[55]

Herodotus reveals the potential of the Athenian regime to make possible the life of the mind in his account of the battle of Marathon in book 6. According to Herodotus, Persian king Darius, ostensibly to punish those

Greeks who took part in the Ionian revolt and the burning of Sardis (V.102, 105), sent a Persian expedition under the command of Datis and his nephew Artaphrenes against Greece, "with instructions to enslave Athens and Eretria and to bring the slaves before him" (VI.94). However, Herodotus says that the real reason for the expedition was Darius' desire to conquer those Greeks who had refused to give him earth and water (VI.48–49), thereby subjugating all of Greece (VI.44, 94). Datis and Artaphrenes headed with their host to Cilicia, where they boarded their horses and men onto ships, setting sail for the coast of Asia Minor (VI.95). Setting out from the island of Samos, they first subdued the Greek island of Naxos, then took the islands of Delos and Carystus (VI.96, 97, 99). Setting off from Carystus, the Persians put in at Euboea in the area of Eretria. They unloaded their horses and men and prepared to attack the city (VI.101).

According to Herodotus, "The Eretrians had no intention of sallying out and fighting, for what they chiefly cared for was to preserve the walls of the city if they could, inasmuch as they had resolved not to quit their city" (VI.101). Unable to distinguish their city from the physical location and visible manifestations of it, the Eretrians were besieged by the Persians for six days. On the seventh day, Euphorbus and Philagrus, two notable Eretrians "who looked to the private gains they would make from the Persians," opened the gates of their city to the Persians who then entered, plundered, and burned the temples, enslaving all the inhabitants (VI.101). After conquering and enslaving the Eretrians, the Persians crossed over from Euboea to Attica, and, accompanied by the recently expelled Pisistrad tyrant Hippias, encamped at Marathon. On receiving this news, Herodotus says that "the Athenians too marched out to Marathon," under the leadership of their "ten generals," the most important of whom was Miltiades (VI.103).[56] The Athenians, unlike the Eretrians, do indeed "quit their city" and sally out to face the Persians. Unlike the Eretrians, the Athenians conceive of their city as something within themselves rather than as something outside of themselves. They are able to make a distinction between it and its physical location and outer manifestations. The Spartans said they would not leave their territory during the Carnea festival—further emphasizing the piety of the Spartans in contrast to the secularism of the Athenians. The Athenians, however, were joined at Marathon by the Plataeans "in full force as a people," (VI.105–6, 108). When it was Miltiades' day to command the troops, the battle lines were drawn up, and the Athenains and Plataeans charged and routed the Persians under Datis and Artaphrenes (VI.111–12).

Herodotus maintains that one of the chief reasons that the Athenians won a great victory over the Persians at Marathon was that, of the Greeks, they were "the first to face the sight of the Median dress and the men who wore it. For till then, the Greeks were terrified even to hear the names of the Medes" (VI.112). The Athenians, with their democratic regime, were able to face the Persians as Persians, or the Persians in their particularity or otherness. The Athenians were able to look on the men underneath Persian clothing without fear as well. They were able to look on the Persians not only as Persians but also as human beings like themselves. In other words, Herodotus indicates that the Athenians at Marathon could look on the other and see the same. They could look on the particular and see the universal, on the different and changing and see that which was at rest.

The Athenians at Marathon, although similar in their grasp of the universal, are still unlike the Persians in crucial respects. The Persians, in their worship of the universal, have a contempt for the particular manifested in their imperial drive to obliterate all distinctions between themselves and others and to make the world one country governed by a single Persian king. On the other hand, at Marathon, the Athenians, looking at the universal, or on men as men, are still defending their own and asserting their particularity as Athenians against the totalizing attempts of the Persians. They combine a universal perspective with an understanding of the importance of the particular. As Herodotus indicates, the Athenians believe that their ability to see men "naked"—or the universality of human nature that lies concealed beneath convention or "clothing"—distinguishes them from the rest of the world. Although unlike the Persians, the Athenians at Marathon resemble Herodotus himself. Herodotus, as revealed in his *Histories*, also uses his eyes and ears to study the particular and changing customs of others—such as the Egyptians, Scythians, and Persians—in order to discover a universal and unchanging human nature that lies beneath. Yet Herodotus also understands the importance of the particular. For example, in book 4, he shows that one can only perceive what is natural from within the conventional. In other words, knowledge of the universal, or what is beyond the political, requires the existence of the political itself. It is in this way that the Athenian regime, in taking account of the whole of human nature, makes possible the life according to the highest human potential, which parallels Herodotus' own activity.[57]

Herodotus shows how Athenian democracy sees things in the way he does, not only in his account of the battle of Marathon in book 6, but also in his account of Themistocles' interpretation of the oracle in book 7. According to Herodotus, upon learning of Xerxes' plan to destroy Athens and enslave

Greece with the might of his entire empire, the Athenians sent envoys to Delphi to inquire about the best plans for their future (VII.140,145). They received instead an oracle that predicted the utter destruction of Athens in the titanic struggle ahead. The oracle encouraged the Athenians to give up notions of resisting the Persians, to abandon their city and the freedom of Greece, and to settle in some distant country. According to Herodotus, the Pythia spoke to the Athenian envoys as follows:

> Wretched ones, why sit you here? Flee and begone to remotest ends of earth, leaving your homes, high places in circular city; For neither the head abides sound, no more than the feet or body; Fire pulls all down, and sharp Ares, driving his Syrian-bred horses. Many a fortress besides and not yours alone shall he ruin. Many the temples of God to devouring flames he shall give them. There they stand now, the sweat of terror streaming down from them. They shake with fear; from the roof-tops black blood in deluging torrents. They have seen the forthcoming destruction, and evil sheerly constraining. Get you gone out of the shrine! Blanket your soul with your sorrows. (VII.140)

The Athenian envoys were greatly distressed when they heard this oracle, but a Delphian named Timon advised them to consult the Pythia a second time, as suppliants (VII.141). The envoys returned to the shrine and said, "My Lord, give us a better oracle about our fatherland; be moved to pity the suppliant boughs with which we come before you, or we will never go away from your shrine but remain right here till we die" (VII.141). As a result of this request, the Pythia uttered a second oracle:

> No: Athena cannot appease great Zeus of Olympus with many eloquent words and all her cunning counsel. To you I declare again this word, and make it as iron: All shall be taken by foeman, whatever within his border Cecrops contains, and whatever the glades of sacred Cithaeron. Yet to you Tritogeneia shall Zeus, loud-voiced, give a present, a wall of wood [*teichos*], which alone shall abide unsacked by the foeman; well shall it serve yourselves and your children in days that shall be. Do not abide the charge of horse and foot that come on you, a mighty host from the land-ward side, but withdraw before it. Turn your back in retreat; on another day you shall face them. Salamis, isle divine [*o theie*], you shall slay many children of women, either when seed is sown or again when the harvest is gathered. (VII.141)

According to Herodotus, this second oracle to the envoys "seemed to be kinder than the earlier, and indeed it was so" (VII.142).[58] The envoys returned to Athens and reported the oracle to the people, upon which a debate arose, made possible by the institution of *isegorie*, over the true meaning of two words or phrases in the oracle: "wall of wood" and "divine" in the phrase "Salamis, isle divine" (VII.142–43). With respect to the meaning of the phrase "wall of wood," two factions arose. The first was some of the elders, who interpreted the phrase to mean the thorn hedge that used to surround the Acropolis in times past. So they urged that the Acropolis be defended (VII.142). The second faction, led by Themistocles, interpreted the "wall of wood" to mean their ships. So they argued that they should be ready to abandon the city and increase the size of their navy in preparation to resist the Persians at sea (VII.142, 143, 144).[59]

Two factions again arose, according to Herodotus, with respect to the meaning of the word "divine." The oracle interpreters asserted that the phrase "Salamis, isle divine, you shall slay many children of women" meant "that the Athenians should prepare themselves for a sea battle at Salamis, which they would certainly lose" (VII.142). The second faction, again led by Themistocles, claimed that the interpreters misinterpreted the meaning of the word "divine" in this phrase. According to Themistocles, because the oracle said "Salamis, isle divine," instead of something like "O cruel Salamis," the oracle should be interpreted as favorable of the Athenians and against the enemy (VII.143). Persians and those serving under them, not Athenians, were the children of women who would be slain in a sea fight off Salamis. Themistocles therefore counseled the Athenians to prepare their ships for a fight at sea, which they would win. According to Herodotus, the Athenians decided in favor of Themistocles' interpretation of the oracle because "it was preferable to that of the oracle-interpreters; for the latter would not have them prepare for a sea-fight or indeed, to tell the truth, put up a hands worth of resistance at all; they should just leave Attica and settle in some other country" (VII.143).

Herodotus reveals the correctness of Themistocles' judgment by interpreting the "wall of wood" to mean the Athenian navy and "Salamis, isle divine" to mean that the Athenians should prepare for a fight at sea which they would win, when he says:

> I am forced to declare an opinion that most people will find offensive; yet, because I think it true, I will not hold back. If the Athenians had taken fright at the approaching danger and had left their own country, or even if they had not left it but had remained and surrendered to Xerxes, no one would have tried to oppose the king at sea . . . So as it stands now, a man who declares that the Athenians were the saviors of Greece would hit the very truth. (VII.139)

In his account of Themistocles' correct interpretation of the oracle, Herodotus shows that the democratic regime of Athens combines not only the Egyptian emphasis on the body and the private with the Persian emphasis on the soul and the public, but that it also makes possible an understanding of speech that combines the principles which underlie Egyptian lying and Persian truth telling. The Egyptians, as "liars," believe that "ideas" cannot be communicated. Words, although representing something unchanging in the mind of the speaker, spawn an infinite variety of interpretations. They are thus constantly changing their meaning, or they are in motion, from the listener's perspective. Words are like Platonic "ideas." They are the cause of the many particular things in the world, yet, for the Egyptians, the many particulars forever obscure the universals from which they proceed. The Egyptians believe that words require interpretation but that interpretation is impossible; words do not reveal the truth. The Persians, as truth tellers, believe, unlike the Egyptians, that words always act as a vehicle for the communication of "ideas" between speaker and listener. The "ideas" are not obscured by the particulars but are immediately apparent. Words therefore require no interpretation, and there is no reason why they cannot reveal the truth. However, this relies on spoken words having the same unchanging meaning for the listener as for the speaker. Thus words themselves, like the "ideas" they express, are universal or at rest. Yet Herodotus reveals the problem with the Persian assumption about human and divine communication when he shows that the names "Smerdis" and "Ecbatana" can have two meanings (III.61-64). Herodotus indicates that although words can express "ideas," or that which is universal and unchanging, they can also incorporate change or motion by having more than one meaning. For Herodotus, interpretation is necessary because words can spawn a variety of meanings, but there is a correct interpretation, since words incorporate rest as well as motion, the universal as well as the particular.

Themistocles, in his interpretation of the oracle, understands, as Herodotus does, that words require interpretation because they can spawn a variety of meanings and incorporate change or motion. The "wall of wood" can mean either the Acropolis, or it can mean the Athenian navy. "Salamis, isle divine" can mean a favorable outcome either for the Persians or for the Athenians in the sea battle off Salamis (VII.142–43). Themistocles also understands, like Herodotus, that words do have one true meaning underlying the variety of meanings that they spawn. They thus incorporate rest as well as motion. Not only is interpretation necessary, but there is a correct interpretation. The true meaning of the "wall of wood" is the Athenian navy, and the true meaning of "Salamis, isle divine" is that the Athenians will be victorious at the battle of Salamis, thereby preventing Greece's absorption into the Persian empire and the loss of their freedom, both internal and external (VII.139). For Themistocles, as for Herodotus, speech, especially divine speech, is a mean between Egyptian lying—which assumes that the "ideas" are forever obscured by the particulars or that the truth can never be known—and Persian truth telling—which assumes that the "ideas" are not obscured by the particulars or that the truth is immediately apparent. Themistocles understands, and persuades the Athenians, of the necessarily complex character of speech. Words can both reveal and conceal, lie and tell the truth—at the same time. For Themistocles and the Athenians, as for Herodotus, there are "ideas," but they can be grasped only through the many particulars of which they are the cause. The truth can be revealed, but only through interpretation.[60]

Given his approach to, and interpretation of, the oracle, it may seem that Themistocles, as represented by Herodotus, is very politically astute, taking his bearings from the necessities that govern politics rather than from the divine—in a way consistent with Athenian secular tendencies. Thus, Themistocles appears as someone who uses appeals to the divine or the oracular simply as a rhetorical device to address the real political problems, such as a Persian invasion, with which he is dealt. Such an interpretation of Themistocles seems to be supported by Herodotus' account in book 8 of the second debate among the Greek naval commanders before the battle of Salamis. Having previously decided to fight the Persians at sea at the Isthmus, Themistocles, who commanded the Athenian contingent of the fleet, tried to persuade the other commanders to remain at Salamis and confront the Persians there. Themistocles began by making three tactical arguments against fighting at the Isthmus. First, at the Isthmus, they would be fighting in open sea, with fewer ships. Second, they would lose Salamis, Megara, and Aegina even if they were victorious. Third, the Persian land forces would follow their fleet, so the Persians would be brought into the Peloponnese, endangering all of Greece (VIII.60). Themistocles then made four arguments in favor of fighting at Salamis. First, they would be fighting in a confined space, as at Artemisium. The confined space would nullify the Persian numerical superiority and ensure a Greek victory. Afterwards, the Persians would depart from Greece in disorder. Second, the defense of Salamis was necessary because Athenian women and children had taken refuge there. Third, if they fought at Salamis, the Greeks would be defending the Peloponnese without bringing the Persian army and navy down into it, and, fourth, they would profit by the survival of Megara, Aegina, and Salamis (VIII.60). Themistocles, after giving this list of reasons, briefly mentions the oracle given to the Athenians and his interpretation of it (VII.141–43,

VIII.60). By having Themistocles briefly mention the oracle as an afterthought, Herodotus seems to indicate that Themistocles' interpretation of it in book 7 is an application of his own, rather than the god's, judgment of how best to defeat the Persians. Themistocles' understanding of the complex character of divine speech appears to provide him the opportunity, or perhaps cover, to apply human reason in the world and to display creative acts of human, rather than divine, intelligence.

Despite his appearance of relying solely on human reason in political and military affairs, which would be consistent with Athenian secular tendencies, Themistocles is nonetheless presented by Herodotus as retaining a substantive connection to the divine. Although it is true that Themistocles most likely interprets the oracle in such a way that it reflects what his own reason has discovered, he and the Athenians treat the words of the oracle with a seriousness and authority that would not be granted to human speech. If an ordinary human being rather than what was believed to be the god had declared that the Athenians should look to their "wall of wood" and that "Salamis, isle divine" would slay many children of women, it is unlikely that a great debate over the meaning of these words would have arisen in the city. It is because they are believed to be the words of Apollo, or the divine presence that Apollo represents, that a struggle over their interpretation ensues. Although recognizing divine speech is fraught with ambiguity and complexity, Themistocles recognizes that the god should be taken seriously, as he is in some sense a speaker of underlying truth.[61]

Given the many stories of oracular communication from Delphi that Herodotus gives us in his *Histories*, we may think it folly for Themistocles to understand the god as a conveyer of deeper truth. For instance, as we saw in the introduction, Herodotus recounts that Croesus, ruler of the Lydian empire, consulted Delphi before attacking Cyrus and the Persian empire. He received oracles foretelling of his destruction of a "mighty empire" and predicted that his rule of Lydia would last until a "mule" became king of the Medes (I.53, 55–56). Despite his confidence in the face of these oracles, when Croesus attacked the Persians he was defeated by Cyrus. The Lydian capital, Sardis, and Croesus himself were captured (I.84–86). Likewise, the Spartans, according to Herodotus, consulted the Delphic oracle before attacking Tegea. They received the following words in reply: "Tegea will I give you, to beat with your feet in dancing, and with a rope to measure, to your fill, her beautiful plainland" (I.66). However, when the Spartans attacked, they were defeated by the Tegeans. As prisoners of war, they were forced to measure Tegean land with a rope. In chapter 3 we also saw Persian king Cambyses' confusion concerning the meaning of an oracle. Herodotus tells us that while in the Syrian city of Ecbatana, Cambyses, intending to rush home to Susa to reclaim his throne from the Magian usurpers, mortally wounded himself with his sword as he mounted his horse (III.64). When told that he was in the Syrian city of Ecbatana, Cambyses realized that he had misunderstood an oracle foretelling his death in Ecbatana. He thought it meant that he would die an old man in the Median city of Ecbatana, whereas it actually foretold his death in the Syrian city of the same name.

Herodotus reveals another important instance of oracular miscommunication, as it were, in his account in book 6 of Spartan king Cleomenes' war against the Argives. According to Herodotus, Cleomenes had consulted the oracle at Delphi and was told by the Pythia that he would capture "Argos" (VI.76). Forthwith Cleomenes, intending to attack the city of Argos, led the Spartan army to the Erasinus river and made preparation to cross it (VI.76).[62] However, when Cleomenes could not get favorable omens for the crossing he withdrew into the territory of Thyreae and "in the sea, cut the throat of a bull," in the hopes of pacifying the gods (VI.76). In the meantime, the Argives marched out of their city to meet the Spartans, and a battle ensued in which many Argives were killed. The rest of the Argives, according to Herodotus, fled to the sacred grove of Argus (VI.78). Cleomenes then ordered the helots who were in his army to surround the grove with firewood. When this was done, he burned it to the ground, killing all the men inside (VI.80). While the grove was burning, however, Cleomenes asked one of the Argive deserters to which of the gods the grove belonged. Upon learning that it belonged to Argus, Cleomenes said, "Apollo of Prophecy . . . how grossly you have deceived me when you said I would capture Argos! For my guess is that this is the Argos in which your prophecy is fulfilled" (VI.80). He then returned to Sparta with his army without capturing the city of Argos (VI.82).

In these stories of encounters with the oracle, Herodotus seems to suggest that the god is ignorant and lacks wisdom, as in the cases of Croesus and the Spartans, or that the god is purposely deceptive, as in the cases of Cambyses and Cleomenes. The god may also be regarded as malicious, as we have seen that Athenian belief in the divine origins of their regime left them susceptible to tyranny (I.60). Thus, it would appear that Herodotus encourages human beings to dismiss completely divine guidance in political affairs. This impression only seems to be furthered by Herodotus' claim that the Alcmaeonidae once successfully bribed the Pythia to get the pronouncement that they wanted (V.63, 66). Yet this interpretation of Herodotus' text lacks subtlety. The god, as expressed by the Pythia at Delphi and represented by Herodotus, is neither simply ignorant nor entirely deceptive. The god knows that Croesus will destroy an empire and that a mule will rule the Medes, yet this empire is Croesus' own—the mule is not an animal but Cyrus himself. The god also knows that the Spartans will be measuring Tegean land with a rope—but as prisoners of war rather than victorious conquerors. Moreover, although the god conceals that Cambyses will die in a Syrian rather than Median city, he does reveal that the name of the city will be Ecbatana. Again, although the god conceals that the territory captured by Cleomenes will be the grove rather than the city, he does reveal that it will belong to Argos. The words of the god both conceal and reveal the truth at the same time. Finally, it was not the god at Delphi, but rather the machinations of Megacles and Pisistratus, that was responsible for Athenian belief in divine support for the Pisistrad tyranny.

Themistocles' encounter with the oracle differs from that of Croesus, Cambyses, Cleomenes, the Spartans, and the Athenians of the Pisistrad era. For Themistocles, the god appears to have knowledge, but he expresses this knowledge ambiguously. The words of the god are complex, and the truth he reveals is not immediately apparent but requires the engagement of human rationality to be understood. When the god declares that the Athenians should look to their "wall of wood" and "Salamis, isle divine, you shall slay many children of women," Themistocles pauses and reflects on what the meaning of the oracle might be. He concludes, perhaps for the reasons later expressed in the debate of the naval commanders before Salamis, that it must mean that the Athenians should look to their ships and that they should prepare for a naval battle against the Persians, which they would win, off the coast of Salamis. As the *Histories* shows, Themistocles' interpretation proves to be correct. Themistocles is initially skeptical toward the oracle, but such rational skepticism is prompted by the god and provides the opportunity to achieve greater clarity about the oracle's deeper meaning. Herodotus' narrative of Themistocles' encounter with the god through the oracle shows that the oracle initiates a rational reflection that leads to a greater understanding of truth.[63]

Sparta in Comparison to Athens

The Spartan regime takes account of both body and soul, private and public—but in a different way than the Athenian regime. For example, Sparta's emphasis on the body is manifested in the custom they share with the Egyptians. They rise from their seats when an older man approaches, and they move out of the way when they encounter their elders on the road (II.82). This great reverence for age, reflected institutionally in the Council of Elders, or *Gerousia,* is a reverence for the bodies out of which they are generated. The Spartans, therefore, like the Egyptians, believe that what Aristotle calls the universal first principles (*hai archai*), are the first things in time and are thus what is oldest. Moreover, the Spartans resemble the Egyptians in their emphasis on the body. The family is rooted in the body in another way as well. Herodotus maintains that in Sparta, as in Egypt, heralds, flute-players, and cooks all inherit their trades from their fathers. Especially in the case of heralds, Herodotus says, "Nor do others bar the hereditary family on the grounds of clarity of voice . . . but they follow their trade as their fathers did before them" (VI.60).

The Spartan regime, however, also emphasizes the soul and the public sphere. This can be seen in the "common meals" instituted by Lycurgus, which sought to make private pleasures public, as well as the "sworn companies" and "regiments of thirty" which emphasized sociability or individual membership in the group (I.65). All three institutions encouraged the Spartans, like the Persians but unlike the Athenians, to repress their own good in favor of dedication to the common good. Furthermore, Spartan king Ariston's illicit love for his friend's wife, who according to Herodotus was "far the most beautiful of all the women in Sparta," reveals that the Spartans, like the Persians, love the beautiful (VI.61). They love the beauty of the body, in contrast to the Egyptians who emphasize only the cleanliness of the body. Thus the Spartans transcend the merely physical part of human beings. This is further reflected by the actions of the Spartans before the battle of Thermopylae. According to Herodotus, Xerxes, encamped in Malis near Trachis, sent a mounted spy to the pass of Thermopylae to see how many Greeks were stationed there and what they were doing (VII.201, 207). When the spy approached the pass, he saw "Some of [the Spartans] . . . exercising and some combing their hair" (VII.208). Wondering at the Spartan concern for their hair, the spy rode back to Xerxes and reported to him what he had seen. Xerxes, baffled by the report, asked Demaratus, exiled king of Sparta, who accompanied him on this expedition against Greece, what they were doing (VII.209). Demaratus responded, "This is their custom [*nomos*]: that when they are going to risk their lives, they make their heads beautiful" (VII.209). In this story Herodotus reveals that, in the face of death, the Spartans can transcend necessity. They place value on unnecessary things such as beautiful hair. They therefore show both their freedom from the body and the beauty of their souls.[64]

Although the Spartan regime takes account of both the body and the soul and therefore the whole of human nature, Herodotus indicates that it is deficient in a number of ways. First, the Spartans do not as adequately combine equality and freedom with the need for political power as the Athenians do. The Spartans, in their need to impose government, sacrifice internal equality and freedom in favor of hierarchical political structures. As noted above, this can be seen in the oligarchical institutions—the small Council of Elders, or *Gerousia*, the Ephorate, and helotry—founded by Lycurgus. However, it can also be seen in the prerogatives of the Spartan kings which Herodotus lists in book 6. For instance, according to Herodotus, Spartan kings have the right to wage war against any country they may choose, and "no Spartiate may stand in their way or he will involve himself in a curse" (VI.56).[65] Also, Spartan kings are reserved seats in the front row at all athletic contests (VI.57). Furthermore, the kings have a right to a double share of everything at public dinners, and, if they are not present at the dinner, then two portions of wheat and two portions of wine must be sent to their homes (VI.57). When the kings attend dinners in private homes, "they are honored in this same way," with a double share of everything (VI.57). Moreover, according to Herodotus, the kings have two votes in the Council of Elders (VI.57).[66] These prerogatives of the Spartan kings may seem paltry when compared with the wealth and power of the Persian kings, but they nonetheless institutionalize the principle of political inequality and hierarchy between kings and subjects.[67]

The justification of such political hierarchy in Sparta, Herodotus implies, is an appeal to the divine just as in the case of Deioces. For instance, Herodotus says that the Spartan kings have two priesthoods, "that of Zeus of Lacedaemon and that of Heavenly Zeus" (VI.56).[68] Second, upon setting out on a military expedition they "have the right to as many animal victims as they will, and, of those sacrificed, they may take the skins and the backs" (VI.56). In peacetime, the kings are the first to begin eating at a public sacrifice, and each of the kings get "a double share of everything . . . over what is given to the other guests" (VI.57). They also have the "right of first libation" and the skins of the sacrificed beasts (VI.57). Finally, "every new moon and on the seventh day of each month there is granted to each king a perfect victim, paid for by the public treasury, for the temple of Apollo" (VI.57). All of these prerogatives serve to fuse politics and religion in Sparta. They bind the kings closely with the gods in whom the Spartans believe, and this perceived relationship legitimizes their rule.

Perhaps as a result of this fusion, the Spartans, Herodotus indicates, cannot see nature. Although the Spartan regime takes account of the whole of human nature, it does not do so in a way that makes possible a life according to the highest human potential, or the life of the mind, as the Athenian regime does. This is the second reason why the Spartan regime is deficient.

Herodotus reveals the inability of the Spartans to see nature in his story of Cleomenes' ascension to one of the Spartan kingships. According to Herodotus, Cleomenes "[came] to possession of [of the throne] not through personal quality but through descent" (V.39). He goes on to explain that Spartan king Anaxandrides, Cleomenes' father, loved his wife very much but had no children with her (V.39). The ephors, in an attempt to save the royal line of Eurysthenes, of which Anaxandrides was a member, and to preserve the dual kingship in Sparta, approached Anaxandrides and said, "Since this wife of yours does not produce children, send her away and take another; by so doing, you will please the people of Sparta" (V.39). Anaxandrides refused to be persuaded by the ephors, and said that he would keep his present wife rather than take another (V.39). Upon this refusal, the ephors consulted with the Council of Elders, and they jointly laid a proposal before Anaxandrides: "We do not now ask you for the dismissal of the wife that you have. No; continue to give her all that now you are giving her, but, besides her, take another wife, one who can bear you children" (V.40). Anaxandrides was persuaded by this second proposal, "and thereafter he had two wives and managed two households, in this acting quite differently from Spartan custom" (V.90).

Herodotus reveals that in order to save one Spartan custom, the dual kingship, the Spartans and Anaxandrides must violate another Spartan custom, monogamy.[69] Anaxandrides married a second wife, and shortly thereafter this second wife bore a child for him and "gave to the Spartiates an heir to the kingship" (V.41). This child was Cleomenes, after whom the second wife had no more children. However, Anaxandrides' first wife, who previous to this had been barren, "now conceived at this very juncture" (V.41). Shortly thereafter she gave birth to triplets, Dorieus being the first to leave the womb, then Leonidas and then Cleombrotus, although "some . . . say that Cleombrotus and Leonidas were twins" (V.41). As the children of Anaxandrides grew to manhood, it became clear that, although Cleomenes "was not quite right in his head and was, indeed, a little mad," Dorieus "was the first of all the young men of his age, and he was certain that, in point of manly quality, he would be made king" (V.42). Yet, rather than being guided by natural merit, the Spartans, "following their custom [*to nomo*]" according to Herodotus, made Cleomenes, the eldest son of Anaxandrides, king (V.42).

Why do the Spartans follow their custom in making Cleomenes king when, to ensure his birth, they had violated their custom in persuading Anaxandrides to have two wives and manage two households? The Spartans, Herodotus indicates, confusing origin (*arche*) with principle (*arche*), or the oldest with the best, refuse to acknowledge the contradiction in their customs and therefore the lawless foundation of their law. Thus, they refuse to see the nature concealed by their customs or refuse to make the distinction between the natural and the conventional; from the Spartan perspective, the oldest should be best, and therefore is or must be so.

The inability to distinguish nature and convention is further revealed in the Spartan account of the origin of their dual kingship. The Spartans, according to Herodotus, say that Aristodemus, when he was their king, brought them as a people from Driopis to that part of the Peloponnese which they now possess (VI.52, VIII.31). Shortly thereafter, Aristodemus' wife Argeia gave birth to twins. However, Aristodemus himself soon died, and "the Lacedaemonians of that day resolved to follow custom [*nomon*] and make the elder of the twins king, but they could not choose which of the two to take, since the children were alike and equal" (V.52). The Spartans, insisting on hierarchy where nature made equality, asked the mother which was the elder of the two. Although "she knew right well," Argeia said that she was as ignorant in this matter as they, because "she wanted both of them somehow to become kings" (VI.52). The Spartans then decided to consult the Pythia at Delphi about what they should do. The Pythia advised them to "make both children kings but honor more the elder" (VI.52). Notice that the Spartans believe that the divine, as well as Argeia, had a hand in instituting the dual kingship. Although intending to obey the Pythia with respect to making both children kings, the Spartans were still at a loss as to which of the two was the elder. To discover this, they devised a plan whereby they would watch the mother, whom they suspected was lying about her ignorance, to see which of the infants she washed and fed first, believing that this one would be the oldest. Accordingly the Spartans "watched the mother of Aristodemus' children and found that she indeed preferred one, always in the same order—the elder-born—in feeding and washing; for she had no knowledge why she was watched" (VI.52). The Spartans, believing that Argeia honored the infant in this way because he was the firstborn, took him and brought him up at public expense (VI.52).

The error the Spartans make, Herodotus implies, is their belief that the mother will naturally be inclined to show more affection for the firstborn son rather than the younger one and thus that her natural inclinations will be in perfect accord with their custom of making the elder son king. Again, Herodotus shows that the Spartans believe that the natural and the conventional are the same thing—or that one cannot make the distinction between nature and convention.[70] In this way the Spartans are unlike the Athenians but like the Scythians, who cannot see an image as an image or who, when looking at the conventional or what is made, believe they are looking at the natural or what is unmade. This inability to see an image as an image and thus the inability to see nature, leads, in contrast to the internal rest of the Athenians, to a permanent internal motion or political instability in Sparta. According to Herodotus, the Spartans named the "elder" of the twins Eurysthenes and the "younger" Procles, and when they reached manhood, "brothers though they were, were, they say, continually at variance with one another all their lives, and so it has continued with all their descendants" (VI.52).

The Spartan inability to see the natural is also manifested in their lesser ability, in contrast to the Athenians at Marathon, to look on or to understand the other. Herodotus reveals this Spartan defect in his account of the Greek mission to Gelon of Syracuse in book 7. This mission occurred after the Athenians, guided by Themistocles, decided to resist the Persians at sea and "all the Greeks who were of the better persuasion assembled together and exchanged their judgments and their pledges with one another" (VII.145). They did away with all enmities and wars between each other, including the most important at the time, the conflict between Athens and Aegina. Secondly, they decided to send envoys to various other Greek cities to form alliances with them against the Persians, one such being Syracuse, ruled by the tyrant Gelon, whose power was "far greater than anything else that was Greek" (VII.145). The purpose of these missions "was that the entire Greek people might somehow unite and take common action, since the [Persians] threatened all Greeks alike" (VII.145).

Upon arriving in Syracuse, the Greek mission put their proposal to Gelon (VII.145). The Spartan envoy Syagrus spoke first, assuring Gelon that Xerxes planned to subdue all of Greece, and that if he defeated the Spartans in battle he would quickly move on to Syracuse and all of Sicily. The only way to repel the attack of the "barbarian" was for all of Greece to draw together, thus being "fighters of consideration for any invader" (VII.157). Gelon initially responded to the speech of Syagrus by berating the Greek mission for selfishness, declaring that the rest of Greece had not previously come to his aid when he had asked them for their assistance in his war against the Carthaginians (VII.158). However, Gelon then said that he was now ready to help the Greek cause against the Persians, offering to send two hundred ships, twenty thousand hoplites, two thousand "slingers," and two thousand light-armed men to support the cavalry (VII.158). However, Gelon made this offer under one condition: "that I [Gelon] shall be the Captain and leader of the Greeks against the barbarian. On no other condition will I myself go or send any others" (VII.158). Infuriated, Syagrus burst out and said:

> Loud will be the lamentation of Agamemnon, son of Pelops, if he heard that the leadership had been taken from the Spartans by Gelon and the Syracusans! Make no further talk about your condition—that we shall surrender the leadership to you. If you are minded to help Greece, know that you will do so under the orders of the men of Lacedaemon. If you do not think fit to obey our orders, do not come to our help. (VII.159)

Gelon, being so angrily rebuffed by the Spartan envoy, modified his condition, proposing that "you [Spartans] lead the land army and I the fleet. Or if it is your pleasure to command the fleet, I am willing to take the land army" (VII.160). However, Herodotus says that "the messenger from Athens answered before he of Lacedaemon could do so" (VII.161). This Athenian envoy spoke to Gelon as follows:

> As long as you were demanding the command of all the Greek host, we of Athens were content to keep silent, *knowing well that the Laconian was able to make an answer for both of us.* But since now, when you are turned aside from the project of commanding the whole, you are demanding the command of the fleet, here is this for you: *even if the Laconian were ready to surrender this to you, we are not.* This command is ours, providing the Lacedaemonians do not want it. If they want to have the command, we will stand down for them, but we will not yield the command at sea to anyone else. (VII.161; italics mine)[71]

Unable to acquire a leadership position and facing another Carthiginian invasion under Hamilcar, Gelon did not join the Greek alliance against the Persians.

Herodotus' account of the Greek mission to Gelon of Syracuse reveals important differences between the Spartans and the Athenians. The Spartans, outraged at the suggestion that they obey the orders of others, rebuff Gelon because under no circumstances will they give up the command that they desire to anyone. The Athenians, on the other hand, although they too rebuff Gelon, are willing to give up the command of the fleet to the Spartans. Herodotus therefore illustrates that in contrast to the Athenians, who are willing to "stand down for them," the Spartans are primarily motivated by pride or their self-regarding character as a group. This self-regarding character of the Spartans is related to the second difference between them and the Athenians that this story reveals. Herodotus indicates that the Athenians, "knowing well that the Laconian was able to make an answer for both," are aware that the Spartans will resist Gelon's demand to command the whole of the forces. The Spartans, however—interrupted by the Athenians before they could respond to Gelon's second proposal because they "were ready to surrender" the command of the fleet to him—are not aware that the Athenians will resist this demand as well. Herodotus therefore illustrates that, whereas the Athenians know and understand the Spartans, the Spartans do not know and understand the Athenians. The Spartans do not know the other or cannot, as the Athenians can, put themselves, intellectually, in the place of another. Moreover, at the beginning of book 8, Herodotus shows that the Athenian ability to put themselves intellectually in another's place, related to their ability to give up their pride, was crucial in keeping the Greek allies united against the totalizing threat from the Persians. According to Herodotus, despite being the premier naval power of Greece and suggesting before the mission that the fleet should be entrusted to them, the Athenians yielded the technical command of the fleet to the Spartan Eurybiades, because the rest of the allies refused to obey their direct orders (VIII.2). The Athenians gave way to the Spartans in this matter, because, Herodotus claims, "they thought what mattered most was the survival of Greece and knew very well that if there was a dispute about the leadership, Greece would perish" (VIII.3).[72]

Not only are the Spartans deficient in their understanding of the other or what is foreign to them, they do not have the same understanding of speech that Themistocles and Herodotus have. Herodotus reveals this deficiency in his account of Spartan king Cleomenes' war against the Argives, which occurred before the battle of Marathon. Consulting the oracle before his invasion and receiving the prediction that he would capture "Argos," Cleomenes, Herodotus indicates, took it for granted that the word "Argos" meant the city rather than the grove just outside the city (VI.76, 78, 80). He thought the meaning of the oracle was immediately apparent. Unlike Themistocles, Cleomenes did not understand, until it was too late, that speech—especially divine speech—is a mean between Egyptian lying and Persian truth telling, and thus that the truth of words, which can spawn a variety of meanings, is not immediately apparent but can only be revealed through interpretation. Herodotus further reveals the Spartan refusal to accept that the gods can "lie," as it were, in his account of Spartan king Leonidas' understanding of the oracle given to the Spartans before the Battle of Thermopylae (VII.20).

The Spartans, upon learning of Xerxes' intention to invade Greece, consulted, as the Athenians did, the Pythia at Delphi about the upcoming war. According to Herodotus, the Pythia spoke as follows:

> For all you people who dwell in Sparta, the city of broad roads, your city is great and glorious, but by the manhood of Persia she shall be sacked—or she shall not, but then Lacedaemon's watcher shall mourn for a king that shall die, from Heracles' race descended. Neither the fury of bulls nor of

> lions shall stem the foeman, though force matches force; the power of Zeus in himself he possesses; and none, I dare say shall restrain him, until the one or the other utterly shall be undone and utterly rent asunder. (VII.220)

Spartan king Leonidas, without any debate as occurred in Athens but thinking to himself and "want[ing] to store up the glory for the Spartiates alone," concluded that the oracle meant that his death at Thermopylae would prevent Xerxes from entering Greece. By dying he would thereby save the city of Sparta from destruction and the whole of Greece from enslavement (VII.220). Leonidas, unlike the Athenian envoys at Delphi and Themistocles in Athens, unequivocally accepts the veracity of the oracle at face value without question. However, the actions of the Spartans at Thermopylae only delayed Xerxes' march into Attica by seven days. According to Herodotus, it was Athenian opposition to Xerxes at sea, especially at Salamis, that prevented the enslavement of Greece and the destruction of Sparta (VII.139). Thus, although Leonidas' understanding of the oracle prepares him for noble self-sacrifice, it does not bring him closer to the truth or allow him, like Themistocles, to see things the way Herodotus does.[73]

Battles on Land and Sea

Herodotus, in books 6 to 9 of the *Histories*, gives an account of the six major battles of the Persian Wars. In book 6, Herodotus deals with the batttle of Marathon, an Athenian land battle against the Persians, led by Datis and Artaphrenes under the auspices of Darius. After the Persian defeat at Marathon, Darius dies and is succeeded by his son Xerxes, who campaigns in person against the Greeks, bringing the force of his entire empire with him. Xerxes' invasion culminates in three battles: Thermopylae, Artemisium, and Salamis. In book 7, Herodotus gives an account of Thermopylae, the famous land battle fought primarily by the Spartans on the Greek side and during which their king Leonidas was killed. In book 8, Herodotus gives an account of the battle of Artemisium, and the battle of Salamis, two sea battles which, on the Greek side, were primarily Athenian. After the Persian defeat at Salamis, Xerxes returns to Asia but leaves three hundred thousand select troops in Greece under the command of his brother-in-law Mardonius. Two more battles ensue, recounted by Herodotus in book 9: Plataea, a land battle which on the Greek side was primarily Spartan and during which Mardonius was killed, and Mycale, which, although a land battle, was fought by both the Greek and Persian fleets in Ionia, and was, on the Greek side, primarily both Spartan and Athenian.

Herodotus' account of these battles shows that the Athenians and Spartans possess two different types of courage and fight for two different reasons. For purposes of brevity, this section will deal briefly with aspects of the battle of Marathon not already discussed, preliminaries to the battle of Artemisium, and preliminaries to the battle of Salamis as well as its immediate effects. With respect to the Spartans, the battle of Thermopylae will be dealt with briefly, and the section will close with short remarks on the effects of the battle of Mycale. The picture that emerges from these battles is of an Athenian regime analogous to, in Herodotus' "cosmological" analysis, the element of water representing motion, and a Spartan regime more analogous to the element of earth representing rest.

According to Herodotus, the Athenians at the battle of Marathon were not only the first Greeks to hear Persian names and see Persian clothing as well as the men who wore it without fear, but they were also the first Greeks "to charge their enemy at a run" (VI.112). Herodotus says that after their battle lines were drawn up and the sacrifices were favorable:

> [T]he Athenians were permitted to charge, and they advanced on the Persians at a run. There was not less than eight stades in the no-man's-land between the two armies. The Persians, seeing them coming at a run, made ready to receive them; but they believed that the Athenians were possessed by some very desperate madness, seeing their small numbers and their running to meet their enemies without support of cavalry or archers. (VI.112)

Herodotus further emphasizes the "running" of the Athenians in his account of what happened after the Persians were routed on the battlefield. The Persians fled to their ships, and with those not burned by the Athenians they "backed water," intending to sail round the Cape of Sunium and take Athens before her soldiers could reach her (VI.113, 115). Although the Persians rounded Sunium, "the Athenians, rushing with all speed to defend their city, reached it first, before the barbarians came, and encamped, moving from one sanctuary of Heracles—the one at Marathon—to another, the one at Cynosargus" (VI.116). Faced with the Athenian army in front of the city, the Persians anchored off Phalerum—the harbor of Athens at this time—but after a few days Datis and Artaphrenes returned to Asia with their Eretrian prisoners, failing in their mission to subjugate the Athenians and the rest of Greece (VI.116).

Herodotus' account of the Athenian run at Marathon shows that the internalization of the regime in Athens leads to an internal rest. The Athenians have an "idea" of the city within themselves that allows them to have an external motion analogous to the element of water; it enabled the Athenians to charge the Persians and then rush back to Athens before the Persians could round the Cape of Sunium. Athenian defense is offense. Thus, Herodotus' account of the Athenian run at Marathon, combined with their ability to hear and look on the Persians without fear, shows that the Athenians are characterized by a type of courage or spiritedness that is directed outwards and leads to the attempt to transcend boundaries. They can look on the foreign other without fear. In this way the Athenians resemble the Persians, whose love of the beautiful drives them not only to look on but also to possess what is foreign to and other than themselves. According to Herodotus, the Persians, more than any other people, welcome foreign customs and adopt the customs of the people they conquer that they regard as more beautiful than their own (I.135). The Athenians at Marathon, although looking on and moving toward the other without fear, do not go as far as the Persians and try to possess the other. At Marathon the Athenians defend their freedom, and therefore their difference, against the homogenizing attempt of the Persians. However, Herodotus indicates that in the absence of such an external threat, the Athenians have the potential to become just as tyrannical or imperial as the Persians. This imperial impulse—not just looking on the other but also desiring to take it and make it one's own—is already manifested by Themistocles in the preliminaries to the battle of Artemisium, as well as what occurs immediately before and after the battle of Salamis.

The external motion and aggressive type of courage shown by the Athenians at Marathon, made possible by the internalization of the regime and resulting ability to look on the other without fear, naturally turns the Athenians toward the sea. This turn to the sea and reliance on naval power to resist Xerxes' attempt to subjugate Greece is furthered by Themistocles' understanding of speech and correct interpretation of the oracle. The Athenians and their allies first decided to encounter the Persians off the coast of Artemisium, in a narrow channel of the Thracian Sea (VII.175–76). Artemisium is a beach in the territory of Histiaea on the coast of northern Euboea, a large Greek island off the Magnesian mainland right across from the pass of Thermopylae (VII.176). The Athenians supplied the largest contingent of ships. They themselves, along with the Plataeans serving with them, manned one hundred and twenty-seven ships, as well as supplying another twenty manned by the Chalcidians, out of a total of two hundred and eighty ships in the Greek fleet (VIII.1). The Persians, however, docked at Aphetae, had nine hundred and twenty-seven ships, having previously lost four hundred ships in a storm off the Sepiad headland (VII.184–85, 190).

The Greeks, realizing that they were badly outnumbered, wanted to flee from Artemisium into the interior of Greece (VIII.4). Knowing this, the

Euboeans begged Eurybiades, a Spartan and overall commander of the entire Greek fleet—despite the fact that the Spartans had provided only ten ships (VIII.1)—to remain at Artemisium until they could remove their families to safety (VIII.4). Failing to persuade Eurybiades, the Euboeans next turned to Themistocles and bribed him with thirty talents of silver, "on condition that the fleet would remain in defense of Euboea" (VIII.4). Themistocles got the fleet to stay where it was by bribing Eurybiades with five talents out of the thirty with which the Euboeans had bribed him, but, according to Herodotus, Themistocles gave the five talents "as though the money came from himself" (VIII.5). Eurybiades was duly "persuaded" not to flee, but Adimantus, commander of the Corinthian contingent, argued against Eurybiades' sudden change of heart and said that he would sail away from Artemisium. Themistocles, however, said, "You will not desert us, for I will give you more money than the king of the Medes would send you for deserting your allies." He had three talents of the Euboean silver sent to Adimantus' ship (VIII.5). Apparently not knowing that he received less bribe money than Eurybiades, Adimantus let go of his resistance, and according to Herodotus:

> [T]hey were all made to change their convictions by gifts, the desires of the Euboeans were met, and Themistocles himself was the one who profited; for no one knew that he kept the rest of the money, but those who had the share in it believed that it had come from Athens for the actual purpose for which it was used. (VIII.5)

Themistocles, in taking the Euboean money and giving some of it to Eurybiades and Adimantus as if it had come from Athens, takes from the other and makes it his own. Thus, Themistocles' actions before the battle of Artemisium reflects the Athenian type of spiritedness displayed at Marathon. It reflects the attempt to transcend boundaries and look on the other, which is similar to Herodotus' own activity. Both move toward the Persian extreme of possessing the other and making it one's own.[74] Nevertheless, Themistocles gets the Greeks to remain and fight at Artemisium. Although encircled by the Persians, the Greeks used the naval tactic of "breaking the line" (*dieplous*), and won a great victory over the Persians (VIII.9–10, 11, 76).

The Greek fleet at Artemisium, however, after hearing of the Spartan defeat at Thermopylae, decided to retreat to the inner part of Greece or to seas nearer home (VIII.18, 22). Upon retreating from Artemisium, the Athenians discovered that the Peloponnesians were not, as had been agreed, in full force in Boeotia waiting to engage the Persians there. Instead, "the Peloponnesians were fortifying the Isthmus [with a wall], which showed that what they were really concerned with was the survival of the Peloponnese;

this is what they were going to guard and let everything else go" (VIII.40). The Athenians therefore asked the rest of the fleet to put in at Salamis, an island off the Athenian harbor of Phalerum, while they put in at Athens itself with the intention of conveying their women and children safely out of Attica by sea. Upon arriving in Athens, a proclamation was made that "every Athenian should save his children and household in any way he could" (VIII.41). Most "sent [their families] off to Troezen, and some to Aegina, and some to Salamis. . . . So when all was conveyed away, [the men] returned to the fleet" (VIII.41). The Athenians—men, women, and children—seeing themselves as the city rather than its visible or outer manifestations are able to forsake their city walls and Athens' physical location. They take to their ships, again pointing to their external motion.

According to Herodotus, when the Greeks who sailed from Artemisium put in at Salamis, the rest of the fleet came from Troezen and joined them there (VIII.42). The overall commander of the entire force was again the Spartan Eurybiades, even though the Athenians again supplied the largest contingent: one hundred and eighty ships out of a total of three hundred and seventy-eight (VIII.44, 48). The Spartans supplied only sixteen (VIII.43). Nevertheless, Eurybiades was overall commander, and when all of the commanders from the allied cities had collected at Salamis, they held a debate over which he presided (VIII.49). Eurybiades opened the debate by bidding "anyone who pleased [to] declare where, among the territories of which the Greeks were master, would be the most suitable place to fight their sea battle; for Attica at this point was already given over for lost" (VIII.49). The majority who spoke, who were Peloponnesians, said that the fleet should sail to the Isthmus and fight for the Peloponnese. They believed that if they were defeated at sea off Salamis they would be trapped on an island without hope for rescue, whereas if they were defeated off the Isthmus "they could put into a coastline that was their own" (VIII.49). Right at this moment in the debate, according to Herodotus, an Athenian messenger arrived with news that Xerxes, arriving in Attica, had entered the city of Athens, entirely empty of its population (VIII.51) and had plundered its temples and put the Acropolis to the torch (VIII.53). When the Greeks at Salamis heard this, some of the commanders immediately "fell into their ships and hoisted the sails," fleeing from Salamis before any official decision was made (VIII.56). The remainder formally decided to leave Salamis the next day, for it was now evening, and fight at sea for the Isthmus (VIII.56). However, when Themistocles returned to his ship from the debate, an Athenian named Mnesiphilus asked him the outcome. When told that they were to withdraw to the Isthmus, Mnesiphilus said to the Themistocles:

> If once they draw off the ships from Salamis, you will never again fight for any fatherland at all; everyone will run off, each one to his own city, and neither Eurybiades nor any other man will be able to keep the [armament] from scattering. Greece will be lost, and all through sheer folly. If there is any means at all by which you can undo this decision, if by any means you can persuade Eurybiades to change his mind and stay here, do so. (VIII.57)

Themistocles, pleased by this advice, made no answer to Mnesiphilus but immediately went to see Eurybiades (VIII.58). Upon getting an audience with Eurybiades on his ship, Themistocles "spelled out all that he had heard from Mnesiphilus, but he recounted it as though it were his own idea, and . . . in his urgency, he persuaded the commander to disembark and to summon the generals to a conference" (VIII.58). Despite his account in book 7 of Themistocles' interpretation of the oracle (VII.143), here in book 8 Herodotus presents Themistocles as taking Mnesiphilus' advice with respect to fighting at Salamis and repeating it to Eurybiades without acknowledging Mnesiphilus as the source.[75] Themistocles, as in the case of the money he took from the Euboeans, is again presented as taking from the other and making it his own—or showing the movement of Athenian spiritedness displayed at Marathon toward the Persian imperialist impulse.

A second debate was held among the Greek commanders at Salamis. Themistocles addressed them but did not repeat what he had said to Eurybiades. Doing so, Herodotus indicates, would surely have insulted the commanders (VIII.60). Rather, abstracting from either the courage or cowardice of the Greek commanders, Themistocles, made three tactical arguments against fighting at the Isthmus and four in favor of fighting at Salamis, concluding with the oracle given to the Athenians and his interpretation of it. According to Herodotus, after Themistocles listed the reasons why the Greeks should fight at Salamis and not sail to the Isthmus, the Corinthian commander Adimantus interrupted him and said, "Hold your tongue . . . you have no country," and argued against putting the question of where to fight to the vote on a motion of a "cityless man" (*apoli andra*) (VIII.61). Themistocles harshly responded by abusing both Adimantus and the Corinthians as a whole, and made it clear that "Athens had a city and land greater than theirs—the Corinthians'—so long as they had two hundred fully manned ships; for . . . there [were] no Greeks able to withstand an attack by [them]" (VIII.61). In this response we see the possibility of Athenian imperialism, inasmuch as it raises the specter of Athens using its fleet to attack and subjugate other Greek cities, after the Persians are defeated and the external threat that unites the Greeks recedes.[76] Athens' potential imperialism is further alluded to by the reversal of the Corinthian attitude in this passage. In book 5, the Corinthians were favorable to Athenian interests, resisting Cleomenes' attempt to impose the tyranny of Isagoras and then the Spartan attempt to impose the tyranny of Hippias on them (V.77, 92). In book 8, however, the Corinthians are against Athenian interests, which suggests that they fear that the Athenians will become to the Greeks what Isagoras and Hippias were to the rest of the Athenians.

Themistocles, in his final argument to Eurybiades, threatens that the Athenians, in whose ships "the whole power of this war is carried," may abandon the cause of Greek freedom altogether and remove themselves and their households to Italy (VIII.62). Eurybiades, fearing that Athenian desertion would result in defeat, finally decided that the fleet should not sail to the Isthmus but should remain at Salamis to prepare to fight the Persians at sea there (VIII.63). Despite the decision of Eurybiades, however, the Peloponnesians at Salamis "were dreadfully afraid . . . for the safety of the Peloponnese" (VIII.74). According to Herodotus, "For a while they would stand close together, man with man, and whispering their bewilderment at the stupidity of Eurybiades. But at last it all burst out into the open" (VIII.74). Eurybiades, at this sign of extreme discontent, held a third debate among the Greeks at Salamis. Again the majority opinion was for sailing to the Isthmus, across which the Peloponnesian land forces under the command of the Spartan Cleombrotus were building a wall, and defending the Peloponnese from there (VIII.74).[77] Themistocles, losing out in the debate but wishing to force the Peloponnesians to resist the Persians at Salamis, secretly left the meeting and had his slave Sicinus take a message to Xerxes and his generals encamped with their fleet at Phalerum.[78] When Sicinus arrived at their camp, he spoke as follows:

> The general of the Greeks has sent me, unknown to the other Greeks; for he is indeed an adherent of the king and wants his side to win rather than the Greeks. I am to tell you that the Greeks are plotting to run away, in their extreme fear, and now you have the chance of achieving the very finest of your actions—unless you stand by and let them run away and escape. (VIII.75)

Themistocles, having himself portrayed as the "general of the Greeks," takes on the identity of Eurybiades, and raises the specter of becoming Persian; he thus again takes what is other and makes it his own. The Persians, "believing in his message," decided to put to sea and encircle the Greeks (VIII.76). Beginning at midnight, so they would not be seen by the Greek forces at Salamis, the Persians extended the western wing of their fleet toward the island of Salamis and the eastern wing into the channel of Munychia (VIII.76). At dawn the next day, when the Greeks realized that they had been encircled by the Persians as they were at Artemisium, they finally made their preparations to fight the Persians at Salamis (VIII.83). A meeting of all the sailors was called, and according to Herodotus, Themistocles spoke

> . . . better than all the others; for all his words were a contrast of the worse and better side in man's nature [*en anthropou phusi*] and position in the world, and he bade them ever choose the better, and wound up his oration by urging them to board their ships. (VIII.83)[79]

Herodotus indicates that just as the Athenians at Marathon required the external threat of the Persians to make their pursuit of private interests coincide with the public good and allow them to see the other without fear, so too the Greeks at Salamis had to be encircled by the Persian fleet to make their concern for their own particular cities coincide with the common good of Greece and allow them to be open to Themistocles' appeal to nature.[80]

After Themistocles finished speaking, the Greeks put their ships out to sea and were attacked by the Persians (VIII.84). Although encircled, as at Artemisium, Herodotus says "the Greeks fought with proper discipline and in ordered ranks," and therefore won a great victory over the Persian fleet, which, although they "fought with zest and in fear of Xerxes," had "no order and no longer [did] anything with a sense of purpose" (VIII.86). Xerxes, after this defeat at sea, was terrified that the Greeks would sail to the Hellespont and destroy his bridges leaving him "caught in Europe and in danger of total destruction" (VIII.97). So he immediately set sail for the Hellespont, intending to cross back into Asia and return to Persia. Xerxes took his entire fleet with him and the bulk of his army, but he left three hundred thousand select troops with the Persian general Mardonius, wrongly believing that he would use these to enslave all of Greece (VIII.100–1).[81]

The next day, when they discovered that Xerxes had fled, the Greeks immediately decided to pursue his fleet (VIII.108). Having pursued them as far as the island of Andros without catching sight of them, the Greeks put in at the island and held another debate. Themistocles argued that the fleet should sail straight to the Hellespont and break the bridges, thereby preventing Xerxes' escape from Greece (VIII.109). Eurybiades, however, argued against this proposition, saying that if Xerxes and his forces were compelled to remain in Europe, they, like a cornered animal, would lash out and conquer Europe and Greece "city by city, and nation by nation . . . and the Persian army would live off the crops that the Greeks would grow yearly" (VIII.108). Eurybiades concluded by saying that if they allowed Xerxes to cross back into Asia, "Henceforth . . . it will be his country and not ours that will be at risk in the war" (VIII.108). Knowing that he could not convince the majority to sail to the Hellespont, Themistocles "changed his position and made his address to the Athenians," as they most of all needed to be dissuaded from attempting to reek vengeance on Xerxes and the Persians. They wished to sail to the Hellespont themselves to break the bridges even if the other Greeks would not follow (VIII.109). Themistocles, presenting Eurybiades' argument as his own, spoke to the Athenians as follows:

> I myself have been present on many occasions, and have heard about far more, where the same thing has happened—that men who were beaten and penned in a corner would fight again and redeem their faint-heartedness. We have found it to our great good luck and that of Greece that we have driven out such a veritable cloud of invaders; let us not pursue men who are in hot flight. It is not we who have done the deed but the gods and the heroes, who grudged that there should be any one man to lord it over both Asia and Europe—a man, moreover, impious and reckless. (VIII.109)[82]

Themistocles, therefore, according to Herodotus, "deceived" the Athenians; believing him wise and of good counsel, they "were ready to listen to everything he said" (VIII.110). Yet immediately after persuading them not to sail to the Hellespont, Themistocles, fearing the future envy of the Athenians and thus his possible need of the Persians, again had Sicinus deliver a message for him to Xerxes (VIII.110).[83] This message ran as follows:

> Themistocles, son of Neocles, general of the Athenians and, of all the allies, the man who is the best and the wisest, has sent me to tell you that Themistocles the Athenian, because he wishes to serve you, has held back the Greek fleet when they would have pursued your ships and destroyed your bridges over the Hellespont. So now take your way back completely at your ease. (VIII.110)

In this message, Themistocles not only takes on once again the persona of Eurybiades and raises the specter of exchanging his Greek identity for a Persian one, but he claims the deed of Eurybiades for himself as well. He presents himself as responsible for preventing the Greek fleet from sailing to the Hellespont and breaking Xerxes' bridges. Themistocles again takes the other and makes it his own.[84]

Herodotus, in the actions and speeches of Themistocles in the preliminaries to the battle of Artemisium, as well as before and after the battle of Salamis, shows the movement of Athenian spiritedness displayed at Marathon towards the Persian imperialist impulse displayed by Themistocles at Salamis.[85] Thus the Athenians, represented by Themistocles, no longer simply attempt to transcend boundaries and look on the other without fear; they try to possess the other and make it their own. At the moment of their highest victory in the service of Greek freedom, Herodotus presents the potential of the Athenians to become as tyrannical or imperial as the Persians.

The battle of Thermopylae, recounted by Herodotus in book 7, reveals both the source and character of the courage possessed by the Spartans. Two sources are given for Spartan courage. The first is law—as described by Demaratus, exiled king of Sparta, in his speeches to Xerxes before the battle of Thermopylae—and the second is pride or the desire for honor—as revealed by the actions of Spartan king Leonidas just prior to and during the fighting at Thermopylae. Although the speeches of Demaratus and the actions of Leonidas reveal two different sources, the character of the courage spoken of and displayed is the same.

According to Herodotus, after Xerxes had crossed the Hellespont and reviewed his land and sea forces at Doriscus, he asked Demaratus, who had accompanied him on his campaign, whether the Greeks would stand their ground and resist his onslaught (VII.100–1). Demaratus, speaking only about the Spartans, responded that "the courage they have comes imported, and it is achieved by a compound of wisdom and the strength of their laws . . . the first thing I say is that in no way will they accept your proposals bearing slavery to Greece, and the second is that they will challenge you to battle . . ." (VII.102). Demaratus, arguing that Spartan courage is derived from wisdom and the firm or lasting character of their laws, makes an indirect reference to their founder Lycurgus and to the stability of the good laws that he instituted in Sparta (I.65). Demaratus further emphasizes the unchanging character of the Spartan laws received from Lycurgus when he responds to Xerxes' second question concerning how the Spartans could fight such a large force as his—the land forces alone totaling one million, one hundred thousand (VII.184–85)—since they were internally free and did not fear the lash or whips of one man. Demaratus qualifies the internal freedom of the Spartans, claiming that the Spartans:

> . . . are free [*eleutheroi*]—but not altogether so. They have as the despot over them Law [*nomos*], and they fear him much more than your men fear you [Xerxes]. At least they do whatever he bids them do; and he bids them always the same thing: not to flee from the fight before any multitude of men whatever but to stand firm in their ranks and either conquer or die. (VII.104)[86]

Demaratus indicates that as the law itself "stands firm" over time, so it orders the Spartans themselves to "stand firm" and never flee, no matter what odds. The Spartans are as unmoving on the battlefield as their law is unmoving over time. Demaratus therefore reveals a strong contrast between Athenian and Spartan courage. The Athenians, ruled by speech, internalize their regime and look on the other without fear. This leads to the external motion of the Athenians, analogous to the element of water, and to their aggressive form of courage. The Athenians on the battlefield move just as much as their speech does in the assembly. The Spartans, on the other hand, are ruled by unchanging laws, which leads to an external rest analogous to the element of earth, or a defensive form of courage. The Spartans on the battlefield are as unmoving as their laws. Whereas the Athenians "run," the Spartans "stand firm." Xerxes however, laughs at Demaratus' claim and dismisses him (VII.105).

Herodotus, after recounting Demaratus' speeches about the source and character of Spartan courage, proceeds to the display of Spartan courage by Leonidas both before and during the battle of Thermopylae. The Greeks who decided not to Medize, refusing to take the Persian side, upon learning that Xerxes was about to cross the Hellespont into Thessaly, gathered at the Isthmus and, after a debate, decided to send their fleet to Artemisium and their land forces to Thermopylae (VII.173, 174–75). They believed that if they guarded the pass at Thermopylae they would prevent the Persians from coming into Greece by land, and they hoped that the narrowness of the pass would neutralize the superior numbers of the Persians (VII.173–75). The Spartans, however, because they were celebrating the Carnean festival—as they were before the battle of Marathon (VII.206, VI.106)—sent only three hundred hoplites to Thermopylae (VII.202). Their Peloponnesian allies, celebrating the Olympic festival (VII.206), sent only five hundred Tegeans; five hundred Mantineans; one thousand one hundred and twenty Andrians; four hundred Corinthians; two hundred Phliusians; and eighty Mycenaeans (VII.202). From Boeotia came seven hundred Thespians and four hundred Thebans—under duress, as they were suspected of wishing to Medize (VII.205)—plus the full force of Opuntian Locrians and one thousand Phocians (VII.203). Herodotus, later in book 8, makes reference to the helots who were present and died at Thermopylae, but he does not mention how many there were (VIII.25). However, in his account of the battle of Plataea in book 9, Herodotus says the Spartans sent seven helots for each hoplite (IX.10). Thus we can speculate that there were two thousand one hundred helots sent to Thermopylae. The total land forces of the Greeks sent to Thermopylae, therefore, was approximately seven thousand three hundred plus the Opuntian Locrians, so they were vastly outnumbered by Xerxes forces.[87] The overall commander of the Greek forces was Spartan king Leonidas, the half-brother of the now deceased Cleomenes and the third son of Anaxandrides (VII.204, V.59).

According to Herodotus, when Xerxes and the Persians marched down from Doriscus and came to Trachis, the Greeks at Thermopylae, much like the Greeks at Salamis, were in "sheer terror" and debated whether they should stay or withdraw off to the Isthmus (VII.201, 207). Although the Phocians, Locrians, and other Peloponnesians wanted to flee to the Isthmus, Leonidas, similar to Themistocles at Salamis, "gave his vote" to stay where they were (VII.207). Herodotus sheds light on the motives of the latter's wish to "stand firm" in his narration of what followed after Leonidas decided to remain at Thermopylae.

While the Greeks were debating whether to stay at Thermopylae or withdraw to the Isthmus, Xerxes sent a mounted spy to see how many Greeks there were and what they were doing (VII.208). When the spy approached the pass, he saw only those Spartans who had been stationed outside the wall, and "some of these men he saw exercising and some combing their hair" (VII.208). Wondering at the Spartan concern to beautify themselves, the spy rode back to Xerxes and reported to him what he had seen. Baffled by the report, Xerxes asked Demaratus what the Spartans were doing. Demaratus responded:

> This is their custom: that when they are going to risk their lives, they make their heads beautiful. Know then, that if you beat these, and those of them who are still in Sparta, there is no other nation in the world, my lord, that will withstand you and lift a hand against you. For now you are making your attack on the fairest [*kallisten*] kingship and fairest city among the Greeks, aye, and the bravest men [*andra aristous*]. (VII.209)[88]

Demaratus draws attention to the Spartan concern for beauty and the nobility of self-sacrifice, which he now says makes them most courageous of all men, not just of the Greeks. However, Demaratus is wrong to believe that this Spartan attachment to beauty and the noble is the only thing that can preserve the external freedom of Greece. Herodotus, as we have seen, shows that the Athenian ability to see the other without fear leads to an external motion and aggressive form of courage that turns them towards the sea and to their victory over Xerxes at Salamis.[89] Yet Herodotus clearly admires Spartan courage, which Demaratus now implies is derived from their attachment to beauty or the noble. Xerxes, again dismissive of Demaratus' words, let four days go by and then, on the fifth, ordered his troops to attack the Spartans in the pass (VII.210). According to Herodotus:

> The Medes charged the Greeks full tilt and had many of their own men killed. Others replaced them, and their attack did not cease, although they were very sorely mauled; but [the Spartans] made it quite clear to everyone, and especially to the King himself, that, though [the Persians] had many men (*anthropoi*) there, there were few *men* [*andres*]. The encounter lasted all day. (VII.210)

The Spartan performance, Herodotus maintains, was that of "skilled soldiers against unskilled," and the Persians, after failing in their repeated attempts to gain control of the pass, ceased operations for that day (VII.211). The Persians tried again the next day, but the Greeks, "now ordered by regiments and nations . . . each fought in turn," and the Persians met with the same lack of success (VII.212). Xerxes, not knowing what to do next, was then approached by a Malian man named Ephialtes. According to Herodotus, Ephialtes, "Thinking that he would get a great reward from the king . . . told him of the path that led over the mountain to Thermopylae, and so he destroyed the Greeks who stood firm there in the pass" (VII.213). Xerxes immediately ordered the Persian general Hydarnes with his men to follow Ephialtes, and the Persians marched all night along this path (VII.215, 217). At dawn, they reached the summit of the pass, where one thousand Phocian hoplites were standing guard on this part of the mountain under the orders of Leonidas (VII.217). When the Phocians realized that the Persians, unexpectedly, had climbed up the mountain, they immediately began to arm, but "under the fire of many arrows that fell upon them," fled to the top of the mountain and prepared to die, "being convinced that the Persian attack had been mounted against themselves in the first place" (VII.218). Yet, the Persians bypassed the Phocians and rushed down the mountain as fast as they could, toward the Greeks in the lower pass at Thermopylae (VII.218).

When they learned that the Persians had climbed the mountain path and made their way around them, the Greeks in the lower pass were divided about what to do (VII.219). The majority, who were in favor of leaving their post, departed, scattering "each to his own city" (VII.219). However, the Thebans, unwillingly, and the Thespians "made their preparations to stand where they were, with Leonidas" (VII.219, 222). Herodotus maintains that "it is said, that Leonidas himself sent [the other Greeks] away out of care that they should not die there" (VII.220). Yet, for himself and the three hundred Spartan hoplites, Leonidas, according to Herodotus,

> . . . thought it disgraceful to quit the post they had come to guard in the first place. I am myself strongly of this opinion; that when Leonidas saw that the allies were faint-hearted and unwilling to run the risk in his company, he bade them be off home; but for himself it would be dishonorable [*ou kalos*] to leave. If he stood his ground, he would leave a great name [*kleos mega*] after him, and the prosperity of Sparta would not be blotted out. For there was a prophecy . . . [that] said that either Sparta would be destroyed by the barbarians or the king of Sparta would be destroyed. . . . I believe that Leonidas thought this over and wanted to store up the glory [*kleos*] for the Spartans alone; and so he sent off the allies. (VII.220)[90]

Herodotus indicates that Leonidas is primarily motivated to stay and fight at Thermopylae out of pride and the desire to achieve honor and glory through a noble death.[91] At sunrise, Xerxes ordered his attack, and the Persians, descending from the mountain, charged the remaining Greeks from two directions, head on and from behind. The Greeks, encircled and putting forth "their very utmost strength against the barbarians [and fighting] in a frenzy with no regard to their lives," were all killed, including Leonidas (VII.223–25).[92] Whereas Themistocles at Salamis is primarily motivated by the desire to defeat Xerxes at sea, thereby saving Athens and the whole of Greece from slavery, Leonidas at Thermopylae is primarily motivated by the desire for a noble death in the hopes of achieving immortal glory for himself and for the Spartans. Moreover, all of the speeches of Demaratus except one indicate that the source of Spartan courage is the stability of their laws, so the actions of Leonidas indicate an alternative source of Spartan courage, their pride or desire to achieve honor.[93] Yet the nature of the courage shown by Leonidas is the same as that described by Demaratus; Spartan courage is defensive, leading to an external rest analogous to the element of earth. On the battlefield, whereas the Athenians "run," the Spartans "stand firm." Thus Spartan courage is animated by a type of spiritedness—unlike Athenian spiritedness—that is self-regarding. It is turned in on itself and seeks to defend its boundaries and what is its own. This defensive and self-regarding character of Spartan courage can be seen in the walls that the Spartans build, first across the pass at Thermopylae (VII.176) and then across the Isthmus. According to Herodotus:

> [A]s soon as the Peloponnesians had word that Leonidas and his men were dead at Thermopylae, they rushed out from their cities and took up their position (under the command of Leonidas' brother Cleombrotus) at the Isthmus . . . and . . . by deliberative decision, they built a wall across the Isthmus. (VIII.71)

Unlike the Athenians, the Spartans cannot fully distinguish their city from the walls at Thermopylae and the Isthmus, which defend their city. They have not fully internalized their regime. Unlike the Athenians, the Spartans rely on something visible and external for the manifestation of their courage. It is at this point where the source of courage for Demaratus and the source of courage for Leonidas converge. According to the speeches of Demaratus, the Spartans are courageous due to their obedience to unchanging laws. Yet the Spartans believe that their laws are supported by the divine. When they obey the laws they obey the gods, who they believe will dispense punishment if they disobey because, being present, the gods can see them. According to the actions of Leonidas, the Spartans are courageous due to their pride or desire for honor. Yet to achieve honor a Spartan must be thought well of by others. This desire for recognition can be seen on the inscription on the pillar set up by the Amphictyons over the grave of the Spartans who died at Thermopylae. The inscription runs as follows:

> Go tell the Spartans, stranger passing by, that here obedient to their words we lie. (VII.228)

For both Demaratus and Leonidas, therefore, the manifestation of Spartan courage requires that it be seen by others, or some external force—either the gods or one's fellow citizens.[94] Unlike the Athenians, Spartan courage relies on being seen rather than seeing the other, on appearance rather than reality.

In his account of the battles of Marathon, Artemisium, Salamis, and Thermopylae, Herodotus shows that Athenians and Spartans possess two different types of courage and fight for two different reasons. Spartan courage is defensive and is characterized by a type of spiritedness that is turned in on itself and seeks to defend its boundaries and what is its own. It is therefore analogous to the element of earth. Also, Spartans are not primarily motivated by the desire to win, but to achieve honor, largely through death, as shown by their "stand" at Thermopylae. The Athenians, on the other hand, possess an aggressive type of courage, as shown by their "run" at Marathon and their turn to the sea at Artemisium and Salamis. Analogous to the element of water, it is characterized by a type of spiritedness directed outwards; it leads to the attempt to transcend boundaries, and it looks on and tries to possess what is foreign or other. The Athenians fight to win and to preserve their internal freedom, along with the external freedom of all of Greece. Herodotus points to his belief in the superiority of Athenian courage in a passage already discussed (VII.139), in which he relativizes the effectiveness of Spartan courage.[95] According to Herodotus:

> If there had been no opposition to Xerxes at sea, what happened on land would have been this: even if the Peloponnesians had drawn many walls across the Isthmus for their defense, the Lacedaemonians would have been betrayed by their allies, not because the allies chose to do so but out of necessity as they were taken city by city, by the fleet of the barbarian; thus the Lacedaemonians would have been isolated and, though isolated, would have done deeds of the greatest valor and died nobly. That would have been what happened; or else they would, before this end, had seen that all the other Greeks had Medized and so themselves would have come to an agreement with Xerxes. In both these cases, all of Greece would have been subdued by the Persians. For I cannot see what value those walls drawn across the Isthmus would be, once the King was master by sea. So . . . a man who declares that the Athenians were the saviors of Greece would hit the very truth. (VII.139)

In this passage Herodotus suggests that Spartan courage, which is noble, was just as good as Medizing, which is base and which is thus ineffective in preserving the external freedom of Greece. Although he recognizes that the Athenians possess a higher or superior form of courage, Herodotus also indicates that this in itself poses the danger that Athens will become as tyrannical as Persia, or, moving from the Herodotean perspective displayed at Marathon to the Persian extreme displayed at Salamis, will come to desire the universal empire that Xerxes did. Herodotus further reveals the imperialist impulse at work in Athens at the close of his work. After their victory against the Persians in the battle of Myclae, the Athenian fleet attacks and subjugates the Greek city of Sestos in the Chersonese—in contrast to the Spartans who had resolved to sail home to the Peloponnese (IX.114–20). The imperialist impulse of Athens is one of the fundamental political problems Herodotus identifies in his *Histories*. What allows Athens to be open to universal truth and preserve the freedom of Greece can also make it imperial and thus destroy the freedom of Greece. The Athenians may attempt to impose on the political world the universality that their regime allows them to grasp in the natural world.

Conclusion

Herodotus and the Role of the Historian

Introduction

The *Histories* provides a solution to the problem of empire. Apparently desired by Athens at the end of the book, empire and the imperialist impulse is a fundamental problem of politics, identified by Herodotus in his work. Herodotus in the *Histories* shows the Athenians, and others like them, that they can satisfy intellectually the desires and dreams that motivate the pursuit of empire politically and militarily—at the same time avoiding the pitfalls and traps that overcame Xerxes and the Persians. Herodotus gives his readers an indication of why he fears imperial expansion: he recounts the many violations of Persian and Egyptian customs committed by Persian king Cambyses in Egypt. In a passage in book 3 of the *Histories*, Herodotus, intending to prove that Cambyses was mad, makes the following claim:

> If there were a proposition put before mankind, according to which each should, after examination, choose the best customs in the world, each nation would certainly think its own customs best. Indeed, it is natural for no one but a madman to make a mockery of such things. That this is how men think about their customs one can see from . . . the following case in particular. Darius, during his own rule, called together some of the Greeks who were in attendance on him and asked them what would they take to eat their dead fathers. They said that no price in the world would make them do so. After that, Darius summoned some of the Indians who are called Callatians, who do eat their parents, and, in the presence of the Greeks (who understood the conversation through an interpreter), asked

> them what price would make them burn their dead fathers with fire. They shouted aloud "Don't mention such horrors!" These are the matters of settled custom, and I think Pindar is right when he says, "Custom is king of all." (III.38)

Herodotus does not posit an absolute relativism in the above passage, however. He points to the difficulty of discovering and studying nature, that which lies concealed beneath custom.[1] Human beings, it would seem, believe their own customs (*nomoi*) to be best or most beautiful (*kallistous*), not because they identify them merely as customary and their own, but rather because they think that their customs are right, that they reflect nature or what is naturally good. When most human beings believe they are looking at nature, they are really looking at what is conventional, or they cannot distinguish between nature and convention.[2] Persian king Darius, as the above passage in book 3 suggests, acquired an insight into the power of custom to present itself as nature because of the Persian conquests that brought him into contact with other cultures. Persian imperialism allowed Darius to see and investigate foreign customs and conventions that differed from his own. Darius thus perceives the mere conventionality of all conventions, pointing him to the reality of a nature distinct from conventions.[3] Herodotus suggests that the identification of a custom as merely a custom occurs only if one looks to, and compares, the particular customs of others with one's own. This comparison makes it possible to discover the existence of a nature distinct from custom; it allows one to distinguish between nature, which is universal, and convention, which is particular. Only then can one begin to study one's true nature, or hope to have self-knowledge. Herodotus aspires to discover and convey such knowledge as he, like Darius, investigates the customs of others, which differ from his own. However, Herodotus does so not through foreign conquest, but through the writing of his *Histories*. He compares the customs of the Greeks with those of the Egyptians, Persians, Scythians, and many others.[4] The danger of the universal empire desired by Xerxes, and apparently desired by Athens at the end of the *Histories*, is therefore this: Xerxes, in his wish to extend his father's empire into a universal one, seeks to destroy all foreign customs and conventions by universalizing the particular customs of Persia (VII.8). In thus denying otherness in the world, he would destroy the ability to identify the natural or to distinguish between nature and convention. He would thereby destroy the possibility of self-knowledge. No one could see oneself in light of the differences between oneself and others. The foundation of Herodotus' own activity would be destroyed as well.

Herodotus' own writing is not merely threatened by empire, but seeks to address it as well. That the *Histories* is a potential solution to the problem of empire can best be seen by comparing Xerxes' gathering of the world's forces to invade Greece in the first half of book 7, with Herodotus' gathering of the world into an intelligible whole, both in book 7 and the *Histories* more generally.

Xerxes' Empire and the Desire for Divinity

According to Herodotus, when Xerxes assumed the Persian throne after the death of Darius, he summoned a special council of the most notable Persians. There he announced his plan to extend his father's empire into a universal one. He would bridge the Hellespont and drive his forces through Europe into Greece, conquering Athens and the other Greek cities in the Peloponnese (VII.8). Xerxes then explained his motive for this campaign, saying:

> [I]f we subdue [the Athenians] and their neighbors who live in the land of the son of Pelops, the Phrygian, we shall show [*apodexomen*] to all a Persian empire that has the same limit as Zeus's sky. For the sun will look down upon no country that has a border with ours, but I shall make them all *one* country, once I have passed in my progress through Europe. For I learn the case is so, that then there will be no city of men nor nation among mankind left that shall be able to come against us. (VII.8)

Xerxes, in his plan to rule the world, wishes to do three things. First, in eliminating distinctions between continents by bridging the Hellespont, Xerxes wishes to make the earth one.[5] By planning to turn the different, and therefore changing, continents into one continent, Xerxes plans to turn motion into rest. Second, paralleling his plan to eliminate physical distinctions between continents, Xerxes intends to eliminate political distinctions between countries through elimination of national boundaries. Xerxes, wishing to make the earth one, wishes to make humanity one as well. His plan to reduce the plurality of countries among human beings into one country, seeks to transform the changing into the unchanging and motion into rest. Third, just as Herodotus, in the first sentence of his work, says he is showing forth (*apodexis*) his history (I.1), Xerxes wishes to show forth (*apodexomen*) a stable universe ruled by the Persians and ultimately by himself.[6] Herodotus thus indicates a connection between his own activity and Xerxes' desire to rule the whole.

The character of the universe or whole that Xerxes plans to rule is revealed by how he orders his forces gathered to invade Greece. According to Herodotus, Xerxes' host "was far the greatest host of any we have heard of" (VII.20). Neither the force gathered by Darius against the Scythians, nor that gathered by the Scythians against the Cimmerians, nor that gathered by Agamemnon against Troy, nor that of the Teucrians and Mysians (before the Trojan War) against the Thracians, was as large as that gathered by Xerxes (VII.20). Xerxes' host included forces from all the nations of Asia and Libya, as well as Egypt. Moreover, while not including the Scythians of Europe nor those Greeks in Attica and the Peloponnese—neither having been subjugated by the Persians at this time—it did include their representatives in Asia. The Sacae, whom Herodotus says are Amyrgian or Asian Scythians, served in Xerxes' army (VII.64), and the Lycians, Dorians, Carians, Ionians, Aeolians—all Greeks in Asia Minor—as well as the Ionian islanders and Hellespontine Greeks, all served in Xerxes' navy (VII.92–95). Xerxes' host, therefore, did, in a sense, represent the entire world, a "world" by which he intended to subjugate Greece.

Xerxes' whole land army gathered in Critalla in Cappodocia and began marching, along with Xerxes himself, to Sardis. From Sardis, they marched to Abydos, on the Hellespont, to cross over the raft-bridge into Europe (VII.26, 37). When marching out of Sardis, Herodotus says that the baggage train and pack animals went first and then, after them, "a mingled host of every nation, with no divisions" (VII.40). After this disordered host there was a large break, and then came the well-ordered and highly adorned Persian contingent. In the front were one thousand horsemen. Immediately behind them were one thousand spearmen, with the points of their spears turned to the ground and golden pomegranates on the other end. After these came ten sacred Nesaean horses and the sacred chariot of Zeus, unmanned and drawn by eight white horses. Xerxes followed in his chariot, drawn by Nesaean horses, and beside him was his charioteer, Patiramphes, son of Otanes (VII.40). Behind Xerxes came another one thousand spearmen, this time with the points of their spears turned towards the sky and golden apples on the other end. After these came another one thousand horsemen, and, after these, ten thousand infantrymen. One thousand of these infantrymen had golden pomegranates instead of points on their spears, and they surrounded the other nine thousand who had silver pomegranates on their spears. Finally, in the rear of the Persian contingent, came ten thousand more horsemen (VII.41). After these Persian horsemen, Herodotus says there was a break of two furlongs, and then followed "the rest of the army, not in divisions" (VII.41).

Like the universe Xerxes wishes to rule, he places the Persian contingent in the middle of his host, and himself in the middle of the Persians.

The Persian forces are extremely well-ordered, divided by function—either cavalry, spear, or infantry. Each function is identified by the different and elaborately adorned weapons they carry—or even by the different ways in which they carry their weapons. However, as to the non-Persian part of Xerxes' host, its inferiority is indicated by the breaks that separate it from the Persian contingent. It marches as a disorderly mob. Xerxes takes no care to divide the rest of his army according to the separate nations which compose it, nor does he divide it by the separate functions which they play, nor the different weapons which they carry.[7] This is again revealed when Herodotus describes their crossing the bridge over the Hellespont into Europe. The first to cross were the ten thousand Persian infantry, but behind them came "a mixed host of all nations" (VII.55). The day after this disorderly mob crossed, the rest of the well-ordered Persian contingent, including Xerxes himself, also crossed the bridge. After these crossed, so did "all the rest of the host" (VII.55). Again, Herodotus mentions no order among them.

Xerxes, in failing to order the non-Persian part of his forces—the overwhelming majority of his host—by their different nations, the different functions which they commonly perform, or the different weapons which they commonly use, ignores the particular customs that distinguish human beings from each other. Rather than trying to preserve the particular customs to which the men in his army adhere, or to divide them into the particular nations to which they belong, Xerxes disperses them into their individual components and then regroups them into one disorderly mass. Xerxes takes no care to preserve the diversity among the nations that he rules in his empire, and which compose his forces gathered against Greece. He has no desire to understand the parts within the whole. Xerxes desires a whole that dispenses with the parts out of which it is composed. He seeks a universal that will crush the particular.

Herodotus indicates that the consequence of Xerxes' desire to rule a whole without parts, if successful, would be to reduce all humanity to slavery. For instance, immediately after announcing that he will reduce all the countries of the world to one country, Xerxes says "so those who are innocent in our sight and those who are guilty will alike bear the yoke of slavery [*doulion*]" (VII.8).[8] After announcing his plans, Xerxes has three dreams. In his third dream, Xerxes thought he was crowned with an olive branch with shoots that sprung out over the entire world—but then this crown suddenly disappeared. The Magi interpreted the dream to mean "that it referred to all the earth and that all mankind should be slaves [*douleusein*] to Xerxes" (VII.19). The Magian interpretation seems questionable, as the olive branch disappears, but the point is that if Xerxes is successful, all human beings will become his slaves. Moreover, before setting out with his host, Xerxes ordered that a channel be dug through the isthmus at Athos, wide enough for two triremes to sail through at the same time (VII.22, 24). The workforce ordered to dig this channel was composed of men "of all nations in the army," and they did their work "under the lash" (VII.22). Xerxes takes men from different nations and melds them into one single workforce. As a result, they do not act out of choice, but out of external compulsion, the fear of the whip. They act like slaves.

Herodotus' account of the incident with Pythius further reveals the radical inequality and slavery that exists under Xerxes' rule. According to Herodotus, on his way from Critalla to Sardis, Xerxes, marching with his entire army, was met by a Lydian man named Pythius in the Phrygian city of Celaenae. Pythius entertained the king as well as his entire host (VII.26–27). After doing so, Pythius offered to contribute money to Xerxes' war effort. Upon inquiry, Xerxes learned that, besides himself, Pythius was the wealthiest man in the world (VII.27). Xerxes then asked this man exactly how much he was worth, and Pythius responded honestly, saying, "I have two thousand talents of silver, and, of Daric staters in gold, I have four million, lacking some seven thousand. All of these now I give you" (VII.28). Xerxes, despite showing delight at Pythius' offer of money freely given, does not accept it but instead, claiming to make him his friend, gives Pythius seven thousand staters of gold to round off his four million (VII.29). Herodotus indicates that Xerxes cannot accept a gift; he cannot be the receiver but only the giver. Everyone must be indebted to him and thus Xerxes rejects any notion of the equality and reciprocity needed for friendship. This is further revealed by the behavior of Xerxes toward Pythius after the eclipse of the sun that took place as the army was marching out of Sardis (VII.37). Pythius, terrified by what he thought the eclipse portended, approached Xerxes and asked him to release the eldest of his five sons from service in his army, "that he may be the caretaker of me and my possessions" (VII.38). Xerxes, furious at this request and calling Pythius a "vile creature" (*kake anthrope*) and his "slave" (*doulos*), reminded him that "[w]hen you did good to me and offered more such, you will never boast that you surpassed your king in deeds of kindness" (VII.39). Forthwith Xerxes ordered that Pythius' eldest son be chopped in two, and the army marched through the two pieces of his body as it left Sardis (VII.39).

Herodotus, in his account of how Xerxes numbered his host at Doriscus, shows that reducing humanity to slavery is ultimately to reduce them solely to their bodies, or to their lowest common denominator. According to Herodotus, when Xerxes and his host had crossed the Hellespont into

Europe, they marched through the Chersonese into Thrace and came to Doriscus, a large plain by the sea (VII.58–59). Here Xerxes decided to count the number of men in his host. Although Herodotus says the total number of the force came out to be one million, seven hundred thousand, he claims that neither he nor anyone else knows how many men each nation contributed to the total force, because Xerxes did not count his host by nation. Rather, Herodotus says:

> This is how [the Persians] counted them: they drew together into one place ten thousand men; and packing them in as tightly as they could, they drew a circle round the outside. Having drawn this and let out their ten thousand, they built a dry-wall on the circumference of the circle, in height reaching to a man's naval. They then pushed others into the walled space until in this fashion they had counted them all. (VII.60)

Xerxes treats his army not as a community of human beings but as a herd of beasts, jammed into a pig-pen-like structure to be counted. This is a consequence of not counting them as members of particular nations but rather as dispersed individuals in groups of ten thousand. In Xerxes' eyes, the human beings he rules are only a mass of bodies. No one has a truly unique individual identity which distinguishes him or her from others. As such, they are like manipulable mathematical objects, each one being interchangeable with all the rest.[9]

Xerxes' tendency to view his host as less than human is also illustrated by his whipping of the Hellespont. According to Herodotus, not one but two bridges were built over the Hellespont, the first one having been destroyed by a violent storm (VII.34). Upon hearing of this destruction while he and his army were in Sardis, Xerxes was furious and outrageously commanded that the Hellespont be given three hundred lashes and a pair of fetters be lowered into the sea (VII.35). Herodotus also claims that one story has it that Xerxes tried to have the Hellespont branded as well (VII.35). Moreover, Xerxes ordered, that while the Hellespont was being whipped, these words should be spoken to it:

> You bitter water, our master lays this punishment upon you because you have wronged him, though he never did you any wrong. King Xerxes will cross you, whether you will or not; it is with justice that no one sacrifices to you, who are a muddy and briny river. (VII.35)

Herodotus illustrates that Xerxes, in trying to convert water, as it were, into land, or motion into rest, has a tendency to animate physical nature in order to exert the kind of absolute control over it that he exerts over human beings. More importantly, however, Herodotus reveals that if Xerxes treats the sea as a human being, this means that he treats human beings like the sea; Xerxes views other humans as beings without souls, as purely inanimate material.[10] They become less than human under his rule. Yet if his men become less than human, then Xerxes must become more than human, or a god. Herodotus shows this tendency to divinization when he records that, after watching Xerxes and his army cross into Europe "under the lash" (VII.56), a man from the Hellespont region spoke thus:

> O Zeus, why did you liken yourself to a man of Persia and take the name of Xerxes instead of Zeus because you wish to destroy Greece, bringing all the people of the world with you? You could have done that without them. (VII.56)

A deeper motive for Xerxes' wish for a universal empire is not simply to "show to all a Persian empire that has the same limit as Zeus's sky" but also to show to all a Persian king who is himself like Zeus. His desire to expand infinitely in space, which would ultimately destroy the possibility of the discovery of nature and self-knowledge, masks a deeper desire to expand himself infinitely in time, or ultimately beyond time. In other words, Xerxes wishes to become divine and therefore to transcend time and the changes it brings. Xerxes again wishes to transform what is in motion—a mortal human being—into what is at rest, an eternal god.

Herodotus records a remarkable incident that took place in Abydos, in which Xerxes shows an awareness of the problematic character of his desire to become divine. Upon arriving in Abydos, before crossing the Hellespont, Xerxes took his seat on a large platform of white stone placed atop a hill. From this elevated position, Xerxes looked down over his entire army, gathered on the beach, and his entire navy, anchored along the shore (VII.44). He was then suddenly overcome with a desire to see an actual race take place between his ships, and forthwith his wish was turned into a reality, in which the Sidonian Phoenician ships won (VII.44). According to Herodotus:

> Xerxes was pleased with the race and with his army. . . . When he saw all the Hellespont covered with ships and all the shores and planes of Abydos full of men, then Xerxes declared himself a happy man; but after that he burst into tears. (VII.44–45)

Xerxes' desire to see his navy in action and the pleasure he feels in seeing his entire host thus arrayed at Abydos reveal his wish to make his own power manifest not simply to others, but to himself as well.[11] Xerxes wishes to know himself and to extend himself beyond time. Xerxes' tears illustrate his awareness that he cannot achieve the latter; he, like his men, is a mortal human being. Artabanus, Xerxes' uncle—who had at first spoken against the king's plan to invade Greece until visited in the night by a dream figure who threatened him if he continued his resistance (VII.10, 17–18)—asked him why he wept (VII.46). Xerxes responded, "[P]ity stole over me as I made my meditation on the shortness of the life of man; here are all these thousands, and not a one of them will be alive a hundred years from now" (VII.46). Showing concern for the plight of his soldiers, Xerxes illustrates his awareness that, although his host may be able to conquer the world, it cannot conquer time. His proposed universal empire, in which Xerxes sees himself, cannot ensure the immortality of the self as it, like the men who will acquire it, will pass away in time. The temporal character of human beings and the things they build through war prevents Xerxes from becoming divine. Despite this insight, Xerxes decides to carry on with his campaign (VII.50). He seems to know of no other alternative course of action or way of life besides continued imperial conquest—the ultimate aim of which he acknowledges is destined to failure. Why does Xerxes persist in this essentially tragic course?[12] Perhaps this can best be answered by looking to Xerxes' continued resistance to the caution of Artabanus.

Xerxes, after meditating on the shortness of human life, asked Artabanus if he would have resisted the plan to invade Greece (VII.47) if the figure in the dream had not come to him (VII.17–18). Artabanus indicates that he would have, and he claims that he is still full of fear as to the final issue of Xerxes' campaign, saying "among the many other matters that occur to me I see that the two greatest things in the world are your bitterest enemies" (VII.47). Thinking that Artabanus means that his army and navy will be inferior in number to those of the Greeks, Xerxes suggests that he immediately muster more men (VII.48). Artabanus then responds, "My lord, no one in his senses would find fault with this army of yours or with the number of your ships. If you were to assemble more men, the two things of which I speak would be but the more your enemies. These two are land and sea" (VII.49). According to Artabanus, the size of Xerxes' forces make both the land and sea his greatest enemies, not the Greeks. The land cannot supply enough food for the army, raising the possibility of famine, and, with respect to the sea, there is no harbor big enough to provide a haven for all of his ships in a storm, raising the possibility that the fleet will be destroyed (VII.49). Unlike Xerxes, Artabanus seeks to understand physical nature rather than to conquer it, and in doing so thinks about the whole in terms of its parts—as composed of earth and water or rest and motion—rather than abstracting from the latter. In this way, Artabanus is similar to Herodotus.[13]

Although acknowledging the wisdom behind Artabanus' cautionary words—"you are altogether reasonable in the way you lay this out, piece by piece" (VII.50)—Xerxes fails to call off his campaign or reduce the size of his host. Rather, Xerxes tells Artabanus, "do not fear everything; do not always take account of everything. As each opportunity arises, if you were to take account of everything that is involved, you would never do anything" (VII.50). Xerxes then says that previous Persian kings would never have established or increased the Persian empire if they had tried to take account of everything, or listened to men like Artabanus who do (VII.50). With this, Xerxes dismisses Artabanus and sends him back to Persia (VII.53). For Xerxes, there is an irreconcilable conflict between understanding and action, or between thought and politics.[14]

Xerxes' meditation on the shortness of life and his exchange with Artabanus before sending him back to Persia have two important implications. The first is that Xerxes reveals a tragic view of both life and politics. For Xerxes, human beings can never achieve their ultimate but necessary aim of transcending time through political conquest. Moreover, Xerxes believes that politics cannot be guided by thought. Speech and deed on the highest level cannot be reconciled. When one is trying to conquer the whole one cannot take time to understand it, especially in terms of its parts. The second important implication, already alluded to by Xerxes' tragic view of politics, is that the Persian regime, a hereditary, imperial monarchy, is not open to a type of thought similar to Herodotus' as manifested in his *Histories*.

Herodotus' Humane Alternative

Despite the fact that the Persian regime is closed to the thought of Herodotus, the *Histories* is both like and unlike the universal empire proposed by Xerxes. In book 4, Herodotus laughs at those previous mapmakers who have set three names on the earth—Libya, Asia, and Europe—because, according to Herodotus, "the earth is all one" (IV.36, 45). Nor can Herodotus learn the names of those who originally divided the world into three conventional, not natural, parts, nor when and how they got the names that they gave them (IV.45). Herodotus understands the earth as a one rather than three, a unity rather than a multiplicity. Herodotus makes the earth one in his writing by eliminating distinctions between continents, just as Xerxes planned to make the earth one in his empire by bridging the Hellespont.[15] By turning the changing continents into one unchanging land mass, Herodotus, like Xerxes, turns motion into rest. However, for ease in communication to his reader, Herodotus concludes his discussion of map-making and world geography by saying, "We will, of course, use the customary names [Libya, Asia, and Europe] for these lands" (IV.45).

Although Herodotus makes the earth one, he, unlike Xerxes, maintains the plurality and diversity among humanity. Herodotus preserves the distinctions between nations in his *Histories* by giving an account of their different customs or *nomoi*. For instance, Herodotus records how Xerxes numbered his host at Doriscus not by particular nation but as a disorderly mass of individual and identical bodies in groups of ten thousand (VII.60). Immediately after this, Herodotus, in his own words and in direct discourse with the reader, gives an account of the unique clothing, weapons, or name of each nation that served in Xerxes army (VII.61–80). He again gives an account of the unique clothing, weapons of war on board the ships, and unique name of each nation that served in Xerxes' navy (VII.89–95). Herodotus, unlike Xerxes, orders Xerxes' host, which represents the "world" in a sense, by what distinguishes the parts from each other rather than by what makes them the same.[16] Unlike Xerxes, Herodotus creates a whole that does not crush the parts out of which it is composed. Xerxes comes to possess and destroy through conquest other peoples and their foreign customs. Herodotus comes to possess and therefore preserve through writing.[17] The *Histories* itself replaces the universal empire dreamed of by Xerxes—but is superior to it. Herodotus, in his writing, can make the world one while also maintaining the otherness of the peoples and their conventions that exist within it. His writing combines the universal with the particular, rest with motion. Herodotus, by maintaining diversity on the level of *nomoi*, makes manifest a higher oneness or universality than the universality of the body. Unlike Xerxes' gathering of the world in book 7, Herodotus' gathering of the world makes manifest and gives room for the soul; his narrative points to that nonmaterial part of human beings by which they can create different customs and regimes.[18] Moreover, whereas Xerxes' empire rules bodies, Herodotus' empire, which exists in speech rather than deed, can rule souls.[19] Thus, Herodotus can rule without enslaving the ruled or attempting to divinize himself; his empire is humane.

The *Histories* not only preserves the diversity of *nomoi*, or the parts within the whole, but, unlike Xerxes, Herodotus puts these parts into an intelligible order. Egyptian customs emphasize rest, Scythian customs emphasize motion, and the Persian and Greek regimes combine both rest and motion. Persia does so in its own unique way, and Sparta and Athens do so each in their own unique ways as well. Yet only Athens combines rest and motion in such a way as to be open to the thought of Herodotus, as seen for instance in Herodotus' account of the battle of Marathon (VI. 111–12) and in Themistocles' interpretation of the oracle (VII.142–43). With the withdrawal of the Persians and the withdrawal of the divine, it is Herodotus who can moderate the Athenian desire for a universal empire modeled on that desired by Xerxes by providing them with a superior, if nonpolitical, one in his *Histories*. The whole which it contains and the way of life necessary for its composition which it points to, allows one to look on the other to see the self without conquering the other or making it one's own—thereby losing both the self and the other at the same time. The *Histories* shows that it is possible to know the self without having to expand the self infinitely in space. Herodotus, in moderating the desire for empire on the political level, maintains the possibility of the discovery of nature and self-knowledge on the intellectual level.

If unsuccessful in moderating the actual Athenian regime in pursuit of empire, as Thucydides' work makes clear, Herodotus' work holds out the possibility of moderating other democratic regimes like Athens in the future, an issue I will address in the epilogue. Herodotus says, in the first sentence of his work, that he is "showing forth" his history so "that time may not draw the color from what [human beings have] brought into being" (I.1). He thus intends his *Histories* to last for all time, just as Thucydides intends his history to do so as well.[20] This points to another way in which Herodotus' empire is superior to Xerxes'. By trying to possess the whole on the intellectual level rather than the political level, Herodotus can "show forth" an empire in writing that will last much longer than the one hundred years Xerxes predicts for his empire. Even if Xerxes were successful in "[showing forth] to all a Persian empire that has the same limit as Zeus's sky" (VII.8), this empire would have disappeared in time. Herodotus' empire, on the other hand, transcends time.

Herodotus, therefore, overcomes—or at least ameliorates—the tragic view of life and politics articulated by Xerxes. For Herodotus, the existence of the Athenian regime makes it possible to believe that politics in the future can be guided by thoughtful inquiry into the whole. As manifested in his *Histories*, one can know oneself and expand oneself beyond time without having to expand oneself infinitely in space. Human beings can thus achieve, if not immortality, then immortal fame, without destroying the possibility of self-knowledge and the foundations of Herodotus' own activity.

Herodotus points to the superiority of his own way of life in the last paragraph of his *Histories*. Here he tells a story in which a notable Persian named Artembares proposes to Cyrus that the Persians "move from this land of ours—for it is little and rocky, too—and take something better than it. There are many lands next to us and many further off, and if we take one of these we shall be more admired for more things. It is natural for those who hold rule to do so" (IX.122). Herodotus writes,

> When Cyrus heard that, he was not amazed at their argument but said that they should do what they said; but in that case they should be prepared to be no longer those who rule but those who would be ruled. "From soft countries come soft men. It is not possible that from the same land stems a growth of wondrous fruit and men who are good soldiers." So the Persians took this to heart and went away; their judgment had been overcome by that of Cyrus, and they chose to rule, living in a wretched land, rather than to sow the level plains and be slaves to others. (IX.122)

Herodotus ends his *Histories* with a warning against the dangers of imperial conquest. His warning extends beyond the Athenians, who are becoming like the Persians, to all regimes in the future.[21] More importantly Herodotus presents Cyrus at the end of book 9 in a very different light from how he presented him in book 1. In the above passage Cyrus associates ease and luxury with slavery and convinces the Persians to reject Artembares' proposal for imperial expansion. In book 1, Cyrus associates ease and luxury with freedom and empire and persuades the Persians to overthrow the Medes and to establish their imperial power (I.126–30). Moreover, it is Harpagus, not Artembares, who urges Cyrus along this path (I.124). Herodotus therefore creates a new Cyrus at the end of his *Histories*—a Cyrus in speech, as it were, as opposed to the actual Cyrus in deed. This new Cyrus prevents the Persians from establishing their empire, the actual expansion of which eventually leads to the war between the Persians and the Greeks that Herodotus records in his *Histories*. Thus, at the end of his work, Herodotus does in speech, or in writing, what is impossible to do in deed, or in history; he goes back in time in order to change the future.[22] If Herodotus "lies" at the end of his *Histories*, he does so only to preserve the possibility of understanding the whole by preventing the conquest of the whole. In other words, Herodotus lies in order to preserve, on a deeper level, the inquiry into truth.

Epilogue

9/11 and the Politics of Empire

The war between "civilization" and "terrorism" has emerged in the eyes of many as the greatest war of our time.[1] Brought most dramatically into public view by the attacks on the World Trade Centers and the Pentagon on September 11, 2001, the "war on terrorism" has given rise in the United States to various pragmatic approaches to making the world safe from the threat of terrorist violence. The arguments reflected in the speeches, writings, and interviews of Paul Wolfowitz, Colin L. Powell, and Joseph S. Nye, Jr. represent three recognizably distinct schools of thought regarding the causes of terrorism and the proper character and projection of American power across the globe in response. While there is much discussion of the concept of empire, or a regime's attempt to govern the world politically or culturally, there is little discussion of philosophy and the attempt to understand the world more generally. A brief consideration of these three approaches illustrates that contemporary reflections on the greatest war of our time tend to privilege pragmatics to the detriment of theory. I will also consider Robert W. Merry's recent critique of the assumptions underlying the positions of Wolfowitz, Powell, and Nye as a representation of the growing body of opposition to mainstream American foreign policy in the post-9/11 era.

Classical sources have been drawn upon by American statesmen and political theorists since the founding to key moments in her history. They can inform our understanding of the current international situation. Herodotus' *Histories*, in particular—with its broad panorama of regimes and analysis of the imperialist impulse at the root of the Persian Wars, has much to teach us about the causes as well as the potentials and dangers of the pursuit of empire. Accordingly, I will conclude by exploring how the *Histories* can be understood to both reflect and transcend contemporary approaches to international politics, war, and global expansion.

The guiding intellectual influence behind the first approach to the new international situation that we will consider is Paul Wolfowitz, Deputy Secretary of Defense in President George W. Bush's first administration and former President of the World Bank. Before serving in these positions he was the Dean of the School of Advanced International Studies at Johns Hopkins University. Between 1989 and 1992, Wolfowitz served as the Undersecretary of Defense in the administration of President George H. W. Bush. It was in the waning months of George H. W. Bush's presidency that Wolfowitz authored the 1992 "Defense Planning Guidance," a classified set of military guidelines that is prepared every few years for the Department of Defense. Subsequently leaked to the *New York Times* and the *Washington Post*, it generated a swirl of controversy. The main sources of contention were the emphasis on maintaining America's newfound status as the sole global superpower in the post-Cold War era and the need to promote America's interests and values in different regions of the world through unilateral military action, if need be.[2] However, it is in President George W. Bush's new *National Security Strategy*, issued to Congress in September of 2002 in response to the attacks of September 11, 2001, where the ideas of Wolfowitz, first percolated in the 1992 "Defense Planning Guidance," find their most robust manifestation.[3] I will therefore explore Wolfowitz's vision for America's role in the world primarily through an analysis of President Bush's *National Security Strategy*, known to the world as the Bush doctrine.

The Bush doctrine begins with the claim that the defeat of Nazism in World War II and of Communism in the Cold War means that the West and liberal democracy have come out as the clear victor at the beginning of the twenty-first century. Thus only "a single sustainable model for national success: freedom, democracy, and free enterprise" has proven to be a viable alternative for organizing human life in the future.[4] Not only is there one best political and economic model for the world; there is also only one right moral code for the world. According to the Bush doctrine, "the United States must defend liberty and justice" because these principles are "right and true for all people everywhere," and although "different circumstances require different methods, [they do] not [require] different moralities."[5]

These assertions of universal political and moral truths rest on an understanding of a universal nature that all human beings share. The Bush doctrine argues that "people everywhere want to say what they think; choose who will govern them; worship as they please; educate their children—male and female; own property; and enjoy the benefits of their labor." Moreover, the defense of such "values of freedom," based on the understanding of a universal human nature, is the "common calling of freedom-loving people across the globe and across the ages." However, despite the United States's "position of unparalleled military strength and great economic and political influence," it should not use this strength to "press for unilateral advantage."[6] In other words, the Bush doctrine explicitly denies that its aim is empire in the traditional territorial sense. Yet it openly promotes the universal expansion of American values or the American way of life, as it asserts that the "United States will use this moment of opportunity to extend the benefits of freedom across the globe. We will actively work to bring the hope of democracy, development, free markets, and free trade to every corner of the world." The ultimate aim of this universal moral and political goal is not simply to do what is right but to protect American national security. According to the Bush doctrine, "defending our nation against its enemies is the first and fundamental commitment of the Federal Government."[7]

The primary focus of the Bush doctrine's expansionist policies are "rogue states" located primarily, but not exclusively, in the Middle East. Rogue states are governed by non-democratic regimes that "brutalize their own people . . . display no regard for international law . . . are determined to acquire weapons of mass destruction [WMD] . . . sponsor terrorism around the globe," and "reject basic human values and hate the United States and everything for which it stands."[8] Rogue states cannot simply be deterred as the Soviet Union was during the Cold War. The strategy of mutually assured destruction was one in which America tolerated the acquisition of WMD by its prime enemy, the Soviet Union. America believed the Soviets would be deterred from using such weapons by the knowledge that America would respond in kind with its own arsenal. This strategy will not work against America's new enemies in the twenty-first century.

The Bush doctrine gives two reasons why rogue states cannot be deterred. First, unlike the Soviet Union, who viewed WMD as weapons of "last resort," rogue states today view them as "weapons of choice," or "as their best means of overcoming the conventional superiority of the United States." Second, rogue states are unlikely to use WMD in their own name but will indirectly use them against the United States by providing them to "a terrorist enemy whose avowed tactics are wanton destruction and the targeting of innocents" and "whose most potent protection is statelessness."[9]

Missile defense is one solution to the problem of rogue states using WMDs as weapons of first choice against their enemies. During an interview conducted by *New York Times* reporter Michael Gordon and FRONTLINE producer Sherry Jones on June 12, 2002, Wolfowitz claimed the Bush administration's purpose in developing missile defense is "to deny these rogue states freedom of action to bully their neighbors." If rogue states were to develop intercontinental ballistic missiles (ICBMs) capable of delivering WMDs to targets on the continental United States, Wolfowitz admitted that "[i]t may take five, ten years to develop that capability against ICBMs. We're well on the way to doing it, but we can't wait until one morning we wake up and someone says "The Iranians are two years away from an ICBM. Let's develop a defense against it." However, in the same interview Wolfowitz also acknowledged that missile defense would not have prevented the terrorist attacks of September 11. In other words it cannot defend the American people against the tactic of "hiding behind terrorists," so to speak, in which rogue states seek to avoid responsibility for committing acts of war against the United States and its allies by using terrorist organizations as their instruments. According to Wolfowitz, "[w]ith 20/20 hindsight, one could clearly wish that we'd taken more preventive action against Al Qaeda and the Taliban in Afghanistan, and prevented Sept. 11. But Sept. 11 was nothing compared to what terrorists or states could do with weapons of mass destruction. . . . So, yes, there are options open to defend the country, instead of just waiting for an attack to come."[10] Wolfowitz therefore suggests that when dealing with the problem of nexus between terrorists and WMDs, America must turn from a defensive strategy, such as missile defense, to an offensive strategy.

Taking the offense against terrorism is therefore at the root of the Bush doctrine's justification of aggressive American action to destroy the "overlap between states that sponsor terror and those that pursue WMD." It brings with it a potential of bringing democracy and American values to all nations and all peoples across the globe.[11] The aim of terrorism, as defined by Wolfowitz in the Bush doctrine, is to inflict mass civilian deaths, primarily in the United States and among its allies, for political purposes, the motive of which is to overcome their inability to inflict mass military deaths against American forces on the battlefield. Terrorists cannot be deterred by mutually assured destruction because terrorists, "who seek martyrdom," do not fear death. The result is that WMDs must be prevented from getting into their hands in the first place. Keeping WMDs out of the hands of terrorists must be accomplished, according to the Bush doctrine, through "preemption," or the use of American military force to effect regime change toward democracy and freedom in rogue states that pursue WMDs and sponsor terrorism.[12] The assumption underlying the justification for military preemption is that nations and peoples who share some semblance of the American way of life will not be hostile to America's existence, power, and prosperity, and so not provide the safe havens that terrorists so depend on.[13]

Colin L. Powell is a loyal ally to Paul Wolfowitz and his ideas as expressed in the Bush doctrine, especially with respect to the priority of fighting terrorism through military preemption, if necessary. However, Powell tends to emphasize the effectiveness of diplomacy in combination with military action to a greater degree than Wolfowitz. Moreover, when it comes to identifying and eliminating the root causes or ultimate sources of terrorism, Powell begins to depart from Wolfowitz in significant ways. Colin L. Powell was Secretary of State in President George W. Bush's first administration, and he served thirty-five years in the United States Army, becoming a four-star General and Chairman of the Joint Chiefs of Staff, under President George H. W. Bush. Powell can be understood to represent a distinct approach to America's role in the post-Cold War era. His address to the Elliott School of International Affairs at George Washington University on September 5, 2003, and his remarks on the occasion of George Kennan's centenary birthday at Princeton University on February 20, 2004, serve as exemplary manifestations of Powell's vision for America in the world.

Like Wolfowitz and the Bush doctrine, Powell, in his remarks at Princeton, agrees that "in the realm of political ideas, there's now no organized, coherent alternative to the liberal triad of democracy, the rule of law and market economics" (Kennan 4). Moreover, Powell's assertion of the universal political truth of liberal democracy and capitalism rests on an assumption of a universal nature that all human beings share. According to Powell, human beings on every continent desire "liberty and the rights of man; . . . intellectual, religious and economic freedom; . . . limited government and the rule of law; . . . tolerance, equality of opportunity and human rights for every man, woman and child on this earth" (Kennan 10). Yet, despite these claims for the universality of American ideals, Powell denies that the Bush administration seeks to lay the foundations for an American empire in the traditional sense: "[t]he United States," according to Powell (in his remarks at George Washington University), "does not seek a territorial empire. We have never been imperialists." However, Powell does acknowledge the desire to expand the American way of life, if not American sovereignty, across the globe. Thus Powell admits, "(w)e seek a world in which liberty, prosperity, and peace become the heritage of all peoples, and not just the exclusive privilege of the few."[14]

Powell also agrees with Wolfowitz's suggestion in the Bush doctrine that the purpose of the globalization of American ideals, with the underlying assumption of regime change in rogue states, is the reduction, if not complete elimination, of terrorism. In his remarks at Princeton, Powell asserts that "defeating terrorism is our number one priority" (Kennan 4). Moreover, it is "the possibility that proliferation of [WMDs] might link up with terrorism," that makes terrorism the preeminent threat that it is, and, as Wolfowitz indicates in the Bush doctrine, this threat justifies the military strategy of preemption (Kennan 4). According to Powell in his remarks at George Washington University, the attacks of 9/11 made clear a certain logic: "if you can see a clear and present threat, a danger coming at you, you do not wait for it to arrive. You deal with it. You preempt. You don't wait for it to strike."[15]

Powell, however, maintains that the United States will not "win the war on terrorism on the battlefield alone" (Kennan 9). Hence the United States must be prepared "to use tough-minded diplomacy that blends power and persuasion in proper measure" (Kennan 8). Powell, therefore, in both his remarks at Princeton and George Washington University, emphasizes diplomacy as a necessary and perhaps more effective instrument than reliance on military solutions to protect America's national security. Diplomacy, as Powell understands it, includes "nurturing relations with the major powers" and maintaining solid partnerships with international and regional organizations such as the United Nations, the European Union, and NATO ("Remarks at Elliot" 7). Also falling under the rubric of diplomacy is Powell's emphasis on the promotion of global free trade and, targeting the Middle East, American provision of assistance for "educational, economic and political reform throughout the Arab world."[16]

Although revealing a shift in emphasis, Powell nonetheless stays within the horizon of the Bush doctrine when he focuses on diplomacy as a necessary if not more effective tool than military force in the war on terror. However, Powell begins to depart from Wolfowitz and the Bush doctrine in significant ways when he distinguishes the fight *against* terrorism from the fight *for* democracy. According to Powell in his remarks at Princeton, "it's not enough to fight against a negative, like terrorism . . . [w]e've got to fight for the positive—for liberty, for freedom, for democracy" (Kennan 11). As opposed to the "negative" goal of destroying terrorism, the "positive" goal of building freedom and democracy around the globe is associated by Powell with the concept of "build[ing] a better world" or "build[ing] a better future" (Kennan 10, 11). Powell gives definition to this vague expression when he claims that "the greatest weapon of mass destruction currently plaguing our world" is not nuclear, chemical, or biological agents as Wolfowitz and the Bush doctrine suggest, but rather HIV/AIDS (Kennan 10). He does not leave it at HIV/AIDS but further characterizes poverty, disease, and starvation as "the really great threats that are out there" (Kennan 14)—America must turn to those if it wants to make herself secure. The alleviation of the appalling physical, social, and economic conditions in the poorer parts of the world through committed humanitarian assistance is essential to America, because the presence of these conditions leads to the failure among vast sections of the world's population to believe in democracy. Powell claims that "democracy . . . doesn't mean anything to people if they get no more food on their table, they're still dying from disease, still don't have access to clean water, healthcare, a better life for their children. . . . We can preach [democracy]. People have to believe it. They'll only believe it if they have a better life from it."[17]

The departure that Powell takes with his advocacy of spreading democracy through humanitarian assistance that eliminates HIV/AIDS, poverty, starvation, and other forms of disease, thereby "build[ing] a better world," focuses on the root causes of terrorism. Wolfowitz, as expressed through the Bush doctrine, implies, I would suggest, that the root cause of terrorism is, as it were, "metaphysical": the absence of the fear of death, which turns into a desire to seek martyrdom in the act of inflicting civilian casualties. Powell, on the other hand, indicates that the root cause of terrorism is, as it were, "material": the endemic presence of poverty, starvation, and disease in vast areas of the world. Thus Wolfowitz and Powell can be understood as articulating a reverse order of causation with respect to the source of the terrorist threat. Wolfowitz suggests that the lack of the fear of death facilitates the turn to terrorism, which in turn either creates or thrives in the social and political instability perpetuated by rogue states; they then are the chief cause of the desperate physical, economic, and social conditions in which their people live. Powell, on the other hand, implies that the desperate physical, economic and social conditions in which many people live leads to the failure of belief in democratic ideals which in turn facilitates the rise of rogue states that either tolerate or actively sponsor terrorism. From these different perspectives on the root causes of terrorism arise two different approaches concerning what America's primary response should be. For Wolfowitz, the "metaphysical" source of terrorism must be confronted by America's use, and demonstrated willingness to use, preemptive military force. Powell, although acknowledging terrorist violence must be met by the use of force, suggests that the "material" causes underlying terrorist violence must be eradicated by American humanitarian assistance.

Moving to the opposite end of the spectrum with respect to the character and projection of American power across the globe is Joseph S. Nye Jr.'s "soft power" doctrine, articulated in *The Paradox of American Power: Why the*

World's Only Superpower Can't Go It Alone and more recently developed in *Soft Power: The Means to Success in World Politics*. Former Assistant Secretary of Defense in President William Clinton's administration and currently the Dean of the Kennedy School of Government at Harvard University, Nye understands his "soft power" doctrine as an alternative to Wolfowitz's emphasis, manifested in the Bush doctrine, on military power. Moreover, Nye intimates that Wolfowitz's "Reaganite variant of Wilsonianism," which he believes is the guiding intellectual force behind the Bush administrations' response to the attacks of September 11, 2001, is guilty of an arrogant unilateralism (*Paradox*, 148, 11, 141). It fails to understand the limits of American military power in defending America's national security, preserving America as "undoubtedly the world's number one power," and spreading American values across the globe (1).[18]

Nye argues that there are a number of reasons why a nation's power, or its "ability to affect the outcomes [it] want[s] . . . and to change the behavior of others to make this happen," has shifted away from military force since the seventeenth and eighteenth centuries. One is the advent of nuclear weapons. The development and proliferation of nuclear weapons points to the deep irony that although the possibility of WMDs falling into the hands of rogue states and their terrorist allies is the primary justification for the preemptive use of military force in the Bush doctrine, in Nye's view this makes such use of force untenable. Also, Nye claims that the use of force can jeopardize economic prosperity in an increasingly interdependent world and maintains that the rise of nationalism as an ideological force makes imperial occupation of weaker peoples by stronger ones more difficult than it was in the nineteenth century. Most interestingly, however, Nye argues that "postindustrial" societies such as America "are focused on welfare rather than glory." Moreover, the attendant lack of a "warrior ethic" in such circumstances means that unlike "preindustrial societies" in Africa and the Middle East and "modernizing industrial" societies in India and China, the publics in Europe, Japan, and North America, according to Nye, "loathe high casualties except when survival is at stake."[19] Hence, such publics tolerate the use of military force to a much diminished degree.

The postindustrial turn to welfare and away from glory means that those who craft American foreign policy must turn to what Nye terms "soft power" in contradistinction to military or "hard power." "Soft Power" according to Nye, "co-opts people rather than coerces them," or, in other words, soft power is an indirect way of using power by "getting others to want what you want." It "shapes the preferences of others." Nye asserts, "if I can get you to *want* to do what I want, then I do not have to force you to do what you do *not* want to do." Such coopting works by inspiring in others an admiration for American values, such that others emulate America's example and aspire to America's "level of prosperity and openness." In short, "soft power" is the ability to get other countries and societies to desire to be like America or to adopt the American way of life—to adopt what Nye would term American "culture."[20]

The spreading of American values across the globe—so that America become John Winthrop's "shining 'city upon a hill'"—can be facilitated, Nye indicates, by the promotion of the already global reach of American popular culture.[21] According to Nye, American films and television express "freedom, individualism, and change." More importantly, in order to ensure the adoption of certain values by others outside their country, Americans must ensure that they protect and promote those same values inside their country. Nye emphasizes that Americans can only influence the policies followed outside their country by "the policies we follow inside our country." For Nye, serious reflection and action with regard to foreign policy requires that one put proper domestic policy first.[22] In other words, in order to effect regime change, as it were, abroad, the American people must elect regimes at home that protect and promote the proper values. The values Nye focuses on are those expressed by "American feminism, open sexuality," and a culture accepting of "individual choices," because such values are "profoundly subversive" of the "patriarchal societies" that Nye suggests are at the root of the dangers America faces in the world today. Nye does not expect terrorist organizations to come under the sway of America's "soft power," but he believes that the states that sponsor them will. Persuading those states that still reject American values and culture to come into the American horizon by way of America's example is the best way to protect Americans against the dangers posed by terrorists as it will "isolate them and diminish the minority of states that give them harbor."[23]

The terrorist threat faced by America in the twenty-first century has a complex combination of causes, according to Nye. Like Wolfowitz's suggestion in the Bush doctrine, Nye implies that one of the sources of this new form of terrorism is, as it were, "metaphysical." According to Nye, the motivations that underlie terrorist violence, especially in the Middle East, are "reinforced by promises of rewards in another world." Nye also identifies, as it were, a "material" cause of terrorism, but—unlike Powell who points to poverty, starvation, and disease—Nye characterizes the material cause of terrorism as the "democratization of technology." By this phrase Nye means that WMDs have become "smaller, cheaper, and more readily available to a far wider range of individuals and groups." Moreover, the Internet, Nye argues, "has reduced the costs of searching for information and making contacts related to instruments of wide scale destruction." The ease with which individuals can potentially find, buy, and use WMDs due to technological advancement has, Nye claims, led to the "privatization of war," in which the monopoly over the use of force has shifted from nation-states to transnational terrorist organizations. However, Nye argues that terrorists ultimately depend for their victory on "soft power," or their "ability to attract support from the crowd," rather than their ability to "destroy the enemy's will to fight."[24] America must therefore place priority on responding with its own "soft power" to ensure that the people in the affected parts of the world choose the values that America stands for rather than those of its terrorist enemies.

Nye's "soft power" doctrine, like the doctrines of Wolfowitz and Powell, explicitly denies that its purpose is to facilitate the creation of an American territorial empire in the traditional sense. Yet, like the Bush doctrine, it openly advocates the spread of American values and culture to all corners of the globe. For instance, Nye indicates that the aim of "soft power" is to maintain the "universality of [America's] culture and to establish a set of favorable rules and institutions that govern areas of international activity." Moreover, Nye explicitly rejects the need for a "balance of power" in international relations in order to preserve international peace. He argues instead for American hegemony, the model of which is British hegemony, or the "Pax Britannica" of the nineteenth century. He looks even beyond Britain, to the near total universalism of the Roman Empire. To this extent, America should engage in "global governance," as international stability "requires a large state to take the lead."[25]

The goals of Nye's "soft power" doctrine are just as universalizing in their tendencies as the goals of Wolfowitz, manifested in the Bush doctrine, and those of Powell, included in his concept of "building a better world." The debate between these three alternatives with regard to the projection of American power in the world is about means, not ends: whether American statesmen spread American values primarily through the use of American military force, as Wolfowitz contends; through a mixture of force, diplomacy, and humanitarian assistance, as Powell contends; or through the spread of American culture by presenting to the world a robust defense of the values of that culture from within, as Nye suggests. If neither the Bush doctrine, Powell's concept of "building a better world," nor Nye's "soft power" doctrine wants to turn the world into one country governed by a single political master—as Herodotus says Persian king Xerxes did when he dreamed of conquering Greece—they do want to turn the world into a global cultural community governed by a single moral code or set of values broadly resembling the American way of life. If America is not to be at the center of an American territorial empire, it is to be at the center of an American "cultural" empire that spans the four corners of the globe.

Is the pursuit of global empire based on American values a positive development in American foreign policy in the post-9/11 world? Robert W. Merry, president and publisher of the *Congressional Quarterly* and former reporter for the conservative *Wall Street Journal*, thinks not. In his book *Sands of Empire: Missionary Zeal, American Foreign Policy, and the Hazards of Global Ambition*, Merry claims that the Bush administration after the September 11, 2001 terrorist attacks, embraced a "humanitarian imperialism" that threatens "to lead [America] toward calamity."[26] The danger of such global ambition is that it posits a world "in which American exceptionalism holds sway everywhere and people's around the globe abandon their own cultures" in the name of universal natural and political truths which are, at bottom, illusory. The failure to recognize the immutable force of cultural outlooks and animosities in international relations in the post-9/11 world is a result, according to Merry, of the administration's misguided acceptance of the thesis put forward by Francis Fukuyama in his 1989 essay, "The End of History," which was later expanded into the book *The End of History and the Last Man*. In brief, Fukuyama argues that the West's victory in the Cold War signals the coming of humanity's highest possible moral and political development: the universalization of democratic liberalism and free market capitalism.

Against the universalism of Fukuyama's argument Merry posits the particularism of distinct cultural outlooks. In sympathy with Samuel P. Huntington's "Clash of Civilizations," Merry argues that a universal culture does not and never will exist because "history is the story of various discrete cultures or civilizations that emerge, develop, reach maturity, and then inevitably decline." This process of cultural growth and decay is largely insulated from alien intellectual forces, as "[n]o body of thought emanating from one culture can be imposed upon another, either peacefully or through force." The cultural boundedness of all thought even applies to the Western mind's inclination to conceive of universal natural and political truth. As Merry claims, "the West's values, its ideas and ideals, its governmental structures and religious sensibilities . . . are not universal. They are distinctly Western."[27] Moreover, the West, now the ascendant civilization, is fated to decline like all the rest.

Consistent with his particular, cultural outlook, Merry is also much more willing than Wolfowitz, Powell, or Nye to explicitly identify Islam as the source of the terrorist threat facing America in the twenty-first century. Merry argues that the first step in confronting and eventually defeating terrorism is to understand the enemy, and the enemy, Merry asserts, "is Islamic fundamentalism." Moreover, Merry does not stop with the fundamentalist version of Islam; he extends his net to almost all who hold some form of Islamic belief. According to Merry, "while most Muslims are not terrorists, anti-Western sentiment is both intense and widespread within Islam—reaching majority status in many Muslim countries." If Muslims around the world are confronted with the choice of fighting to preserve their own culture or adopting Western culture, "few," according to Merry, "will choose the West." Thus, far from taking preemptive action to effect regime change in "rogue states," Merry argues that American governments should give such states their full support. According to Merry, "[o]ur friends are those within the Islamic lands who are seeking to destroy or contain Islamic fundamentalism—even including strongman dictators, corrupt royal families, military bureaucrats. . . . In this context it can be seen that Saddam Hussein was not a prime enemy of the United States in the war with Islam."[28]

Barring the presence of secular authoritarian governments able to contain the Islamic threats within their own countries, Merry does what appears to be an about face and encourages American administrations to promote the emergence of "Islamic core states" in the Middle East as the key to peaceful relations. An "Islamic core state," according to Merry, would be able and willing to "provide stability and enforcement of norms" within that "roiling civilization" which is Islam, as well as to "negotiate on behalf of their civilization(s) when conflicts arise with outside cultures." Merry identifies the Islamic theocracy of Iran as a prime candidate for development as the "Islamic core state" of the Middle East. For Merry, this may require America to "accept Iran into the nuclear club." He thus dismisses Wolfowitz's concerns about Iran's nuclear capabilities and, it seems, the latter's belief that American missile defense must be developed to defend against it. Of crucial importance, however, to Merry's idea of developing "Islamic core states," whose moral and political realities would differ so widely from those possessed by the United States, is that it implies rather strongly that America should not seek—as the Wolfowitz, Powell, and Nye doctrines urge—a universal, "cultural" empire that extends American values to all four corners of the globe.

If the Bush Doctrine's embrace of military preemption to spread democracy is adopted, Merry warns that America will be transformed into a "Crusader State" that "promot[es] a universal culture and extol[s] presumed universal values that must be spread throughout the world in the righteous cause of peace." Two dangers lurk if America decides on such a course. Although American statesmen have repeatedly denied any interest in an American territorial empire in the traditional sense, Merry argues that, as clashes between the West and the world of Islam and other non-Western cultures intensify, America, seeking to impose its values on others, will increasingly "find itself reaching for the tools of imperialism" to stabilize "enflamed regions." However, the resulting domestic stresses and strains produced by such "imperial or hegemonic ambition" would threaten to destroy republican institutions within America itself. Pointing to the overturning of the Roman republic and the ushering in of Caesarism due to imperial overreach, Merry asks, "could that never really happen in America?" Merry points to the irony that spreading democracy abroad could actually lead to the destruction of democracy at home. Another danger that Merry believes will result from such "missionary zeal" in the name of universalizing democracy is that it will "spread conflict and turmoil" across the globe as America collides with other world cultures.[29] Merry implies that the Bush Doctrine and other doctrines—such as those of Powell and Nye that embrace the idea of an American "cultural" empire that spans the four corners of the globe—commit America to a near perpetual warfare that threatens American lives—and possibly the existence of America itself.

Herodotus is particularly relevant to our situation today. The more we explore the regimes presented to us in the *Histories*, the more we begin to see the understanding of America and the world manifested in the arguments of Wolfowitz, Powell, Nye, and Merry reflected back to us. For instance, Merry argues that the human condition does not allow for unity under a single set of values. It inevitably manifests division as particular cultural communities are resistant to foreign ways of life and ways of thinking. The existence of such cultural distinctiveness is also reflected in the *Histories* in Herodotus' narrative of Egypt and Scythia, two regimes that represent opposing but parallel ways of life. Herodotus' Egyptians believe themselves to be the oldest of human beings; they thus emphasize social stability and reverence for age and the past. For Herodotus, Egyptian emphasis on stability and on the ancestral reinforces the strict piety that governs every aspect of their lives. Herodotus' Scythians, on the other hand, are a nomadic people without a city; they are thus in constant motion. Herodotus links Scythian motion with their reverence for youth rather than age, as well as a lack of intellectual development that he does not admire. Most important, however—in terms of reflecting Merry's assumption of the resistance of particular cultures to influences from other cultures—is that both the Egyptians and the Scythians, according to Herodotus, resist—through killing if need be—the introduction of all foreign customs into their community. Ironically, therefore, what makes Egyptians and Scythians similar is their self-conscious rejection of the difference of the other.

In contrast to Merry's thesis of the immutability of cultural difference, Wolfowitz and Powell explicitly, and Nye implicitly, assume a universal human nature upon which is based their confidence in the possibility of a single set of political and moral principles governing the peoples of the world. If Merry's particularist assumptions are foreshadowed in Herodotus' Egyptians and Scythians, the universalist assumptions of Wolfowitz, Powell, and Nye are foreshadowed in the Persian and Athenian regimes that Herodotus describes. Herodotus' Persians, for example, worship the universal objects of nature, such as the sky, sun, moon, stars, and the earth, air, fire, and water. Also, in the Persian debate on government that takes place after Persian customs, political succession, and religious authority have been overturned, each participant argues for the regime that he believes would be best for Persia, in light of what he regards as the universal nature of human beings unclothed by custom or law. The tendency of Herodotus' Persians toward nature is matched by their tendency toward empire; Persian kings desire to impose a universality on the political world that reflects the universality of the natural world.

Herodotus' Athenians also grasp a universal human nature that informs their regime. This can be seen in the victory of the Athenians in the battle of Marathon, one of the chief reasons of which, Herodotus maintains, was that the Athenians were the first Greeks who could bear the sight of Persian clothing and the sound of Persian names without fear. The Athenians could show such fearlessness toward the invading Persian army because they did not view the Persians as superhuman warriors destined to rule the world; they saw them as human beings who shared a common nature with themselves. Moreover, the Athenian ability to see a universal human nature leads to an aggressive form of courage displayed by their charge against the Persians at Marathon. This courage ultimately allows them to turn to their ships and the sea to defeat Persian imperial designs. For Herodotus, Athenians look on the other without fear and move toward it. This Athenian form of courage has reflections in the Bush Doctrine's vision of an outward looking American regime prepared to use preemptive military force to spread American values abroad.

The motion and daring of Herodotus' Athenians are in contradistinction to the stability and conservatism of Herodotus' Spartans. For instance, whereas the Athenians possess an aggressive and outward-looking form of courage displayed by their "run" at Marathon, the Spartans possess a defensive and inward-looking form of courage, displayed by their "standing firm" at Thermopylae. Spartans seek to defend their boundaries and prevent their unique way of life from being destroyed. The self-regarding character of Herodotus' Spartan regime has metaphorical similarities to Merry's vision of the cultural autonomy of great peoples in history and to Nye's vision of an American regime attentive to its "soft power." "Soft power," or the dominance of American values across the globe, requires that Americans take care to preserve their values at home. Americans must look internally before they can project themselves externally; the proper domestic agenda is the necessary precondition for effective foreign relations.

Nye is also most Spartan in the caution that he displays toward the outside world. For instance, he criticizes his intellectual opponents behind the Bush doctrine for their immoderation, claiming that they "exaggerate the degree to which the United States is able to get the outcomes it wants in a changing world" and that "their foreign policy is all accelerator and no brakes."[30] This lack of cautious restraint on the part of those behind the Bush doctrine is, Nye emphasizes, partly due to their failure to "allow others a voice" in multilateral institutions and consequently to "participate in decisions."[31] Nye's emphasis, shared by Powell and Merry, on giving a voice to others, points to his sensitivity not toward the universal nature that makes human beings the same but toward the cultural diversity that distinguishes them. Nye, like Merry, suggests that the opinions of others from different cultures must be listened to because the diversity of cultures will necessarily spawn a diversity of perspectives on the world that can inform our own.

Reading the *Histories* reveals many similarities between the various regimes Herodotus describes and the alternative visions of Wolfowitz, Powell, Nye, and Merry, concerning the character of America and projection of its power across the globe. Yet the most important way in which reading Herodotus can shed light on our situation in the world today is his conception of the deepest motives—and hence greatest possibilities and dangers—of the drive toward universal empire. As we have seen, the Wolfowitz, Powell, and Nye doctrines all explicitly eschew the idea of an American attempt to acquire a universal territorial empire in the traditional sense—as Persia did, when it invaded Greece, and Athens did two generations later, when it invaded Sicily. Yet all three doctrines openly advocate the universal spread of American values either through "hard power," humanitarian assistance, or "soft power"—and hence the universal "empire" of American culture or the American way of life with the American government in the lead.[32] However, for all three doctrines, the primary, although not exclusive, motive—and hence fundamental justification for establishing this empire—is national security. Moreover, Merry's critique of American imperial ambitions is also motivated by security concerns. According to Wolfowitz in the Bush doctrine, "the first and fundamental commitment of the Federal Government" is to defend the American people against its enemies. For Powell, "defeating terrorism is our number one priority." According to Nye, "national strategic interests are vital and deserve priority, because if we fail to protect them, our very survival would be at stake." According to Merry, "Bush [has] embraced a post-9/11 foreign policy destined . . . to lead his country toward calamity."[33] The universal projection of American power to establish the universality of American values, and the argument against it, are ultimately in the service of protecting American lives. Thus the justification of "empire" and its critique, in the final analysis, is pragmatic; it is about the safety of the body, or the preservation of bodily life.

Although Herodotus would not disagree with the importance and justice of the preservation of bodily life, he reveals in his *Histories* the drive toward empire, as well as the desire to moderate such imperial ambitions, is not simply pragmatic but also philosophic. The motive of both is not only to protect the body but also to elevate the soul. The regime's attempt to rule the world masks the deeper desire of the mind's attempt to understand the world. Empire, Herodotus illustrates, makes possible and manifests the attempt to expand the mind. Empire allows the intellect to make contact with, and feeds its desire to understand, the natural whole, or cosmos, of which it is a part. Yet Herodotus points to the deeply ironic and troubling suggestion that the drive toward universal empire on the political level, if it were ultimately to succeed, would actually cut off the mind's access to nature and therefore foreclose the possibility of self-knowledge, on the intellectual level. Universal empire, in the end, places politics above philosophy. However, in order to understand this highest possibility and guard against this gravest danger of empire, Herodotus suggests that one must be open to his thought as manifested in his *Histories.*

The intellectual empire manifested in the *Histories* that shows Herodotus making contact with, and ordering the world through, mind, is an achievement that stands above not only the tragic attempt by Xerxes to conquer the world but also above the new world order envisioned by modern thinkers and actors in the post-9/11 era. As I have argued, Wolfowitz, Powell, and Nye wish to protect American interests by spreading American values across the globe either through the "hard power" of the American military, the humanitarian assistance of the American people, or the cultural seductiveness of America's "soft power." Like Xerxes—who wishes to create a whole that dispenses with the parts by universalizing the particular Persian regime—Wolfowitz, Powell, and Nye wish to do the same by universalizing the liberal democracy of the American regime. They wish to transform the world into a single community, adhering to a single culture or set of values broadly resembling the American way of life. The *Histories*, on the other hand, at the same time that it binds the world together and gives it a rational order, also preserves the multiplicity of customs or cultures that exist within it. Moreover, Herodotus does not simply maintain diversity—despite the apparent oneness of the world—by recording the smallest of idiosyncrasies of the most unknown of peoples in Xerxes' army or in far-flung parts of the earth. Herodotus also creates unity *through* diversity by showing the intricate interplay of the principles of rest and motion as they manifest themselves and move through the customs and regimes of Egypt, Scythia, Persia, and Greece.

Unlike Merry's insistence, therefore, on the irreducibility of cultural differences that should preclude any notion of the universalization of certain ways of thinking and acting on the part of American statesmen, Herodotus' respect for the diversity of *nomoi* among the peoples of his world points to his belief in, and desire to make manifest, a higher oneness—the oneness or common possession of a soul, or nonmaterial nature, by which human beings create different customs and regimes. Herodotus, in his writing, creates not only unity *through* diversity; he also suggests that diversity is created *through* unity, by the common sharing of a soul that is creative and from which flows the multiplicity of *nomoi* we see in our world. For Herodotus, if it is both impossible and undesirable for human beings to share a common political life, it may be possible for them, or at least some of them, to share a common intellectual life.

Herodotus thus combines the universalism or focus on nature in the thought of scholars and statesmen such as Wolfowitz, Powell, and Nye, with the particularism or focus on culture in the thought of scholars such as Merry. However, Herodotus grasps and makes manifest the power of both nature and culture, the universal and particular, in a way that transcends these various modern approaches to the possibility of empire in our world today. As I have argued, the end that Wolfowitz, Powell, and Nye want to achieve by the universal projection of American power to establish the universality of American culture, as well as the end that Merry desires by attempting to moderate these imperial ambitions, is security. What justifies an American "empire," as well as the argument which counsels against it, is the concern for the protection of American lives. Imperialism, and the desire to moderate it, is ultimately about the body and the preservation of bodily life. Herodotus, however, in his narrative of Xerxes' marshalling of the world's forces to invade Greece, shows that the drive toward empire is, in its deepest sense, about the longings in the soul for knowledge of self and transcendence of time. Moreover, the *Histories* itself, by making the world one while also maintaining the multiplicity of *nomoi* that exists within it, is a universal empire in thought and speech superior to the universal empire that Xerxes attempted to realize in action and deed. In this way Herodotus' writing allows for empire, or for the grasping of the universal on a higher level than that offered by Wolfowitz, Powell, or Nye. Herodotus holds out the possibility that the whole can be grasped intellectually in the mind of the human being, rather than spatially in the world of the human being.

Finally, in holding out the possibility of empire on the intellectual level, Herodotus provides an internal principle of moderation more effective than Merry's appeal to external principles, such as the irreducible cultural diversity of the world or the threats to one's own regime—or even bodily existence, when one wages war against foreign peoples loyal to their own way of life. Herodotus does not point outward to "externals" such as culture or physicality, but inward to the soul. He reveals that the deepest motivation of empire is the desire of the soul to know the soul itself and to preserve the soul in some form beyond bodily death. Herodotus then proceeds to show how these two longings of the soul can really only be addressed by following the path that he has illuminated by going there before. Rational inquiry into the whole and communication of one's discoveries through writing, both of which preclude the conquest of the whole, are the tasks ahead. If one wants to *understand* the world in order to understand and transcend the self, one cannot govern the world in order to protect the self; in the end one must choose philosophy over politics.

Notes

Chapter 1

1 Herodotus, *The History*, trans. David Grene (Chicago: University of Chicago Press), 1987. All subsequent citations from this edition will follow a book/paragraph format.

2 I owe this insight—that the different ways in which people speak and understand speech is crucial to Herodotus—to Norma Thompson, *Herodotus and the Origins of the Political Community: Arion's Leap* (New Haven: Yale University Press), 1996.

3 For the complexity of Herodotus' speech, see Christiane Sourvinou-Inwood, "Herodotus (and others) on Pelasgians: Some Perceptions of Ethnicity," in *Herodotus and His World: Essays from a Conference in Memory of George Forrest*, eds. Peter Derow and Robert Parker (Oxford: Oxford University Press), 2003.

4 For an alternative view, see John K. Davies, "Democracy without Theory," in *Herodotus and His World*, ed. Derow and Parker, 2003. Benardete suggests that since a relation to the fourth and highest cut of Plato's divided line, called *noesis* or "intellection," cannot be found in the *Histories*, Herodotus, unlike Plato, does not philosophize. See Seth Benardete, *Herodotean Inquiries* (The Hague: Martinus Nijhoff), 1969.

5 For a similar view, see Henry P. Immerwahr, *Form and Thought in Herodotus* (Cleveland: Press of Western Reserve University, 1966).

6 Michael Palmer, *Love of Glory and the Common Good: Aspects of the Political Thought of Thucydides* (Lanham, Md.: Rowman & Littlefield, 1992), 10–11.

7 Palmer, 11, 111, 113–14, 117.

8 Clifford Orwin, *The Humanity of Thucydides* (Princeton: Princeton University Press, 1994), 194–95, 200–201.

9 Orwin, 195, 198, 200, 204.

10 See Steven Forde, *The Ambition to Rule: Alcibiades and the Politics of Imperialism in Thucydides* (Ithaca: Cornell University Press, 1989), 6, 198–99.

11 Forde, 7, 196–98, 208, 210.

12 See Gregory Crane, *Thucydides and the Ancient Simplicity: The Limits of Political Realism* (Berkeley: University of California Press, 1998), 241, 247–50, 254.

13 Crane, 239–41, 252.

14 See Laurie M. Johnson, *Thucydides, Hobbes, and the Interpretation of Realism* (DeKalb: Northern Illinois University Press, 1993), xii, 28, 214.

15 Johnson, xii, 27, 29, 31–32, 214.

16 Jack Riley, "Freedom and Empire: The Politics of Athenian Imperialism," in *Thucydides' Theory of International Relations: A Lasting Possession*, ed. Lowell S. Gustafson (Baton Rouge: Louisiana State University Press, 2000), 122–23, 138–39, 142–45, 148–49.

17 Riley, 120–21, 144.

18 Leo Strauss, "On Thucydides' War of the Peloponnesians and the Athenians," in *The City and Man* (Chicago: University of Chicago Press, 1964), 192–93, 209.

19 Strauss, "On Thucydides' War," 228–29.

20 For an alternative view see Francois Hartog, *The Mirror of Herodotus: The Representation of the Other in the Writing of History*, trans. Janet Lloyd (Berkeley: University of California Press), 1978.

21 Strauss uses the categories of rest and motion to analyze Thucydides' history of the Peloponnesian war. See Strauss, "On Thucydides' War," 140, 156–57, 159, 160.

22 Most scholars who study Herodotus' understanding of the best regime focus on either the theoretical regimes expressed in the Persian debate on government in book 3, or on Herodotus' discussion of the actual historical regimes that come to be and exist in time in books 5–9. For scholars who focus on the theoretical regimes of the Persian debate, see Stanley Rosen, *The Quarrel Between Philosophy and Poetry* (New York: Routledge, 1988); and Stewart Flory, *The Archaic Smile of Herodotus* (Detroit: Wayne State University Press, 1987). For scholars who focus on Herodotus' account of regimes in history, see Carl Page, "Thumos and Thermopylae: Herodotus vii: 238," *Ancient Philosophy* 16:2 (1996): 301–31; Binyamin Shimron, *Politics and Belief in Herodotus* (Stuttgart: Franz Steiner Verlag Wiesbaden, 1989); Charles W. Fornara, *Herodotus: An Interpretive Essay* (Oxford: Oxford University Press, 1971); Martin Ostwald, *Nomos and the Beginnings of the Athenian Democracy* (Oxford: Oxford University Press, 1969); and E. N. Tigerstedt, *The Legend of Sparta in Classical Antiquity* (Stockholm: Almquist & Wiksell, 1965). Donald Lateiner, as I do, provides an insightful analysis of Herodotus' understanding of the best regime in light of the *Histories* as a whole. See Donald Lateiner, *The Historical Method of Herodotus* (Toronto: University of Toronto Press, 1989).

23 See, for instance, Aristotle, *Poetics*, trans. Gerald F. Else (Ann Arbor: University of Michigan Press, 1967), 1451b1–10.

24 For a similar argument see John Marincola, "Herodotus and the Poetry of the Past," in *The Cambridge Companion to Herodotus,* ed. Carolyn Dewald and John Marincola (Cambridge: Cambridge University Press, 2006), 23–24.

25 For a discussion of how Herodotus is indebted to and distinguished from his poetic predecessors, especially Homer, see Marincola, 13, 15–16; Alan Griffiths, "Stories and Storytelling in Herodotus," in *The Cambridge Companion to Herodotus,* ed. Dewald and Marincola, 135; and John Gould, *Herodotus* (London: Weidenfeld & Nicholson, 1989), 119. Also, for Herodotus' relationship to Greek tragedy, see Jasper Griffin, "Herodotus and Tragedy," in *The Cambridge Companion to Herodotus*, ed. Dewald and Marincola, 46–47, 49. For an alternative argument, see Virginia Hunter (*Past and Process in Herodotus and Thucydides* [Princeton: Princeton University Press, 1982], 68–69, 75, 85–86, 87), who maintains that Herodotus' Egyptian narrative in book 2 of the *Histories* is a major challenge to the Greek poets, as it is meant to undermine the entire Greek poetic tradition with respect to both religious and historical matters.

26 Hugh Bowden (*Classical Athens and the Delphic Oracle: Divination and Democracy* [Cambridge: Cambridge University Press, 2005], 33–34, 37–38, 73) argues that it is unlikely that verse oracles would have been spoken by the Pythia at Delphi and maintains that Herodotus' account of Croesus and the oracle is completely fictitious. Also see Griffin (51), who maintains that Herodotus' story of Croesus, in style and theme, follows the pattern of Greek tragedy.

27 Stadter points to the story of Sparta's Tegean campaign to argue that Herodotus presents Sparta as a city that desires to be and eventually succeeds in becoming an imperial power. See Phillip Stadter, "Herodotus and the Cities of Mainland Greece," in *The Cambridge Companion to Herodotus*, ed. Dewald and Marincola, 244.

28 Bowden (51) denies any deliberate ambiguity on the part of Greek oracles. The issue focused on here, however, is not whether Herodotus gives a literal account of, or believes, in oracles, or even whether he believes in gods. Rather, the purpose of these examples is to show that Herodotus' discussion of oracles illustrates to his readers how he would like his own work to be approached. Also see Christopher Pelling ("Speech and Narrative in the *Histories,*" in *The Cambridge Companion to Herodotus,* ed. Dewald and Marincola, 116) for a similar argument that Herodotus' text requires the interpretive engagement of its readers to be understood.

29 For Herodotus' understanding of the truth of the phrase "black doves," see Rosaria Vignolo Munson, *Black Doves Speak: Herodotus and the Languages of Barbarians* (Cambridge: Harvard University Press, 2005), 68–69.

30 With respect to the preceding discussion, see Thomas L. Pangle in his "Introduction" to Leo Strauss, *Studies in Platonic Political Philosophy* (Chicago: University of Chicago Press, 1983), 3–4.

Chapter 2

1 See Ann Ward, "Self-reflection, Egyptian Beliefs, Scythians and Greek 'Ideas': Reconsidering Greeks and Barbarians in Herodotus," *The European Legacy: Toward New Paradigms* 11:1 (2006): 3–4. For a similar argument, see Hunter, 70, 72, 74–75, 76, 89.

2 Martin Bernal, *Black Athena: The Afroasiatic Roots of Classical Civilization*, vol. 1 (New Brunswick: Rutgers University Press, 1987), 1, 33, 76, 79, 98–101. Also see Ward, 1–2.

3 Mary Lefkowitz, *Not out of Africa: How Afrocentrism Became an Excuse to Teach Myth as History* (New York: Basic Books, 1996), 22–23, 27–52, 124–25, 134–35, 137, 161. Also see Ward, 2.

4 Robert Palter, "Black Athena, Afro-Centrism, and the History of Science," *History of Science* 31, no. 93 (1993): 227–28, 231, 233, 235, 252, 258, 268, 273–74. Also see Ward, 2.

5 Herodotus represents the Pelasgians as a single "barbarian" or non-Doric ethnic group with their own language, some of whom became "Greek"—the Ionians and Athenians—when they adopted the Greek language brought by the Dorians when the latter migrated from the north into the Peloponnese (I.57–58). Sourvinou-Inwood (122–23, 131) argues that Herodotus constructs the Pelasgians as a single ethnic group over against the Dorians in order to construct the Dorians as a single ethnic group, thereby establishing an antithesis between "Greeks" and "barbarians" which he nonetheless quickly moves to deconstruct by claiming, "though the [Dorians or "Greek stock"] was weak when it split off from the Pelasgians, it has grown from something small to be a multitude of peoples by the accretion chiefly of the Pelasgians but of many other barbarian peoples as well."

6 My translation. Sourvinou-Inwood (139–40) and Thomas Harrison (*Divinity and History: The Religion of Herodotus* [Oxford: Oxford University Press, 2000], 252) point out that Herodotus gives a Greek etymology for the word *theous* despite having claimed in *Histories* II.57 that the Pelasgians spoke a non-Greek language. Sourvinou-Inwood interprets this apparent contradiction to mean that Herodotus uses the word "Pelasgian" to mean two different things: those Pelasgians who became Ionian and Athenian when they adopted the Greek language—implying that it is this group whom Herodotus is talking about in the passage concerned—and those Pelasgians who remained "barbarians" with their own "barbarian" language. Munson (*Black Dov*e, 12–13) suggests that Pelasgians are presented as a bridge between the barbarian and Greek identities, at once barbarian and Greek-speaking. Also see Scott Scullion ("Herodotus and Greek Religion," in *The Cambridge Companion to Herodotus*, ed. Dewald and Marincola, 195), who argues that the Pelasgian gods spoken about in this passage reflect a rationalized or moralized understanding of chance that is cognate with Herodotus' conception of an abstract and impersonal divine force that maintains balance in the natural and human worlds.

7 Lefkowitz (25) appears to deny that for Herodotus even the god Heracles in the Greek pantheon comes from Egypt. According to Lefkowitz, Herodotus asserts that Heracles was descended not from the country of *Aigyptos*, but from the man named *Aigyptos* who was Greek. For an alternative argument see Hunter (68–69) who claims that Herodotus discusses and attests to the truthfulness of the much older Egyptian god Heracles in order to show the unreliability of Greek tradition. For Herodotus, according to Hunter, Egyptian tradition seriously undermined Greek beliefs. Also see Gould (11).

8 See Ivan M. Linforth, "Greek and Egyptian Gods (Herodotus II.50 and 52)," *Classical Philology* 35, no. 3 (1940): 301; and Rosalind Thomas, *Herodotus in Context: Ethnography, Science and the Art of Persuasion* (Cambridge: Cambridge University Press, 2000), 277–79. For an alternative argument, see Scullion (199), Hunter (71), and Harrison ("Divinity," 252, 256). The latter suggests that Herodotus, aware that language can change, means that the Egyptians gave the Pelasgians the actual Greek names now in use in Greece, but, "having imparted these to the Greeks, and the names having fallen out of use in Egypt, [the Egyptians] had begun to use different names" (256).

9 Alan B. Lloyd (*Herodotus, Book II: Introduction* [Leiden: Brill, 1975], 141) argues that Herodotus' intellectual predilection for wonder is crucial for the choice of subject matter in book 2, and that the opposition of Egyptian customs to Greek customs is a source of wonder to Herodotus. Also see Rosalind Thomas ("The Intellectual Milieu of Herodotus," in *The Cambridge Companion to Herodotus*, ed. Dewald and Marincola, 67, 70), who argues that Herodotus' presentation of Egyptian customs in oppositional form is similar to sophistic modes of argumentation, especially as found in the works of Protagoras.

10 To show that they do not care how they look, Egyptians in mourning let their hair grow, implying that they believe the body, or what proceeds from it, is in its very nature shameful. Also, that Egyptians, and all people in general, need customary ways to express internal natural passions such as grief suggests that nature can only be revealed through convention.

11 Thomas ("Intellectual Milieu," 66) points to this passage as an illustration of Herodotus' interest in the early medical writings that often referred to Egypt as a source of medical lore.

12 The Egyptians are not only lacking in their knowledge of the whole of the human but are also lacking in their knowledge of the whole of the body, that part of the human which they take as the whole. It seems that there is no one in Egypt who knows the health of the body as a whole, or who identifies which disease, and hence which kind of doctor is appropriate, when a person is sick. Similarly, the Babylonian practice is based on the individual or particular experience of community members with respect to some disease. In Egypt specialization is too great and in Babylon there is not enough specialization—or none at all.

13 Perhaps it is their belief in this doctrine that allows the Egyptians to say that their king Rhampsinitus descended into Hades, played dice with Demeter, and

then returned. See Benardete (51–52) for a discussion of how Herodotus' story of Rhampsinitus is related to Odysseus in Homer's *Odyssey*, and how Greek poetry in general makes public and less pious what is secret and holy in Egypt, or turns the ugly and profane into the beautiful.

14 Plutarch maintains that Apis is Osiris, thus the Egyptian Dionysus. See Plutarch, "Of Isis and Osiris, Or of the Ancient Religion and Philosophy of Egypt," in *Plutarch's Essays and Miscellanies*, vol. 4, ed. Arthur Hugh Clough and William W. Goodwin (New York: The Colonial Company, 1905), 95.

15 Benardete, 46.

16 Hegel, although noticing the striking character of Egyptian worship of animals, does not see that this is only the worship of, first, what the Egyptians believe is more beloved of the gods than themselves, and second, the form or outer appearance which the gods choose to adopt. For Hegel, animals in Egypt are actually manifestations of the divine. See G. W. F. Hegel, *The Philosophy of History* (New York: Dover Publications, 1956), 211–12.

17 Thompson (106, 110) persuasively argues that Heracles, adopted by and the inspiration for the Athenians, shows in this story an intelligence that seeks to go behind convention to discover the "truth about the ultimate." In doing so "Heracles represents qualities that define humanity: free and knowledge-seeking, yet fated" (106). He is therefore an example of what Herodotus regards as exceptional individuals, "who manage to assert their freedom and self-sufficiency in the face of overpowering necessities" (111).

18 Thompson (47–48) makes an interesting connection between Psammetichus' attempt "to discover the natural language" and the impulse behind the state of nature theories in such modern political philosophers as Hobbes, Locke, and Rousseau.

19 See Thompson, 33; and Munson, *Black Doves Speak*, 22.

20 Benardete, 35. Also see Aristotle, *Nicomachean Ethics*, trans. H. Rackham (Cambridge: Harvard University Press, 1926), 1139a6, 1139b27–30.

21 Benardete, 58–59.

22 Not only do the Spartans share the reverence for age with the Egyptians, but they also hold artisans or tradesmen in the lowest contempt, yet holding men solely dedicated to the art of war in the highest honor (II.167). Herodotus indicates that this opinion originated in Egypt, coming to Sparta from there.

23 See Benardete (34, 35) who explains that the previous story of Psammetichus' experiment was a discussion of the divine, because looking for the first language is looking for the language of the gods. Also see Munson, *Black Doves Speak*, 22. But see Scullion (200–201) who interprets Herodotus to mean that he will avoid any discussion of theology, reflecting his sophistic or Protagorean skepticism about the gods.

24 James Romm ("Herodotus and the Natural World," in *The Cambridge Companion to Herodotus*, ed. Dewald and Marincola, 178, 180) argues that Herodotus' interest in the relationship between the Nile and Egypt's land reflects his larger

interest in physical geography that is quite unique among the Greek art and literature of his day, the latter focusing on the unnatural space of the *polis*.

25 The verb Herodotus uses here to indicate that the Nile floods the fields, *arse*, can also mean "come upon," and that which he uses to indicate that it makes the land fertile, *apoupas*, can also be used as a metaphor, according to Liddell and Scott, for a woman giving birth to children.

26 Having noted the fact that the land in the Delta region is actually produced by the constant motion of the Nile, therefore indicating that some land can actually move, Herodotus seems to be suggesting that much of what initially looks to be at rest in nature, is actually in motion, and that what is really at rest, the unchanging and universal, may be more difficult to find than at first appears.

27 The principles of rest and motion, represented in book 2 by the earth and the Nile, are referred to by Thomas (Herodotus, 42–43) as the categories of "the wet and the dry" that are also found in the early medical writings and speculations of the natural philosophers.

28 Keith connects the Egyptian belief that their sexuality is determined by something outside themselves, leading to a moderation that makes possible a decent social life, to the Egyptian doctrine of the soul (II.123). Keith calls this "the myth of the soul," which is the Egyptian contribution to the world, the soul being that form which human being takes when our inner beings are understood as dependent on something external to the human which has created it. See Sidney Keith, "Herodotus: The First Political Scientist" (University of Toronto: Ph.D. Dissertation, 1989), 119. I would only add to this insightful discussion by Keith by noting that Herodotus emphasizes the Egyptian invention of the doctrine of the *immortality* of the soul and not simply of the existence of the soul itself.

29 See II.156 as an example of Egyptian belief that the gods are generators, and II.42, which reveals that Egyptian priests believe the sexual nature of the gods cannot be looked at directly. Also Hegel (210) has a similar view about the relationship between Egyptian gods and the Egyptian people.

30 Plutarch, "Of Isis and Osiris," 92. Also note that Herodotus and Plutarch have a minor disagreement, Herodotus not admitting that even the belief that Osiris is an allegory for the Nile is taught publicly in Egypt.

31 Plutarch, "Of Isis and Osiris," 94, 95. Plutarch also says that the Greeks call Dionysus, who comes from Egypt and is called Osiris, *hues*, meaning "the wetter," and "a son" they call *huios*, from *hudor*, meaning "water." See also Vasunia, who maintains that for the Greek authors in antiquity the Nile was often associated with male fertility as represented not by Dionysus (Osiris) but by Zeus (Ammon). Phiroze Vasunia, *The Gift of the Nile: Hellenizing Egypt from Aeschylus to Alexander* (Berkeley: University of California Press, 2001), 43, 45.

32 Hegel, 209–10.

33 See Keith (113–16) who persuasively argues that at their religious festivals, the Egyptians enact their gods, or for brief moments "merge their identity with the gods." Keith argues that the whole principle of Egyptian religion is an alternation between moderating human distance from the gods and shameless ecstatic

union with them for brief moments. For further examples of this see II.42, II.46, II.48, II.61, and II.63.

34 Thomas (*Herodotus*, 135–39; "Intellectual Milieu," 62–65) claims that Herodotus' discussion of the flooding of the Nile is within the intellectual milieu of the natural philosophers of the late fifth and early fourth centuries BCE. Also see Gould (9) and Robert Fowler ("Herodotus and His Prose Predecessors," in *The Cambridge Companion to Herodotus*, ed. Dewald and Marincola, 32), the latter arguing that Herodotus' search for the "cause" (*aitie*) of the Nile's flooding reflects his concern for the abstract principle of cause and effect in nature, signifying a considerable advance over the concern of the writers of the sixth century BCE for the "beginnings" (*archai*) of the natural world.

35 Benardete, 39.

36 See Ward, 9.

37 Benardete, 48.

38 Benardete, 48.

39 This is not to say that Proteus' actions are in themselves motivated by a selfish concern for himself, but rather that in being outraged at Alexander and keeping Helen safe in Egypt until Menelaus comes to reclaim her, Proteus understands and approves of the importance which men in general place on their selfish desires, such as a husband's desire to keep and protect a wife for himself.

40 It can be objected that the thief not only conceals himself but reveals himself as well; he has the daring to tell the truth about his most unholy deed and his wisest deed to the king's daughter. However, to counter this objection, it should be noted that although the thief speaks truthfully to the king's daughter about what he has done, this is not the truth that Rhampsinitus is trying to discover—he already knows what the thief has done. Rather, Rhampsinitus is trying to discover who the thief is. In this respect the thief still "lies" or prevents the discovery of his true identity by hiding behind the arm of a dead man, which he gives the king's daughter instead of his own. It is this final deception that Rhampsinitus greatly admires and wants to reward the thief for, not for speaking the truth to his daughter. Moreover, Herodotus indicates the distrust in words—or, in the extreme case, the silence, which results when lying is the highest form of speech—when he has Rhampsinitus ask the thief to come into his "sight" (*opsin*) in order to be made known to him and to receive his reward. For Rhampsinitus, only "seeing is believing." Or he can only discover the truth with his eyes, not his ears.

41 Egyptian king Amasis commits a lie of omission by sending the former Egyptian king Apries' daughter in place of his own daughter to Persian king Cambyses to be his concubine (III.1). Herodotus says the Egyptians claim that Persian king Cambyses was actually the son of Apries' daughter and the Persian king Cyrus, knowing this to be a lie (III.2). Herodotus also says that the Egyptians lie about which corpse was mutilated and burned by Cambyses, knowing full well that it was Amasis' corpse and not that of some other man as they claim (III.16). See also Benardete, 69–70. But see Hunter (76, 83), who claims that Herodotus

accepted the stories of the Egyptian priests and the indigenous traditions of Egypt as truthful and more reliable than Greek traditions.

42 Plato, *Republic*, trans. Allan Bloom (New York: Basic Books, 1968), 476a–b, 479a. Also see Mary Nichols, *Socrates and the Political Community: An Ancient Debate* (New York: State University of New York Press, 1987), 112.

43 Hunter (62, 65) argues that Herodotus in this passage is not trying to undermine the example of his predecessor, but rather refers to Hecataeus' experience with the priests in Thebes to corroborate his own story about the 345 statues, representing 345 generations, and thus in support of his larger argument concerning the longevity of human history in Egypt and the Egyptian preservation or "memory" of this history.

44 Nunez makes a similar argument with respect to the relationship between Herodotus' Egyptians and Scythians. Jose-Miguel Alonso-Nunez, "Herodotus' Conception of Historical Space and the Beginnings of Universal History," in *Herodotus and His World,* ed. Derow and Parker, 150. Also see Tim Rood, "Herodotus and Foreign Lands," in *The Cambridge Companion to Herodotus*, ed. Dewald and Marincola, 302; and Hunter, 273.

45 Benardete, 99

46 Strauss, *City and Man*, 140–41.

47 See III.132–34 for alternative reasons for Darius' invasion of Scythia.

48 *The Sea of Azov.*

49 Benardete, 101.

50 *The Dnieper.*

51 Hartog, 20–21.

52 See Munson, *Black Doves Speak*, 44.

53 Benardete, 104.

54 Although the Pontine Greek story is fantastic or poetic, they can use these poetic images to represent the natural or the real. The Scythian story is also fantastic or poetic, but it in no way leads them back to nature or reality. The Scythians cannot distinguish an image from that of which it is an image, and they thus confound the conventional with the natural.

55 In the Scythian account of their own origins, the female is not simply absent; Zeus marries the daughter of the river Borysthenes, the progeny of such union being Targitaus. Despite this however, the Scythian account makes no mention of the wife of Targitaus, or the wives of his three sons. Moreover, the Pontine Greek account of Scythian origins gives a much greater role to the snake woman than the Scythian account gives to the daughter of the Borysthenes river. Whereas the latter is simply noted as one of the parents of Targitaus, the snake woman is shown to have power over Heracles, stealing his mares and commanding him to have intimate relations with her. She is clearly the one responsible for the birth of the first king of the Scythians, from whom all the other Scythians are descended. Furthermore, whereas in the Scythian account the daughter of the Borysthenes remains silent, in the Pontine Greek account the snake woman is shown in both indirect and direct discourse with Heracles.

56 *The Bug.*
57 See Ward, 11–14.
58 Benardete argues that the Scythians, due to the imitation in their way of life of the constant flow of their rivers, "cannot have any of the wisdom that comes with rest. Whatever requires memory—that is, all learning—escapes them" (114). Rosen however, maintains that the motion of the Scythians "is a crude imitation of the wisdom and motion of Herodotus . . . a level of 'wisdom' that surpasses the wisdom of the civilized Greeks" (36–38). Rosaria Vignolo Munson (*Telling Wonders: Ethnographic and Political Discourse in the Work of Herodotus* [Ann Arbor: University of Michigan Press, 2001], 117), in contrast, argues that the Scythians are associated with an "Athenian" type of wisdom.
59 Taylor (14) insightfully points out that this strategy, which Herodotus so admires in IV.46, is for the Scythians "like Plan B," or is their second choice, adopted only after their first choice, waging a pitched battle with their allies, is realized to be impossible.
60 Taylor, 14.
61 Benardete, 118.
62 Hunter (184–85, 189, 196) argues that Darius' invasion and eventual retreat from Scythia serves as a pattern or process in the *Histories* that illustrates the inherent problems of empire, the dangers and injustices of expansionism, and the real possibility that a ruler, or despot, will fail in his attempt to conquer distant lands.
63 Benardete, 118.
64 Paradoxically, the Scythians suppose that the Persians are at rest, during the night, but only their mules are tied down. When the Scythians determine to stand their ground and fight, the Persians decide to imitate the Scythians and retreat.
65 Hartog, 203. Also see Rood (296–97) and Hunter (197, 214). Hartog's position is that Herodotus distorts the reality (the Scythians were both nomads and cultivators) and calls them nomads for the sake of making the metaphor with the Athenians. If Hartog is correct, then, just as the Scythians collapse reality with symbol, so does Herodotus with the Scythians, although understanding that he does so consciously (he reveals the diversity among the Scythian tribes as well as assimilates them together as nomads), thus distinguishing himself from the Scythians. The Scythians in reality "wander" between nomadism and cultivation, but Herodotus ties them down symbolically, or locates them in "nomadism."
66 Hartog, 203.
67 Hartog, 203.
68 Thucydides, *History of the Peloponnesian War,* trans. Rex Warner (London: Penguin Books, 1954), I.143.
69 Hartog, 3, 56.

70 Sourvinou-Inwood makes a similar argument with respect to "Greekness," stating that "the people who shared in the Greek ethnic identity were the people who perceived themselves to be Greeks . . . " (140).

71 Sourvinou-Inwood, 60.

72 Keith (165–67) argues that Herodotus, in showing spiritedness or will to be at the root of Scythian political society, reveals his opposition to the tradition of modern philosophy, beginning with Hobbes, that abstracts from or seeks to repress spiritedness. If the heart of being a Scythian, however, is an individual act of will, then Herodotus' discussion of the Scythians in book 4, I would suggest, may be more akin to elements of Hobbesian philosophy—especially Hobbes' discussion in his *Leviathan* of the condition of human beings in the "state of nature" and how they pull themselves out of this predicament—than Keith perhaps would accept.

73 Notice the resemblance between the noun *histie* and the verb *histemi*, which means "to make stand." See Henry George Liddell and Robert Scott, *Greek-English Lexicon: Abridged Edition* (Oxford: Oxford University Press, 1997), 335.

74 Hartog, 121.

75 The goddess Hestia represents the stable and permanent, but the Scythians neither make images to her nor build her any altars or shrines; she remains invisible. Moreover, whereas their invisible goddess Hestia is not in their own image—she represents rest, not motion—the god Ares, whom they do try to make visible is in their own image, represents war, the greatest of motions.

76 Benardete, 116.

77 Herodotus says that "these are native-born Scythians, for the servants of the king are those he bids to serve him; he has no purchased slaves" (IV.72). If the reason there are no purchased slaves in Scythia is that all who serve the king are native born, Herodotus suggests that the Scythians themselves are slaves.

78 Benardete, 116. The Scythians, therefore, do not kill so many of the king's attendants because they believe they will serve him in an afterlife, which would indicate that the Scythians do believe in a soul or something beyond the body and the material world. Rather, the point of Herodotus' description of royal burial customs is to show that the Scythians, wishing to memorialize their dead king and his power but unable to distinguish between the natural and the conventional, turn natural things—human beings and their bodies—into conventional things—statues to memorialize the dead.

79 In contrast, the pile of 700,000 stones, which Darius has his army construct at the river Artescus, is a memorial to Darius' army as individual men (IV.92). This is unlike Ariantas' great bronze cauldron, which, in destroying the individual arrowheads, destroys the individual identity of the Scythians who brought them.

80 This is not in contradiction with everything becoming skin or body in Scythia, as this is also what happens in Socrates' speech in the *Republic*. Although

Socrates denies the body and thus the separate identity of its members by introducing the equality of the sexes and communism into the city, his eugenics program reduces all to manipulable material bodies, which far from restoring their individual identities, reduces them to simplified mathematical objects. See Nichols, *Socrates and the Political Community,* 99, 106, 121.

Chapter 3

1 Griffiths (131, 136) suggests that the Persian chroniclers are a purely fictitious creation by Herodotus, telling a story that represents the audience as Io and Herodotus himself as the Phoenicians who carry Io off to Egypt, a reference to book 2 of the *Histories.*

2 Hesiod, *Aegimius,* trans. Hugh G. Evelyn-White (Cambridge: Harvard University Press, 1914), 3.

3 Hesiod, *Aegimius,* 5. Also, see Aeschylus, *Prometheus Bound,* trans. David Grene (Chicago: University of Chicago Press, 1956), 681.

4 Hesiod, *Aegimius,* 6. Also, see Aeschylus, *The Suppliant Maidens,* trans. Seth Benardete (Chicago: University of Chicago Press, 1956), 305.

5 Hesiod, *Aegimius,* 306–8, 530–90. Also, that the Greeks believe Io was restored to human form in Egypt and bore Zeus a son there called Epaphus shows that they believe that the Egyptians derived their gods from the Greeks, not vice versa as Herodotus claims in book 2.

6 See Thompson (32, 35) who argues that Herodotus uses the Persian chroniclers' rationalization of Greek myths to identify them as a people, or culture, who "resolutely will not attend to the utterances of others," and are therefore "not philosophical." Flory (26) also notes the demythologized nature of the Persian account in the proem and claims that Herodotus tries to show through this account that economic concerns are what really motivate international relations. Scullion (192) argues that the exclusion of myth from the proem distinguishes the *Histories* from Homer's *Iliad.*

7 Benardete (21) argues that the motives and actions of both Xerxes and Artaynte in this story have a close relationship to those of Candaules (I.8–12). Xerxes' love made him forget that, as a gift from his wife Amestris, the cloak belonged to him and no one else. In giving the cloak to Artaynte, he had Candaules' contradictory desire to share the beautiful, to make what was essentially private and therefore beautiful, public. Artaynte, on the other hand, does the opposite of Candaules. Whereas Candaules delighted in his wife not only because she was his, but also because she was beautiful, Artaynte delighted in the robe not only because it was beautiful, but also because it was hers; Xerxes had given it to her.

8 The Persians again demythologize a Greek myth. According to Greek mythology, Zeus, charmed with Europa's beauty, transformed himself this time—rather than his beloved in the case of Io—into the shape of a bull, and mingled with a herd as Europa and her maidens were playing along the seashore. Europa, deceived by the gentleness of the bull, mounted his back. Forthwith Zeus, with

Europa on his back, rushed into the sea and swam with her to Crete, where she became mother by Zeus to Minos, Rhadamanthus, and Sarpedon. See Hesiod, *Catalogues of Women and Eoiae*, trans. Hugh G. Evelyn-White (Cambridge: Harvard University Press, 1914), 19. Also, notice that Herodotus, in identifying the Cretans as the Greeks who carried off Europa, shows himself to agree with the Persian chroniclers in their judgment of the falsehood of Greek myths. Thus, when Herodotus points to the danger of demythologizing the world by contrasting the Greek mythical story of Io with the story of Xerxes' love and Masistes' death, he does not criticize the Persian chroniclers for seeing the falsehood of the myth, but rather for failing to understand the function that myths perform for human understanding—and thus for a failure in their understanding of human nature. Herodotus suggests that human beings should not observe the world directly, but rather indirectly through poetry, which perhaps reveals more profound truths on a deeper level.

9 For the Persian desire to exonerate themselves and blame the Greeks for the beginning of the enmity between Asia and Greece, see Carolyn Dewald, "'I Didn't give My Own Genealogy': Herodotus and the Authorial Persona," in *Brill's Companion to Herodotus*, ed. Egbert J. Bakker, Irene J. F. De Jong, and Hans Van Wees (Leiden: Brill, 2002), 270.

10 See Heleen Sancisi-Weerdenberg, "The Personality of Xerxes," in *Brill's Companion to Herodotus*, ed. Bakker, et al. (Leiden: Brill, 2002), 586.

11 That Herodotus refers to the theme of empire in I.5, see Benardete, 8–9, Immerwahr, 306–7, and J. A. S. Evans, *Herodotus, Explorer of the Past* (Princeton: Princeton University Press, 1991), 3. Dewald (270–71) argues that in this passage Herodotus distinguishes his own narrative voice from those of his sources or informants.

12 See Hunter (112, 224–25) for the use of analogical reasoning as an important methodological tool used by Herodotus.

13 Benardete, 73.

14 Evans (26–28) argues that Xerxes is wrong to attribute this *nomos* or law to a god, as it is the result of a deliberate human choice, as all customs or conventions are. Cyrus, according to Evans, had given the Persians a choice, and they freely chose the *nomos* of imperialism. Xerxes, however, is governed by this *nomos* freely chosen by his ancestors, and thus has no choice. Choice creates necessity, as a *nomos*, although elected freely, once chosen cannot be overturned without severe cost. Also see Pelling ("Speech and Narrative," 109) and Sancisi-Weerdenberg (583–84). For an alternative argument, see Thomas Harrison, "The Persian Invasions," in *Brill's Companion to Herodotus*, ed. Bakker, et al. (Leiden: Brill, 2002), 558. Scullion (196) argues that Xerxes' use of *nomos* in this passage makes it equivalent to Herodotus' conception of the divine, representing "moralized chance." Also see Hunter (203–7) who argues that although the drive to expansion may be inherent in empire, Herodotus shows that this drive must find expression through the imperial despot, or Persian king himself, and that this drive or psychological urge is implanted by the gods. Forsdyke suggests

that in this passage Herodotus draws a negative parallel between Persian imperial expansion and Athenian imperial expansion, as Athenians of Herodotus' generation appealed to the exploits of their ancestors in the Persian Wars to justify maintenance and extension of the Athenian empire. See Sara Forsdyke, "Herodotus, Political History and Political Thought," in *The Cambridge Companion to Herodotus*, ed. Dewald and Marincola, 229–30.

15 Benardete (8) argues that Herodotus leaves ambiguous as to who was the first, Croesus or Gyges. If payment of tribute is considered unjust, it was Croesus, or if the capture of a city is considered always unjust, as the Persians do, then it was Gyges.

16 According to Griffiths (140) Herodotus adopts the purely rational perspective of the "Persian chroniclers" in the telling of the Gyges story.

17 Perhaps related to the false story spread by his parents that Cyrus was suckled by a "bitch," meaning a female dog (I.122).

18 See Aristotle, *Nicomachean Ethics,* 1141a31–1141b7.

19 Benardete (72) argues that the Persians worship what is constantly in motion: "fire, water and winds are either formless or invisible," and because "the moon wanes, the sun sinks, the sky is one through day and night," they never have the same look. I argue, however, that because these natural elements and cosmological bodies do not change their character from place to place or among different peoples, they are universal, and therefore the Persians worship what is at rest.

20 Benardete, 72.

21 See Munson, *Black Doves Speak*, 26–27.

22 Plato, *Republic*, 474b–e.

23 Nichols, *Socrates and the Political Community*, 112.

24 Nichols, *Socrates and the Political Community*, 112.

25 Benardete, 69, 27, 72.

26 Benardete, 72.

27 Benardete, 42.

28 Benardete, 43.

29 Xerxes violates this custom at IV.43, as does Amestris at IX.112.

30 Benardete, 72.

31 Persian class structure resembles the class structure within the good city in speech, articulated by Socrates in books 2 to 7 of Plato's *Republic*, which parallels the class structure within the well-ordered soul. According to Socrates, in the good city the first class is composed of philosophic rulers, the second underneath them is composed of spirited warriors, and the third and bottom class is composed of desiring artisans. Flory (121, 128–36) argues that Herodotus believes Persian kings such as Darius are like Plato's philosopher-kings.

32 Benardete, 71.

33 Benardete (71) points out that Persian truth telling which collapses speech and law requires the Persians to deny the existence of tragedy, such as that surrounding the stories of Orestes and Oedipus.

34 Kenneth H. Waters (*Herodotus on Tyrants and Despots: A Study in Objectivity* [Weisbaden: Franz Steiner Verlag, 1971], 54) maintains that this Persian story is simply a pretext, not a real cause, for the armed invasion of Egypt. Evans (19–20) argues that Herodotus does not believe vengeance for a wrong is ever a causal agent for imperial expansion. Vengeance or retribution was only used in public discussion as a respectable cause to conceal aggression. Benardete (71) notes that the Persian account of why Cambyses invaded Egypt is similar to the reason why the Greeks attacked Troy, mocked by the Persian chroniclers in the proem. However, Benardete then argues, "we soon realize that neither the beauty of Nitetis nor her being a woman decided Cambyses; it was the way Amasis lied that enraged him" (71).

35 For a discussion of how these actions are related to Egyptian lying and thus their distrust in speech, see Benardete, 70.

36 Benardete, 75.

37 Hunter (179, 182–83) argues that Herodotus' narrative of Cambyses' Ethiopian campaign is actually a paradigm that illustrates the dangers of empire, particularly when imperial expansion involves injustice toward others in the form of taking territory that is not one's own and enslaving innocent people. As such, Cambyses' Ethiopian campaign prefigures Darius' Scythian campaign in book 4 of the *Histories* and Xerxes' campaign against Greece in books 7–9.

38 See Benardete (80) for a similar discussion.

39 Bernadete, 80. Also note that, in neglecting the body, Cambyses also neglected what was "Sacred." The connection between the body and the sacred seems to be that both fall outside the law, or the political, and therefore cannot be brought into speech by the Persians, who collapse law and truth telling. The Persians, therefore, in their commitment to speech or rationality, come very close to atheism, which can be seen by the fact that they do not worship "gods" as such, but rather the universal elements of nature and the cosmological bodies in the heavens.

40 McGlew argues that Cambyses' incest with his sister represents the Greek belief in the unlimited freedom from law, especially as regards sexual matters, of the tyrant. James F. McGlew, *Tyranny and Political Culture in Ancient Greece* (Ithaca: Cornell University Press, 1993), 26–30. Herodotus' portrayal of Cambyses therefore offers a perfect historical complement to Plato's theoretical account of tyranny in book 8 of Plato's *Republic.*

41 See Benardete (80) who argues that, in killing Prexaspes' son, Cambyses confounded soul and body, believing that they were interchangeable.

42 Rosen (39–40) argues that the ambiguity in the logos of the dream and the oracle in this case shows that "there is no real harmony between the divine and human intellect." According to Rosen, Herodotus indicates that if the gods do speak to human beings, they cannot do so clearly—and thus human action cannot be fashioned around their messages. Religion and politics should remain separate.

43 Immerwahr (168) claims that the destruction of relatives is a major motif of Herodotus' Cambyses' story. Cambyses' murder of his brother Smerdis actually makes possible the revolt of the Magi against him, and his murder of his sister/wife and, if she was indeed pregnant, of his offspring, actually makes possible the future rise of Darius and the debate on the best regime in theory (III.80–83).

44 Notice that the Persian conspirators exclude the Persian people from any say in their deliberations.

45 Strauss notes the tension between religious authority and the search for what is right or best by nature when he says, "Some time before Plato, Herodotus had indicated that this state of things, (the search for natural right replaces the cave of Zeus), by the place of the only debate which he recorded concerning the principles of politics: he tells us that free discussion took place in truth-loving Persia after the slaughter of the Magi . . . if man knows by divine revelation what the right path is, he does not have to discover that path by his unassisted efforts" (Leo Strauss, *Natural Right and History* [Chicago: University of Chicago Press, 1953], 85). Thomas ("Intellectual Mileu, 67–68) raises the possibility that Herodotus' "Persian debate" may actually be linked with the sophist Protagoras.

46 Benardete, 87. Also see Lateiner, 165.

47 Many commentators point to the fact that Otanes never actually uses the word *democracy* in his speech. For instance, see Arlene W. Saxonhouse, *Athenian Democracy: Modern Mythmakers and Ancient Theorists* (Notre Dame: University of Notre Dame Press, 1996), 50; and Keith, 298. However, Vlastos notes that Herodotus, in book 6, calls the regime that is favored by Otanes in book 3, "democracy." According to Herodotus, "When Mardonius, coasting along Asia, came to Ionia, I will tell you of the most wonderful thing that happened—most wonderful, that is, for those Greeks who do not believe that among the Seven Persians Otanes *did* give his judgment that Persia should be ruled by democracy (*os chreon eie demokratesthai Persas*)" (VI.43). Gregory Vlastos, *Platonic Studies* (Princeton: Princeton University Press, 1973), 170.

48 Saxonhouse (*Athenian Democracy*, 50) argues that the arrogance and hubris shown by the monarch offends the principle of equality underlying Otanes' speech. For Otanes, Saxonhouse implies, freedom, shown by the monarch, may be at odds with equality.

49 See also Keith, 296.

50 Rosen (44) maintains that Otanes attributes change and violence to the regime against which he argues, something which all three speeches—that of Otanes, Megabyzus, and Darius—have in common.

51 Keith (299) claims that Otanes is appealing to the Persian ancestral way of life (I.71), before Cyrus turned them toward empire (I.125–26).

52 See Saxonhouse, *Athenian Democracy*, 50.

53 Saxonhouse (*Athenian Democracy*, 37, 52–53) argues that for Otanes, decision-making by all is not a good in itself, but rather an institutional mechanism for preventing the inequality of tyranny, or at least for negating the bad effects of

the inequality necessary for political leadership. Otanes' reliance on institutions is the real contribution to democratic theory, and, furthermore, according to Saxonhouse, the principle of equality underlying Otanes' speech makes him the closest of speakers to Herodotus' own political perspective. Also see Lateiner, 170–71, 185. Flory (132) on the other hand, argues that for Herodotus democracy is not the best but the worst regime. According to Flory, Otanes' speech comes first so that the cumulative arguments in the speeches of Megabyzus and Darius can prove Otanes wrong.

54 Keith (302) argues that the regime of Megabyzus seeks the rule of gentlemen who by education and experience can distinguish between the noble and the base, and for this purpose, one of the main tasks of the regime will be "the education of the populace or a group within it, selected for merit, in order to ensure the supply of perfect gentlemen to become rulers." Megabyzus' "meritocracy" or "aristocracy" therefore, according to Keith, resembles Socrates' ideal republic.

55 Benardete (86) points out that of the three speakers, only Megabyzus uses a poetic simile—"like a river in winter spate"—and a verb of knowing (*ginoskein*).

56 Benardete, 86.

57 Plato, *Republic*, 558c.

58 Aristotle, *Nicomachean Ethics*, 1131a10–1131b2.

59 Keith, 313–14.

60 Keith (313) insightfully points out that according to Darius, the person of the king is a more powerful object of wonder than the laws, and thus that the people's "natural propensity to worship what they perceive as superior to themselves," will most likely be directed towards a living human being rather than something so impersonal as the laws.

61 Keith, 315.

62 Pelling suggests that Darius' argument for the inevitability of monarchy (tyranny) and the praise of Cyrus is strictly a Persian perspective without wider applicability to the experience or moral horizon of the Greek world. See Christopher Pelling, "Speech and Action: Herodotus' Debate on the Constitutions," *Proceedings of the Cambridge Philological Society* 48 (2002): 146–47.

63 Benardete (213) who argues that for Herodotus the political perspective is freedom and empire, Flory (128) who believes that for Herodotus the best regime is the rule of one man who resembles Plato's philosopher-king, and Rosen (47) who argues that Herodotus is a Machiavellian, all maintain that of the three speakers in the debate, Darius comes closest to representing Herodotus' own political views. Keith (318–35), following Benardete, Flory, and Rosen, finds Herodotus' political science revealed in the Persian debate on the best regime. Keith concludes that the oligarchic regime articulated by Megabyzus, based on exceptional individuals, is regarded by Herodotus as the best regime in theory. On the other hand, according to Keith, the despotic regime articulated by Darius, which reduces all human beings ultimately to their sexual or bodily desires and seeks to elevate a ruler who best knows how to govern human beings as if they were cattle, is regarded by Herodotus as the best regime in practice.

64 For an argument different from my own, see Lateiner, 165, 182–83.

65 For a reading similar to my own, see Pelling ("Speech and Action," 132, 154).

66 See Benardete, 85, and Rosen, 42.

67 Corinth, which is explicitly referred to by Socles as having been an oligarchy, did degenerate into being ruled by tyrants, first by Cypselus and then by his son Periander (V.52). However, it should be noted that the oligarchy in Corinth seems to have been of the more traditional kind—characterized by rule of the rich and pursuit of wealth (II.167)—rather than resembling the more aristocratic regime described by Megabyzus.

68 See Keith, 303–4.

69 For a thoughtful reading that is different from my own see Vlastos (172–77) who argues that *isonomia* expresses the moral norm of equality by which regimes can be evaluated, and that for Herodotus it serves as the name of democracy (*demokratia*) because the democratic regime comes closest to adhering to this norm. Also see Pelling ("Speech and Action," 136–39) who argues that Otanes' use of *isonomia* does not signify a democratic "constitution," but rather a slogan that connotes the absence of tyranny, and which can embrace Greek states that are not democratic, such as Sparta.

70 In book 5 of Plato's *Republic*, Socrates distinguishes between things that can, in the precise sense, be known and therefore thought, and those things that can only be opined (476e–479e). The easiest way to explain Socrates' distinction between that which can be known and that which can merely be opined is to consider his description of the philosopher in contrast to the lover of sights and sounds. The lover of sights and sounds loves the many sensible and particular things that come to be and pass away in the world, which "participate in" but are not the thing "itself." The philosopher, on the other hand, loves the thing "itself," not its particular manifestations, and thus loves the "one" rather than the "many," that which cannot be sensed but only grasped by the mind (476a–476d, 478d). Socrates calls the thing "itself" as opposed to the many particulars that participate in it, the "idea . . . which always stays the same in all respects" (479a). Thus, whereas the particular manifestations of the "idea" come to be and pass away and are therefore changing, the "idea" is unchanging and therefore universal; the "idea" is the universal characteristic that all the particular examples of the thing share. For instance, with respect to the "idea" of the beautiful, examples of particular manifestations would be a beautiful man, a beautiful woman, a beautiful tree, and a beautiful poem. The "idea" of the beautiful is the universal characteristic that all these particular examples of beauty share and allow us to call them beautiful; it is the quality of beauty that makes the particulars what they are. According to Socrates, it is only the "ideas" which can be fully known whereas the particulars can only be opined, and thus, whereas the philosopher is a lover of knowledge, the lover of sights and sounds is merely a lover of opinion (480a).

71 See Pelling ("Speech and Action," 131, 150–53) for an alternative reading. He argues that the Persian experience of tyranny in comparison to the Greek tyr-

anny of Polycrates of Samos and Periander of Corinth in book 3 is the immediate context of the debate.

72 For the importance Herodotus places on the multiplicity of meaning in names such as *Smerdis*, see Munson (*Black Doves Speak*, 41 n. 48). Also, for other examples of key words in the *Histories* having two meanings, see the word *empire* (I.53, 91), the word *Ecbatana* (III.64–65), the word *paean* (V.1), and the word *Argos* (VI.76, 80).

73 For Herodotus' focus on the particular see Marincola (23) and Gould (115).

74 Things change rather than remain the same. Yet, if this were simply true, no word could refer, in the strict sense, to anything except perhaps "flux." Thus, things should be understood as complex mixtures of change and continuity, and the words that refer to these things as containing this complexity. Aristotle, for example, addresses this issue in book 3 of the *Politics*, when he asks whether the city changes or remains the same when either the regime or the generations change with the passage of time. According to Aristotle, because "it is looking to the regime above all that the city must be said to be the same," if a city such as Athens experiences regime change from tyranny to democracy, the city also changes (1276b10). However, we would still be right to refer to the city as "Athens," as something, if not the regime, has clearly remained the same—its people. Yet, what if the regime remains the same but the people change? Must it, Aristotle asks, "be asserted that the city is the same as long as the stock of inhabitants remains the same, even though some are always passing away and being born . . . ?" (1276a34–35). In the case of generational as opposed to regime change, Aristotle indicates that the city remains the same. However, the word "Athens" would still refer to something that has clearly changed—the generations. The word *Athens* contains a complex mixture of continuity and change, because it refers to a city composed of regime and people, who themselves are complex mixtures of continuity and change.

75 See Pelling ("Speech and Narrative," 110).

76 Otanes withdraws from the contest, asserting, "I will not rule or be ruled. But I withdraw from any chance of rule on one condition: that I shall not be ruled by any one of you, neither myself nor my descendents" (III.83).

77 Thompson, 81.

78 It should be noted that there is a difference in the type of deceit practiced when one lies intentionally in speech and when one "lies" in deed through remaining silent or unintentionally in speech. In this sense, Herodotus' Persians can be contrasted to his Egyptians. Herodotus indicates that the Egyptians regularly practice the first form of lying, intentionally in speech. For example, the Egyptians say that Persian king Cambyses was the son of Nitetis, daughter of Egyptian king Apries, and Persian king Cyrus. But, Herodotus claims "[the Egyptian] story is not true. For they know well . . . that Cambyses was the son of Cassandane, the daughter of Pharnaspes . . . and certainly not any Egyptian woman. The Egyptians have twisted this story because they want to lay claim to be connected with the house of Cyrus as true kinsfolk" (III.2). For another

example of intentional Egyptian lying in speech, see Herodotus' assessment of their story concerning the burning of Egyptian king Amasis' corpse (III.16). The Persians, on the other hand, appear only to lie intentionally in deed by remaining silent about the truth—such as Darius' failure to inform his fellow conspirators that he had rigged the outcome of the contest for the throne—or unintentionally in speech. The Persian debaters illustrate the latter form of concealing the truth when they use words to express that which they believe is universal, unchanging, and simple, when in reality these things are particular, changing and complex.

79 Benardete, 27, 69, 72.

80 Benardete, 84.

81 Rosen (80) argues that Otanes' last sentence in this passage shows that he "prefers the many to the few," or democracy to either oligarchy or monarchy, consistent with the position Otanes takes in the debate on the best regime (III.80).

82 Rosen (41) claims that in this speech Darius, who—Rosen believes—represents Herodotus' political point of view, shows that the establishment of political order, or justice and freedom, depends upon self-interest, or lies and murder, and not the gods. Therefore, according to Rosen, for Darius, and thus for Herodotus, "Gain replaces the gods," meaning that both Darius and Herodotus have a Machiavellian understanding of politics.

83 Sourvinou-Inwood (139–41, 144) argues that Herodotus himself uses the word "Pelasgian" to mean different things in different places in his narrative, in order to deconstruct the assumptions underlying the traditional belief in the strict ethnic divide between "barbarians" and Greeks. Also see Rood (303) and Munson (*Black Doves Speak*, 9–10).

Chapter 4

1 For an alternative understanding of Herodotus' methodology, see Waters (1–3) who maintains that Herodotus lacks a political science (or notion of a best regime) that he tries to convey in his *Histories*. Waters (41–42) argues that Herodotus is an "objective historian," unconcerned with what is right and wrong, and that he makes no moral judgments with respect to the historical material with which he is dealing.

2 Forsdyke, "Herodotus," 224–26. Also see Robin Osborne, "Archaic Greek History," in *Brill's Companion to Herodotus*, ed. Bakker, et al. (Leiden: Brill, 2002), 514.

3 Forsdyke, "Herodotus," 230. Also see John Moles, "Herodotus and Athens," in *Brill's Companion to Herodotus*, ed. Bakker, et al. (Leiden: Brill, 2002), 36–39, 42, 51. He argues that Herodotus draws tacit parallels between the Athenians of the *Histories* and the Athenians of his own day.

4 See Rosen, 47, and Flory, 128.

5 Fornara, 48–49.

6 Pelling, "Speech and Action," 136–39.

7 Page, 328; and Tigerstedt, 92, 100.

8 Forsdyke, "Herodotus," 233; idem., "Athenian Democratic Ideology and Herodotus' *Histories*," *American Journal of Philology* 122:3 (2001): 348; and Kurt Raaflaub, *The Discovery of Freedom in Ancient Greece* (Chicago: University of Chicago Press, 2004), 59, 95.

9 Shimron, 84–91.

10 Peter Euben, "The Battle of Salamis and the Origins of Political Theory," *Political Theory* 14:3 (1986): 368–69.

11 Arlene W. Saxonhouse, *Free Speech and Democracy in Ancient Athens* (Cambridge: Cambridge University Press, 2006), 30, 35–36.

12 Saxonhouse, *Athenian Democracy*, 31–57; and Lateiner, 170–71, 185. Also see Munson, *Black Doves Speak*, 4–5.

13 See Plutarch for the democratic and commercial character of the regime that Solon founded in Athens. Plutarch, "Solon," in *Plutarch's Lives*, trans. John Dryden (New York: The Modern Library, 1905), 107–8, 110.

14 For instance, Herodotus says that in the time of the bad laws before Lycurgus, "Leon and Hegisicles were kings at Sparta," indicating that they ruled simultaneously (I.65). Herodotus discusses the origin of the dual kingship in book 6, which I will analyze later in this chapter. Also, Plutarch, in contrast to Herodotus, attributes the creation of the ephors to King Theopompus one hundred and thirty years after Lycurgus' death. Plutarch, "Lycurgus," in *Plutarch's Lives*, trans. John Dryden (New York: The Modern Library, 1905), 54.

15 See John Hart (*Herodotus and Greek History* [New York: St. Martin's Press, 1982], 67) for the age requirement and term of office of the nonroyal members of the Council of Elders.

16 For the number and tenure of the ephors, see Hart (67) and Kevin Mark Cragg, "Herodotus' Presentation of Sparta" (University of Michigan: Ph.D. Dissertation, 1976), 87.

17 With respect to the abundance of leisure that the institution of "helotry," imposed by Lycurgus, gave to the Spartans, Plutarch says "that in Sparta he who was free was most so, and he that was a slave there, the greatest slave in the world" ("Lycurgus," 68, 71, 93).

18 For instance, Plutarch, following Plato, argues that the small Council of Elders was the structure of greatest importance that Lycurgus founded, resisting both the rise of tyranny and the rise of democracy in Sparta ("Lycurgus," 53).

19 According to Socrates in the *Minos*, it is said that the Cretans received their laws from Minos, who in turn was educated by Zeus. Plato, *Minos*, trans. Thomas L. Pangle. In *The Roots of Political Philosophy: Ten Forgotten Socratic Dialogues*, ed. Thomas L. Pangle (Ithaca: Cornell University Press, 1987), 319c–320b. Thus, it seems that if the Spartans believed their laws came from Crete, via Lycurgus via Minos, they still believed that they had their origin in the divine.

20 Hart (5) maintains that the "Hill" party gathered and championed by Pisistratus were the poorer peasantry of eastern Attica who ought to have benefited from Solon's laws but could not, due to their remoteness from the city. Hart also says

that the "Coast" party, the stronghold of the Alcmaeonidae, was commercial in character and did indeed reap the benefits of Solon's laws. The "Plain" party, stronghold of the "Philiad" family and traditional rivals of the Alcmaeonidae, was composed of the landed gentry, who had suffered economically and politically by Solon's reforms.

21 According to Socrates, in book 8 of Plato's *Republic*, the first action of the tyrant is to ask the people to provide him with his own private contingent of bodyguards (566b–c).

22 Waters (21–23) argues that this is one of the passages that illustrates that Herodotus has no moral animus against the Pisistrads or against tyranny as such.

23 Although Herodotus indicates in book 2 of the *Histories* that the anthropomorphization of the Egyptian gods by Hesiod and Homer is an advance above the Egyptian belief in gods of animal form, Herodotus indicates here the problems of such an anthropomorphization. However, see Forsdyke ("Herodotus," 236), who claims that Herodotus misrepresents this episode with Pisistratus.

24 For a thoughtful reading that is different from my own regarding the place of the irrational in Herodotus' narrative, see Thompson (28–30), who argues that Herodotus includes both "serious" or factual and "ridiculous" or mythical stories in his *Histories*, because they both serve to found the various political communities to which such stories belong. They define that community's culture, and guide that community or culture into the future.

25 Herodotus discusses the supposed "curse" of the Almaeonidae in book 5 of the *Histories*. According to Herodotus, before the time of Pisistratus a young man named Cylon, having won an Olympic victory, attempted to make himself tyrant of Athens (V.71). He and a small band of his supporters tried to seize the Acropolis for this purpose but failed. They then fled as suppliants to the sanctuary of Athena. The authorities in Athens at this time then persuaded Cylon and his party to leave the sanctuary and stand trial, on the promise that they would not receive the death penalty. However, Herodotus says that when they left the sanctuary they were murdered, and it was rumored that the Alcmaeonidae were responsible and were thus placed under a curse (V.71). According to Hart (2), it is likely that Megacles I, grandfather to the Megacles involved with Pisistratus and one of the "Nine Archons" at the time of Cylon's attempted coup, is the Alcmaeonid referred to by Herodotus in V.71. Herodotus thus reveals an irony in the political motivations of the Alcmaeonidae family. Megacles' grandfather—Megacles I—killed Cylon, thus saving Athens from a potential tyrant. The Megacles of the present story, however, helps restore Pisistratus and tries to entwine his family with the tyrant's, by marrying his daughter. It seems that the Alcmaeonidae can be both tyranicides and supporters of tyranny.

26 Herodotus here draws a strong contrast between internal freedom and tyranny. Also, Pisistratus' encampment at Marathon, accompanied by his son Hippias, foreshadows the Persian encampment at Marathon under Datis and Artaphrenes, accompanied by Hippias as well, in book 6 (VI.102). So

Herodotus draws a parallel between Pisistratus' tyranny over Athens with, if it were successful, Persia's subjection of that city to her empire. Native tyranny and foreign domination seem to pose the same threat to internal freedom.

27 Plutarch, however, tells us that Solon did return to Athens and saw the rise of Pisistratus ("Solon," 115–17).

28 Hart (5) says of this passage that "what Solon's legislation required was not amendment but enforcement."

29 Immerwahr (156) maintains that Solon's point in this speech is to show the insecurity of riches, and the danger in thinking that one is happy (*holbos*) when one is merely wealthy (*plousios*), therefore drawing the distinction between material wealth and real happiness. Munson (*Black Doves Speak*, 71) argues that, for Herodotus, the miscommunication between Croesus and Solon shows that cultural misunderstandings have a linguistic component.

30 See the discussion of tyranny in Hart, 62.

31 Plutarch indicates the antinomian character of Solon's founding activity when he says that Solon was more likely to soften or repeal laws already in existence—such as Draco's laws—rather than impose harsh new ones. Furthermore, according to Plutarch, Solon purposely gave his laws obscure and ambiguous wording so disputes between the citizens could not be settled by the letter of the law, so that all cases would have to be brought to the courts. As a result, the judges and jurors—the poorest and therefore the majority of men—"were in a manner master of the laws," leading to tyranny of the majority, rather than the rule of law ("Solon," 107–8).

32 Havelock argues that the injustice Herodotus refers to in this passage implies cannibalism, the kind practiced by Homer's Cyclops "who knew not justice or laws." See Eric A. Havelock, *The Greek Concept of Justice: From Its Shadow in Homer to Its Substance in Plato* (Cambridge: Harvard University Press, 1978), 298.

33 Interestingly Havelock (306) argues that the word *dikaiosune*, used here to refer to the practices of Deioces as well as elsewhere in the *Histories* (II.141–52, VI.73, 85–87, VII.163–64), refers to justice in the soul, as opposed to the word *dike*, which refers to justice in the city. The former is related to a total selflessness, the latter is related to a selfishness that assumes selflessness on the part of the one dispensing *dike*. If Havelock is correct, then Deioces was not just divided between his internal intentions and his external appearances, but within his soul as well. He possessed both justice (*dikaiosune*) as well as a desire (*erastheis*) for tyranny.

34 Deioces' rise to power resembles Glaucon's description of the origin of justice in Plato's *Republic*, with the exception that, whereas in Glaucon's story the naturally weaker become the conventionally stronger. In Herodotus, Deioces, the naturally stronger, becomes the conventionally stronger as well (358e–359a). Furthermore, it also resembles Hobbes' description of the contract of every man with every man to bring the Leviathan into being. See Thomas Hobbes, *Leviathan*, ed. Edwin Curly (Indianapolis: Hackett Publishing, 1994), 109.

35 Xenophon makes a similar point at the beginning of his *Cyropaedia* at I.i.2. Xenophon, *Cyropaedia*, ed. Walter Miller (Cambridge: Harvard University Press, 1914), 5.

36 Saxonhouse (*Athenian Democracy*, 45–49), argues, as I do, that, for Herodotus, there is a tension between equality and authority.

37 See Benardete, 25.

38 Shimron, 3, 26–28, 55. For an alternative to the argument that Herodotus approaches human events from a strictly rational perspective, see Thomas Harrison, who claims that Herodotus' narrative is "underpinned by theological assumptions" ("'Prophecy in Reverse'? Herodotus and the Origins of History," in *Herodotus and His World*, ed. Derow and Parker, 238, 240).

39 Again, Herodotus draws a strong contrast between tyranny and internal freedom, as he did when discussing Pisistratus' third attempt to establish his tyranny in Athens in book 1 (I.62).

40 See the discussion in Benardete, 145.

41 See the discussion in Hart, 13.

42 Although Herodotus maintains that the democratic regime founded by Cleisthenes was an advance, he does not share Hegel's "philosophic" view of history. Herodotus, unlike Hegel, does not believe in the necessarily progressive character of the historical process nor that it is governed by a rational or divine will seeking to make itself manifest in the world. See Hegel, 1–103. Although he does not share Hegel's view of history, which has no room for chance, Herodotus does not swing to the other extreme, to Solon's view of history, which sees the totality of history as governed completely by chance—which leads to the conclusion that death is better than life. Rather, Herodotus indicates that chance is certainly a part, but not the whole, of history, and that chance events may have beneficial effects that make life worthwhile.

43 This is deeply ironic, as the name *Isagoras* means "equality of speech" and Herodotus indicates that from this man's defeat emerges a regime that will be characterized by *isegorie* and that equality of speech will arise. Moreover, Herodotus' account of Cleisthenes' struggle with Isagoras again shows the role of accident in history. First, if Cleisthenes had been winning in his struggle for power, there would have been no reason for him to have wooed the commonality to his side. Second, Cleisthenes' father, losing out to his rival Lycurgus and his "Plain" faction in a similar situation in book 1, took Pisistratus, the tyrant, into partnership after having driven him out once before, rather than the *demos* or the common people of Athens (I.60). Perhaps the only reason that Cleisthenes, unlike his father Megacles, did not recall the Pisistrads rather than take the people into his own party to defeat Isagoras, is that he did not want to share power and prestige with the Pisistrads and be second to Hippias. Thus, the democratic regime that he founds is only an incidental if beneficial result of Cleisthenes' primary desire for power and influence. Also, see Hart (11), who argues that there is a discrepancy between the short-term motives of

Cleisthenes—to secure his personal position rather than high-minded devotion to the common good—and the great, long-term benefits, and that Cleisthenes himself probably did not foresee what his reforms would bring to Athens.

44 See Ostwald, 151. Also see discussion in Hart, 11; and Aristotle, *Politics*, 1257b36–37.

45 See the discussion in Benardete, 146.

46 This is similar to the two origins of the city that Aristotle describes in book 1 of the *Politics*. According to Aristotle, the city develops naturally but violently out of the conjunction of master and slave—for the sake of preservation and out of the conjunction of male and female—for the sake of reproduction. Thus, the first origin of the city is in the family, which is rooted in necessity and the body. Yet, Aristotle says "the one who first constituted a city is responsible for the greatest of goods." He suggests the second origin of the city, through the founding of a wise lawgiver and the deliberation and choice implied in such a founding—made possible by the uniquely human capacity for reason and speech. Aristotle, *Politics*, 1252a, 26–1252b, 30; 253a, 30–31; 1253a, 6–19. Also see Mary P. Nichols, *Citizens and Statesmen: A Study of Aristotle's Politics* (Lanham, Md.: Rowman & Littlefield, 1992), 9–10, 15–19.

47 For an alternative understanding of the refounding of the Athenian democracy in book 5, see Ostwald (147, 153–57), who argues that Cleisthenes appealed to the slogan *isonomia*—"equality before the law"—to gain the people's support. However, Ostwald (159–60) insightfully distinguishes between the founding activity of Solon and the refounding activity of Cleisthenes, arguing that Cleisthenes "made it clear that he was not acting as a law*giver* in the sense in which Lycurgus or Solon had imposed their legislation on Sparta and Athens, respectively, but that the people were themselves to take the responsibility of accepting and implementing the measures proposed by him." As a result, Cleisthenes substituted in Athens the notion of *nomos*—understood as measures regarded as valid and binding for all classes of society because all classes of society had an equal opportunity to propose and ratify them—for the notion of *thesmos*—understood as measures imposed on the city by a third party. In other words, under Cleisthenes' reforms, the people were understood as the makers of the laws rather than the receivers of the laws; the source of law was human rather than divine.

48 For instance, see the speech of the Athenians to the Spartans in book 1 of Thucydides, when, speaking of Salamis, the Athenian says, "But we left behind us a city that was a city no longer, and staked our lives for a city that had an existence only in desperate hope. . . ." (*History of the Peloponnesian War*, trans. Richard Crawley and ed. Robert B. Strassler [New York: Free Press, 1996], I.74, 2). Also, see Aeschylus, *The Persians*, trans. Seth Benardete (Chicago: University of Chicago Press, 1956), 345–49.

49 According to Ostwald (144) the "Council" referred to by Herodotus in this passage "was still the old Solonian Council of Four Hundred." Ostwald also

maintains that Cleomenes' entrusting of the government to three hundred of Isagoras' partisans "was an attempt to establish an oligarchy and not merely to reduce the number of Councilors. . . ."

50 In this passage Herodotus points to the remarkable singularity of purpose or thought that Cleisthenes' reforms allowed the Athenians to have.

51 According to Herodotus, as a result of this break (*dichostasies*) between Cleomenes and Demaratus in Eleusis, a new law (*nomos*) was established in Sparta that prescribed "when the army went on campaign, both kings were not allowed to go with it at the same time" (V.75). So the Spartan regime is not as stable or unchanging as Herodotus presents it.

52 Fornara (48–49) argues that the key word in this passage is not *isegorie* but *eleutherothenton*, and that Herodotus does not intend to endorse Athenian democracy or one form of government against another. Instead, according to Fornara, Herodotus wants to show the antithesis between freedom and despotism, and thus his admiration for free government, "whatever its more particular form." According to Fornara, "in this respect it is clear that his admiration for the Spartan government was even more intense than any feeling he evinced for Athenian democracy."I disagree. It is *isegorie* which is the key word in this passage (V.78). Herodotus calls *isegorie*, equality of speech, a good thing (*spoudaion*), not *eleutheria*, freedom. The freedom that Herodotus distinguishes from despotism near the end of the passage must be understood as subordinate to and flowing from *isegorie*, which Herodotus praises at the beginning of the passage. Internal freedom, the freedom coming from the equal right to speak rather than the rule of law as in Sparta, is the freedom which Herodotus is admiring in this passage, and it only pertains to the Athenian regime, not the Spartan one. For a discussion of what is technically meant by *isegorie* and why it is a phenomenon peculiar to Athens, see Hart, 67. Also see Forsdyke ("Athenian Democratic Ideology," 348), who argues that this passage in Herodotus reveals that Athenian military strength depended on Athenian democratic ideology. Also, see Raaflaub (59–61, 86), who maintains that political freedom as an ideology arose after the Persian Wars were complete. Euben (368–69) argues that Herodotus recognized the political freedom referred to in this passage not only as the foundation of Athenian victory at Salamis but also of his own activity of writing history.

53 See discussion in Benardete, 146. Also, the Athenian democracy and its unique kind of internal freedom is related to tyranny because Athens is *anomia*, ruled by speech rather than law. To this extent, every Athenian, as potentially having an equal right to make the laws, is above the law as the tyrant is. Thus in some ways, the Athenian democracy is characterized by the "tyranny of the majority," as Megabyzus says in his speech in book 3 (III.81).

54 See Benardete, 146–47.

55 For examples of the defective way in which Herodotus believed Athens usually combined private and public, body and soul, unless pressed by a powerful external force, see the stories of Alcmaeon (VI.125), Hippoclides (VI. 126–30),

Aristagoras in Sparta and Athens (V.49–50, 97), and Miltiades' siege of Paros (VI. 132–36).

56 One of Cleisthenes' reforms was the establishment of the "Board of Ten Generals," one general being elected from each of the ten new tribes to serve for one year (Grene, 449–50, n. 47). Miltiades was the most important of the ten. The Athenian generals, once at Marathon, quarreled over whether or not to fight the Persians. Miltiades resolved the question in favor of fighting, and the battle of Marathon was fought on the day Miltiades was in command. Miltiades was a member of the Philaidae family who were the chief rivals of the Alcmaeonidae family in Athens (VI.109–11). For a further discussion of the Philaidae family tree and Miltiades' supposed contempt for democracy, see Hart, 17–22.

57 Thompson (37–40) argues that Herodotus' account of Marathon "revealed nothing less than the unfolding of Athenian identity. Marathon seems to represent for Herodotus the moment in which Athenian political identity is first haltingly enunciated . . . Herodotus can thus be seen identifying the deepest causes of [Athenian] victory." According to Thompson, there were two causes, for Herodotus, of the Athenian victory at Marathon. First, the secular nature of the regime, and second, the coexistence of "nobility and baseness . . . side by side" in Athens, or the combination of the defense of freedom and the common good with the pursuit of private gain. Although generally agreeing with Thompson's analysis, I would add a third cause, which flows from the first two. The Athenians can use their eyes and ears to look on the other and see themselves, and thus to see that "national character" (Thompson, 80) is a product of convention, not nature. In other words I argue that the Athenians at Marathon share a similar perspective with Herodotus.

58 Robertson argues that the two oracles given to the Athenians actually mean the same thing: both foretell the loss of Attica to a foreign invader and both advise the Athenians to withdraw to the Peloponnese behind the safety of the Isthmus wall, built by the Peloponnesians after the defeat of Leonidas at Thermopylae. Yet the latter alternative is explicitly acknowledged by neither of the two main parties to the debate that arose in Athens over the meaning of the second oracle. See Noel Robertson, "The True Meaning of the 'Wooden Wall,'" *Classical Philology* 82:1 (1987): 2, 9–10.

59 Bowden (73, 103–4, 106–7) argues that both oracle verses quoted by Herodotus and the debate over the meaning of the reference to the wooden wall were "post-eventum" creations by Herodotus, designed to emphasize the wisdom of Themistocles, one of the key figures of his history, and to remind his readers of divine involvement in human affairs.

60 See Benardete (199) who argues that Themistocles' interpretation of the oracle "left [the Athenians] freedom of choice; they learned that the word 'divine' did not spell their necessary defeat." Also, see Thompson (100–103), who insightfully points out that "Themistocles stands out as an admirable leader in shaping positive responses to the god," because "Herodotus seems to be impressed with

a people's active structuring of its religious beliefs, and this is where Athens comes in for praise." Furthermore, Thompson (105–8) argues that the different ways in which the Greeks—especially the Athenians represented by Themistocles—and the Persians receive divine communication is indicative of their different political structures. Divine communications usually come indirectly to the Athenians through the Delphic oracle whose ambiguous language is open to competing interpretations. This need for interpretation presupposes the freedom of speech of a democratic regime. The Persians, or more precisely their kings, usually receive divine communication through dreams (e.g., Xerxes' dream in VII.12–18). This kind of communication leaves no room for debate or for a "human counterstroke" against the gods. This situation reflects the obliteration of the exercise of free will in the tyrannical political structure of Persia. Moreover, Thompson (81) argues that the more positive stance that the Greeks have towards the divine, which presupposes the high value that they place on free discourse, is a sign that they, and not the Persians, are the real "truth-tellers" in Herodotus' *Histories*. I am indebted to, and in agreement with, Thompson's argument that the different ways in which people speak and understand speech is of crucial importance to Herodotus and that "Persian truth telling is . . . [Herodotus'] broadest subject of attack" (81). Yet I come to the same conclusion for different reasons. First, I argue that Herodotus criticizes the Persian dedication to "truth telling" not because the Persians fail to tell the truth despite their pretensions to do so but because they do indeed attempt to tell the truth absolutely and at all times. They are the "truth tellers," not the Greeks. Herodotus indicates it can lead either to madness, as in the case of Cambyses, or to the total collapse of the belief in the distinction between truth and falsehood, as in the case of Darius. The second way in which my argument diverges from Thompson's is related to her understanding of Herodotus' definition of truth telling. According to Thompson, "Herodotus provides in the History his own definition of truth telling: how a society characterizes and perpetuates the truest version of itself, in its ability to absorb criticism, to be open to change, and to show depth in its creative resources. In effect, truth telling represents the larger human predicament of demarcating and establishing a spot for oneself in the world" (81). According to Thompson (3), Herodotus has affinities with Heidegger. Thus, "truth" is not an "idea" or an objective reality, but rather a subjective view of the world or cultural cave. Some are better than others in sustaining a community, such as the Greeks over the Persians. I argue, however, that for Herodotus, who has affinities with Plato and Aristotle rather than Heidegger, there are "truths" that are not merely subjective, but rather represent an objective reality. For Herodotus, there are "ideas," or objective realities, but they are not immediately apparent. As the Persian dedication to truth telling implies, "ideas" are obscured by the many particular and changing things in the world. For example, Herodotus declares, knowing that many will disagree, that it is objectively true that the Athenians were the saviors of Greece because they resisted the Persians at sea and therefore that Themistocles' interpretation of the ambiguous language in the oracle was the correct one (VII.139, 142–43). Themistocles sees that all speech, but especially divine speech, can both conceal and reveal the truth simultaneously. It is impossible for the divine to speak without lying and telling the truth at the same time. This fact makes the Athenians, but not all Greeks, superior to the truth telling Persians.

61 This discussion of Themistocles' relation to the Delphic oracle in the *Histories* has been guided by Howland's (59–68) analysis of Socrates' relation to the same oracle in Plato's *Apology of Socrates.* See Jacob Howland, *Kierkegaard and Socrates: A Study in Philosophy and Faith* (Cambridge: Cambridge University Press, 2006). Also see Scullion (196–97, 202), who suggests that Herodotus sees the "divine" or "the god" as an abstract force representing moralized chance that stands behind the usual anthropomorphized Greek god, e.g., Apollo speaks through the Pythia at Delphi.

62 According to Stadter (245) Cleomenes' desire to dominate the Argives is an illustration of his personification of the imperialist side of Sparta.

63 For a similar discussion of Socrates' encounter with the oracle in Plato's *Apology of Socrates,* see Howland, 63.

64 For further analysis of Spartan actions before Thermopylae, their relationship to the Persian political structure, and their attempt to extend their empire, see Page, 324.

65 This custom seems to be at odds with what Herodotus says at V.75. There Herodotus claims that, as a result of King Demaratus' desertion of King Cleomenes' when he was attempting to impose Isagoras as tyrant on Athens, a new law was established in Sparta that required one king to remain at home while the other king went on campaign with the army (V.75).

66 It is commonly believed that Thucydides criticizes Herodotus and wishes to establish the superiority of his mode of inquiry to that of the *Histories* when he says, "There are many . . . unfounded ideas current among the rest of the Hellenes, even on matters of contemporary history which have not been obscured by time. For instance, there is the notion that the Spartan kings have two votes each, the fact being that they have only one . . ." (Thucydides, I.20, 3). Yet, Cragg (88) notes that Herodotus expresses himself ambiguously in this passage, indicating that either each king had two votes or that the combined votes of the kings equaled two.

67 Cragg argues that Herodotus makes clear that Spartan kings are not absolute. According to Cragg (93) the kings are often subject to the ephors acting as a judicial body, for instance in VI.82, where Cleomenes is arraigned before them on bribery charges, as well as to the ephors and the Council of Elders acting jointly—for instance in V.40, when they coerce Anaxandrides into taking a second wife. Thus Cragg implies that Spartan kings were subject to the courts made up of the ephors and the Council of Elders and that they were thus subject to the law. See also Demaratus' impeachment (VI.65) and the trial of Leotychides for abusing the Aeginetans (VI.85). For an alternative view, see Stadter (243),

who claims that the Spartan dual kingship assimilated Sparta to the Asian kingdoms of Lydia and Persia, thus distinguishing it from other Greek cities.

68 Benardete argues that Zeus of Lacedaemon is a local god who takes care of the Spartans during peacetime and that heavenly Zeus is a universal god who takes care of the Spartans when they campaign against another city. The former, according to Benardete (172), is reminiscent of the Egyptian Zeus of Thebes who concealed his true identity in a ram's skin, and the latter is reminiscent of the Persian Zeus who represented "the whole disc of heaven," or the sky. Therefore, Benardete argues, "the Spartans recapitulate the two major barbarian peoples, who contributed as well to two major parts of Herodotus' own logos . . . Books II and III."

69 Herodotus never gives an account of Athenian "customs," as distinguished from "laws" self-consciously made, except perhaps for a very brief mention of two before the battle of Salamis, at VIII.41 and VIII.54.

70 See Benardete (170–71), who concludes that this story of the origin of the Spartan dual kingship shows that "Spartan 'sophrosune' or sobriety rest[s] on their ability to fit what ought to be to what is, and what is to what ought to be." To the extent that they are unable to adjust convention to nature and nature to convention, it would lead the Spartans away from sobriety toward madness, as happened to Cleomenes, whose birth is due to the failure to adjust what is to what ought to be.

71 Emphasis mine.

72 Harrison ("The Persian Invasions," 574) believes this claim is spurious, reflecting a pro-Athenian bias on the part of Herodotus.

73 For a contrary argument with respect to Herodotus' belief in the veracity of oracles, see Jon D. Mikalson, "Religion in Herodotus," in *Brill's Companion to Herodotus*, ed. Bakker, et al. (Leiden: Brill, 2002), 195.

74 Blosel argues that in his account of Themistocles' acquisition and use of Euboean bribe money before Artemisium, Herodotus intends to foreshadow and critique Athenian imperial mistreatment of their allies in the Delian League. See Wolfgang Blosel, "The Herodotean Picture of Themistocles: A Mirror of Fifth-century Athens," in *The Historian's Craft in the Age of Herodotus*, ed. Nino Luraghi (Oxford: Oxford University Press, 2007), 186–87, 196.

75 See Moles, 45–46.

76 Moles, 46.

77 Harrison ("The Persian Invasions," 567) argues that the disagreement over strategy regarding how to repel the Persians from Greece reflects the tension between its two leading cities—Athens and Sparta—a theme running throughout the *Histories*.

78 Themistocles, Herodotus tells us, later made Sicinus a citizen of Thespia (VIII.75).

79 Thomas ("The Intellectual Milieu," 68) claims that Themistocles' speech is reminiscent of the sophistic methodology used by Protagoras.

80 Herodotus also shows the limits of speech and the necessity of compulsion to effect the action and unite the Greeks. When words, in contrast to the Persian understanding, are understood to lie or conceal the truth as well as to reveal it, persuasion must be combined with force, choice with necessity, or freedom with slavery. See Themistocles' speech to the Andrians (VIII.111). Also see Marincola (22) and Griffin (55), who argue that Herodotus' account of the dissension among the Greeks before the battle of Salamis clearly distinguishes the *Histories* from its tragic predecessor, Aeschylus' *Persians*, and serves to obscure the contrast between Greek and barbarian. Also see Munson (*Black Doves Speak*, 16, 18). For an alternative argument see Hunter (269–70), who claims that in the *Histories* we see the struggle of the Greek mind to conceive of one Hellas as a unity of equals, the latter differing markedly from the imperial unity under either Agamemnon in the past or Xerxes in the present.

81 Mardonius and his troops are defeated at the battle of Plataea that Herodotus describes in book 9 (IX.16–85).

82 Themistocles not only repeats the argument of Eurybiades but now also says that the gods and heroes, rather than the better side of human nature (VIII.83), were responsible for their victory at Salamis. When he wants to dissuade the Athenians from attacking the Persians, Themistocles appeals to the divine—in contrast to his appeal to human nature when he wanted to persuade the Greeks to fight the Persians at Salamis. Herodotus therefore indicates that the divine, or men's concern for piety—both of which are lacking in Athens after its regime is refounded by Cleisthenes—moderates aggressiveness, or the imperialist impulse. Mikalson (187–88, 192) argues that this passage exemplifies Herodotus' message that both the cause of the Persian Wars and the Persian failure against Greece have a religious explanation. See also Harrison ("The Persian Invasions," 561).

83 For examples of the envy felt towards Themistocles after the battle of Salamis, see the refusal of the Greek commanders gathered at the Isthmus to award Themistocles the first place in honor, as well as the exchange between Themistocles and Timodemus in Athens (VIII.123–24; 125).

84 For further examples of Themistocles taking the other and making it his own after the battle of Salamis, see Herodotus' account of the siege of the Andrians, where Herodotus says Themistocles' "greed for money was insatiable" (VIII.111–12).

85 For a similar interpretation of Herodotus' presentation of Themistolces, see Forsdyke ("Herodotus," 232), and Stadter (248). Moles (46–48) argues that Themistocles' ability to take from the other and make it his own is presented by Herodotus as a positive character trait that makes him the savior of Greece.

86 Page (327–39), argues that this exchange between Xerxes and Demaratus shows that whereas Xerxes rules over bodies, the Spartan law rules over, and becomes part of, the Spartan soldiers' soul. Page suggests that the Spartans, having internalized their law, feel the command to stand and fight even against hopeless

odds, not as a compulsion from outside, as the Persian soldiers do, but from within, as part of their own character. I would only add to these persuasive arguments by Page that the Spartans seem not to internalize their law to the same extent as the Athenians do. They continue to believe that it is a product of divine providence or of something outside themselves. Thus they obey the law not only because they fear betraying themselves but also because they fear betraying the gods. Also, see Forsdyke ("Athenian Democratic Ideology," 348), who maintains that this representation of Spartan courage as a product of "law and fear of social censure" is actually a reflection of the Athenian perspective embodied by the *Histories*. Thomas ("The Intellectual Milieu," 69) argues that the implicit contrast between *nomos* and *physis* in Demaratus' exchange with Xerxes has a distinctly sophistic flavor.

87 For seven thousand as a rough estimate of the number of Greek forces at Thermopylae, see Lawrence Tritle, "Warfare in Herodotus," in *The Cambridge Companion to Herodotus*, ed. Dewald and Marincola, 215.

88 See my previous discussion of this passage in the present chapter.

89 For an alternative reading of the role of Sparta in the *Histories*, see Tigerstedt (95–100), who maintains that the speeches of Demaratus and the actions of the Spartans at Thermopylae show that Demaratus is the foil to Xerxes and Sparta is the foil to the Persians. Thus it is Sparta, not Athens, that is, for Herodotus, the first representative of and highest exponent for Greekness. According to Tigerstedt, the "eulogy of Spartan heroism at Thermopylae . . . more than counterbalances the praise of Athenian courage and skill at Marathon and Salamis," and, contrary to his direct speech in VII.139, Herodotus indicates that Greece's fate depended on the Spartans.

90 With regards to allies, Leonidas, at Thermopylae, acts very differently than Themistocles, at Salamis. Leonidas sends them home, but Themistocles gets them to stay.

91 Tritle (216) suggests that, at Thermopylae, life imitates art, as Leonidas and his Spartans are driven in their actions by the stories told of the heroes at Troy in Homer's *Iliad.*

92 All except the Thebans, who ignobly turned themselves over to the Persians when they saw them gain the upper hand against the Greeks (VII.233).

93 For further proof that an alternative source of Spartan courage is pride, or the desire for honor (largely) through death, see Herodotus' discussion of Eurytus, Aristodemus, and Pantites, three of the Spartan "Three Hundred" who missed the fighting at Thermopylae—and Aristodemus' future fate at the battle of Plataea (VII.229–32, IX.71).

94 For a further discussion of this issue, see Page (326–29), who argues that courage in both the Spartan and Persian regimes relies, in different ways, "on seeing and being seen."

95 Benardete (191–93) and Page (328) both argue that Herodotus has one notion of the virtue of courage, not two, and that its highest manifestation exists in Sparta and is displayed at the battle of Thermopylae. Shimron (84–91), on

the other hand, argues that the core of Herodotus' political thought is his appreciation of the importance of sea power in war, and hence concludes that Herodotus preferred Athens to Sparta and Persia. Finally, Tigerstedt (92, 100) acknowledges that Herodotus has two conceptions of courage, Athenian and Spartan, but argues that Herodotus' admiration for Spartan courage outweighs his admiration for that of the Athenians.

Conclusion

1 Thompson argues that this passage "reveals [Herodotus] thinking like a Greek," portraying the "intellectual" Greeks as superior to the "traditional" Indians and the "cynical" Persians (137). This is consistent with Thompson's argument that for Herodotus, all thought, including his own, is bound by cultural subjectivity. Yet this does not mean that Herodotus "retire[s] in relativistic despair; cultures make out better and worse in his portrayal" (86). Also see Marincola (19), Rood (298–300), and Munson (*Black Doves Speak*, 78). Kass, on the other hand, argues that in spite of its explicit relativistic conclusion, this passage does point to universal, natural truths about human beings. First, all human beings—Greeks, Indians, and Persians—die, and therefore become simply a body. Second, all peoples have burial customs for dead bodies. See Leon Kass, *Toward a More Natural Science: Biology and Human Affairs* (New York: Free Press, 1985), 227. Scullion (196) suggests that the word *nomos* in the line from Pindar quoted at the end of this passage refers to Herodotus' abstract understanding of the divine.

2 For Hunter (265) the interrelationship between *nomos* and *physis* is a central theme in the *Histories*. Also see Thomas ("The Intellectual Milieu," 69–70) for the prominence of this theme among the sophists.

3 See Kass, 296.

4 Descartes follows a similar path. In the *Discourse on th Method*, Descartes claims that only after he left home and traveled abroad did he observe such a diversity of customs among men, that allowed him to recognize that everything he had previously come to accept as true was merely a result of his own customs. He resolved to use only the "natural light" of his reason to investigate himself and his own human nature. Rene Descartes, *Discourse on the Method*, trans. Robert Stoothoff (Cambridge: Cambridge University Press, 1985), 115–16.

5 See Xerxes' third dream after he announces his plans—interpreted by the Magi to mean that Xerxes' rule would extend over the entire earth (*pasan gen*) and that all human beings would be his slaves (VII.19). Romm (178, 187, 189, 190) points to VII.8 to suggest that the Persian Wars were fought not just between human beings but against the natural world as well. Thus, there is a parallel between empire, expanded through force, and technological control or conquest of nature, achieved through creative human intellect.

6 Page (316–17) argues that Xerxes' wish that his empire be seen and his power recognized reveals his craving for glory. Moreover, Xerxes' reflective wish to

see his own empire himself, or to contemplate "the outward show of his power actually at work"—see for instance the viewing of his army and navy at Abydos (VII.44)—reveals a deeper desire to see the self, or to have self-knowledge.

7 Xerxes' indifference toward the distinctions among nations, functions, or weaponry among his non-Persian host parallels Darius' indifference toward the distinctions in burial customs among his Greek and Indian subjects (III.38).

8 Notice that Xerxes acknowledges that his proposed universal empire will be unjust. Moreover, Mardonius, Xerxes' cousin, points out that the Persian Empire as it presently stands is built on injustice as well. In response to Xerxes' announcement of his plans, Mardonius approvingly says, "For it would certainly be a terrible thing if, for no injury done to Persia but simply to increase our power, we should have subdued and taken for our slaves the Sacae, the Indians, the Ethiopians, the Assyrians, and many other great nations, and then did not punish the Greeks, who on their side began the wrongdoing" (VII.9). Also see Hunter, 204, 206–7.

9 Page argues that the counting of the host at Doriscus illustrates Xerxes' tendency to abstraction, or his tendency to reach for the universal and suppress the particular. According to Page, "Xerxes' ultimate abstraction is his hope for an empire that has the 'same limit as Zeus's sky.' He aims at a unification that lacks political nuance, as if the homogeneity of the sky should immediately be the measure for human community" (322).

10 See Page, 319–20.

11 See Page, 317.

12 Griffin (53) argues that Xerxes' references to decline, reversal of fortune, and the fragility of human life are major themes in Greek tragedy.

13 Artabanus' theory of how one learns also makes him similar to Herodotus. Artabanus prefaces his speech in opposition to Xerxes' plan to invade Greece by saying:

> My lord, when no opposing opinions are presented, it is impossible to choose the better, but one must accept what is proposed. When such opposites are stated, it is as it is with gold, the purity of which one cannot judge in itself, but only if you rub it along side other gold on the touchstone to see the difference. (VII.10)

Thus, just as Herodotus believes that one set of customs must be considered in light of another set of customs for the natural to become manifest (III.38), so Artabanus believes that a good opinion must be set against a bad opinion for the goodness of the former to become known—just as one piece of gold must be placed alongside another piece of gold for the purity of each to be revealed. Artabanus is not exactly like Herodotus, however. Whereas Artabanus only takes account of the principles of rest and motion as manifested in physical nature, Herodotus takes account of these principles as they are manifested in human nature and the things of human beings—such as the regime and speech—as well. In thinking more broadly about what constitutes the whole of rest and motion, Herodotus, unlike Artabanus, concludes that not simply the land and sea but the Greeks, especially the Athenians, were indeed Xerxes' greatest enemies, and not due to their superior numbers, but rather due to their superior regimes. Moreover, responding to Xerxes' anguish on the shortness of human life, Artabanus responds "Life gives us greater occasion for pity than this. Short as his life is, no man is so happy . . . that it shall not be his lot, not only once but many times, to wish himself dead rather than alive. . . . So death comes to be for man a most desirable escape from a life of wretchedness" (VII.46). Artabanus thus articulates a Solonian conception of human life and history rather than a Herodotean one (I.31–32). Lastly, Artabanus proves wrong in his judgment of the Ionians. He advises Xerxes to release them from service in his navy, arguing that they would play false to his cause and help the Athenians and the rest of the Greeks preserve their freedom (VII.51). Herodotus, by contrast, shows that the majority of the Ionians did not prove false to Xerxes. They fought against the Greeks with ardor in the battle of Salamis (VIII.22, 85–86). Despite these differences, however, Artabanus is still a thoughtful man and, taking account of the principles of rest and motion within the whole, he is more like Herodotus than he is like Xerxes.

14 See Pelling ("Speech and Narrative," 106) and Harrison ("The Persian Invasions," 569). For an alternative argument, see Sancisi-Weerdenberg, 587.

15 See Scullion, 193. Immerwahr (300) on the other hand, argues that Herodotus believed in a natural territorial boundary or separation between Asia and Europe, which served as a unifying theme of his *Histories*. Also see Mikalson, 194.

16 It is true that, after Xerxes finished counting his host in terms of the number of individual bodies in it, he had it arranged by nation and took particular interest in contemplating the uniqueness of each. According to Herodotus:

> Xerxes, when the host had been numbered and ranged in formation, was set on driving through them in person and seeing them all . . . driving through in his chariot, nation by nation, he inquired about each one, and his secretaries wrote down the information until he had gone down from one end to the other, both of horse and foot . . . Xerxes, transferring from his chariot to a Sidonian ship, sat there under a golden canopy and sailed past the prows of the ships, putting his questions to them just as he had done with the army and recording it all. (VII.100)

Yet, in Herodotus' narrative, Xerxes only takes an interest in the particularity of the nations serving in his host *after* Herodotus himself gives an account of the unique customs and names of each (VII.61–80, 89–95). It is almost as if Herodotus gives Xerxes his cue. Moreover, Xerxes still sees his host primarily in terms of the number of bodies it composes. See, for example, Xerxes' exchange with Demaratus before the battle of Thermopylae (VII.101–3), in which Xerxes articulates his belief that strength resides in numbers, not in the superior quality of one's soul. Herodotus shows Xerxes painfully learning that this is a mistaken belief when he fights the Spartans at Thermopylae (VII.209–25) and the Athenians at Salamis (VIII.41, 83–86).

17 For a similar view of the relationship between Herodotus' fascination with foreign customs and Persian imperialism, see Rood, 294.

18 See Leo Strauss, who argues, "A hundred pages—no, ten pages—of Herodotus introduce us immeasurably better into the mysterious unity of oneness and variety in human things than many volumes written in the spirit predominant in our age" ("Liberal Education and Responsibility," in *An Introduction to Political Philosophy: Ten Essays by Leo Strauss*, ed. Hilail Gilden (Detroit: Wayne State University Press, 1989), 343). Also see Marincola, 24.

19 Page (328) argues that Spartan law rules the Spartan soul (VII.104), but it is precisely for this reason that Sparta is not open to the thought of Herodotus; the hold of the law on the soul of the Spartan is too great for Herodotus to compete with. The Athenians, however, are ruled by speech, and Herodotus can become, as it were, another voice in the assembly.

20 Thucydides, I.22.

21 See Forsdyke ("Herodotus," 231) for this passage as a warning to the Athenians. Also see Hunter, 216. As directed to regimes in the future, see Moles, 49–50, 52. For a contrary argument see Gould, 116–19.

22 Herodotus thereby substitutes justice for injustice. See, Mardonius' speech on the injustice of the Persian Empire (VII.9).

Epilogue

1 See Colin L. Powell, "Remarks at the Elliot School of International Affairs," http://www.state.gov/secretary/rm/2003/2386.htm.

2 See Paul Wolfowitz "Defense Planning Guidance," in "Frontline: The War Behind Closed Doors," http://www.pbs.org/wgbh/pages/frontline/shows/iraq/etc. wolf.html.

3 For Wolfowitz and the 1992 "Defense Planning Guidance" as the guiding intellectual influence behind President George W. Bush's *National Security Strategy*, see William Kristol, John Lewis Gaddis, Barton Gellman, and Dennis Ross in "Frontline: The War Behind Closed Doors," http://www.pbs.org/wgbh/pages/frontline/Shows/iraq/themes/1992.html.

4 See the *The National Security Strategy of the United States of America* (September 2002), i.

5 *The National Security Strategy*, 3.

6 *The National Security Strategy*, i.

7 *The National Security Strategy*, i, ii.

8 *The National Security Strategy*, 14.

9 *The National Security Strategy*, 15.

10 See "Frontline: Missile Wars: Interview: Paul Wolfowitz," http://www.pbs.org/wgbh/pages/frontline/shows/missile/interviews/wolfowitz.html.

11 *The National Security Strategy*, 15.

12 *The National Security Strategy*, 15.

13 The main thrust of the criticism of the Bush doctrine involves its rationale for preemption. For instance, Bruce Ackerman claims that the doctrine of preemption violates Article 51 of the United Nations Charter, thereby violating international law. Ackerman believes it seeks to create an "imperial presidency," exercising a "double unilateralism" that repudiates the restraints of the U.N. Security Council abroad and the U.S. Congress at home. Moreover, the justification for preemption thinly veils the real desire to wage "aggressive war" that departs from the traditions of American statesmen. Bruce Ackerman, "The Legality of Using Force," http://www.law.yale.edu/outside/htnl/Public Affairs/293/yls article.htm; and "But What's the Legal Case for Preemption," http://www.law.yale.edu/outside/html/Public Affairs/282/yls article.htm. Malcolm Brailey argues that what the Bush doctrine terms "pre-emptive self-defence" intentionally conceals the actual strategy of "preventive self-defence," that, according to Brailey, is both immoral, according to international norms, and illegal, according to international law, as set out in Article 51 of the U.N. Charter. See Malcolm Brailey, "Pre-Emption and Prevention: An Ethical and Legal Critique of the Bush Doctrine and Anticipatory Use of Force in Defence of the State," paper presented at the Institute of Defence and Strategic Studies, Singapore (November 2003), 2–3, 17–18. For a range of views that spans the assertion of the transparent illegality of preemption as framed by the Bush doctrine with respect to Article 51 of the U.N. Charter, to the assertion of its limited acceptability in attempting to deal with proliferation of weapons of mass destruction, see Thomas Franck, Martti Koskenniemi, Michael Byers, Eyal Benvinisti, and Terence Taylor in "Iraq and the 'Bush Doctrine' of Pre-Emptive Self-Defence," in "Crimes of War Project," http://www.crimesofwar.org/print/expert/bush-intoBush-print.html (last updated August 20, 2002; accessed August 12, 2007). Also, see George Lopez, who argues that the Bush administration's "pre-emptive war doctrine" violates not simply international law but the "traditionalist" view of Christian just war theory as well. George Lopez, "Just? Unjust?" in *Sojourner's Magazine*, online at http://www.sojo.net/index.cfm?action&mode=printerfriendly&issue=soj.

14 See Colin L. Powell, "Remarks on the Occasion of George Kennan's Centenary Birthday," http://www.state.gov/secretary/rm/29683.htm; and "Remarks at the Elliott School of International Affairs" (2).

15 Powell, "Remarks on the Occasion of George Kennan's Centenary Birthday," and "Remarks at the Elliott School of International Affairs" (2).

16 Powell, "Remarks on the Occasion of George Kennan's Centenary Birthday," and "Remarks at the Elliott School of International Affairs" (3).

17 Powell, "Remarks on the Occasion of George Kennan's Centenary Birthday," and "Remarks at the Elliott School of International Affairs" (14).

18 Joseph S. Nye Jr., *The Paradox of American Power: Why the World's Only Superpower Can't Go It Alone* (Oxford: Oxford University Press, 2002), 1, 11, 140, 148. Also see Nye, *Soft Power: The Means to Success in World Politics* (New

York: Public Affairs, 2004), x–xii. Also see Shah, who argues that the way in which the Bush administration projects power is often seen in the third world as a new form of imperialism and may actually contribute to acts and threats of terrorism against the United States. See Anup Shah, "Military Expansion: The Bush Doctrine of Pre-emptive Strikes; A Global Pax Americana," http://www.globalissues.org/Geopolitics?Empire?Bush.asp?p=1.

19 Nye, *Paradox of American Power*, 5–6. Also, see Nye, *Soft Power*, 18–19.

20 Nye, *Paradox of American Power*, 8, 9. Also, See Nye, 2004, x, 5–8.

21 See Ferguson, who dismisses "soft power" as an effective foreign policy tool, arguing that even if young people, especially in the "Islamic world, "enjoy [or would like to enjoy] bottles of Coke, Big Macs, CDs by Brittney Spears and DVDs starring Tom Cruise," none of these things seem to increase their love for the United States (Niall Ferguson, "Think Again: Power," *Foreign Policy* [2003]: 21).

22 Nye, *Paradox of American Power*, 9, 141; *Soft Power*, 8, 11.

23 Nye, *Paradox of American Power*, 11, 145.

24 Nye, *Soft Power*, 22–24.

25 Nye, *Paradox of American Power*, 1, 10, 15, 16.

26 See Robert W. Merry, *Sands of Empire: Missionary Zeal, American Foreign Policy, and the Hazards of Global Ambition* (New York: Simon & Schuster, 2005), 195.

27 Merry, *Sands of Empire*, xii, 158, 254.

28 Merry, *Sands of Empire*, 233–35.

29 Merry, *Sands of Empire*, xiv–xv.

30 Nye, *Paradox of American Power*, 140.

31 Nye, *Paradox of American Power*, 17, xii, xiv, 137, 138.

32 This discussion leaves aside, of course, the disagreement that the supporters of the Bush administration and the supporters of the Powell and Nye doctrines may have concerning the character of American values or the American way of life.

33 See *The National Security Strategy*, i; Powell, "Remarks on the Occasion of George Kennan's Centenary Birthday"; Nye, *Paradox of American Power*, 138; and Merry, 195.

Bibliography

Ackerman, Bruce. "The Legality of Using Force," http://www.law.yale.edu/outside/htnl/Public Affairs/293/yls article.htm (last updated September 23, 2002: accessed August 12, 2007).

———. "But What's the Legal Case for Preemption." http://www.law.yale.edu/outside/html/Public Affairs/282/yls article.htm (last updated August 20, 2002, accessed August 12, 2007).

Aeschylus. *The Suppliant Maidens*. Translated by Seth Benardete. Chicago: University of Chicago Press, 1956.

———. *The Persians*. Translated by Seth Benardete. Chicago: University of Chicago Press, 1956.

———. *Prometheus Bound*. Translated by David Grene. Chicago: University of Chicago Press, 1956.

Alonso-Nunez, Jose-Miguel. "Herodotus' Conception of Historical Space and the Beginnings of Universal History." In *Herodotus and His World: Essays from a Conference in Memory of George Forrest*. Edited by Peter Derow and Robert Parker. 145–52. Oxford: Oxford University Press, 2003.

Aristotle. *The Politics*. Translated by Carnes Lord. Chicago: University of Chicago Press, 1984.

———. *Poetics*. Translated by Gerald F. Else. Ann Arbor: University of Michigan Press, 1967.

———. *Nicomachean Ethics*. Translated by H. Rackham. Cambridge: Harvard University Press, 1926.

Benardete, Seth. *Herodotean Inquiries*. The Hague: Martinus Nijhoff, 1969.

Bernal, Martin. *Black Athena: The Afroasiatic Roots of Classical Civilization*. Vol. 1. New Brunswick: Rutgers University Press, 1987.

Blosel, Wolfgang. "The Herodotean Picture of Themistocles: A Mirror of Fifth-century Athens." In *The Historian's Craft in the Age of Herodotus*. Edited by Nino Luraghi. Oxford: Oxford University Press, 2007.

Bowden, Hugh. *Classical Athens and the Delphic Oracle: Divination and Democracy*. Cambridge: Cambridge University Press, 2005.

Brailey, Malcolm. "Pre-Emption and Prevention: An Ethical and Legal Critique of the Bush Doctrine and Anticipatory Use of Force in Defence of the State." Paper presented at the Institute of Defence and Strategic Studies, Singapore, November 2003.

Cragg, Kevin Mark. "Herodotus' Presentation of Sparta." Ph.D. Dissertation, University of Michigan, 1976.

Crane, Gregory. *Thucydides and the Ancient Simplicity: The Limits of Political Realism*. Berkeley: University of California Press, 1998.

Davies, John K. "Democracy without Theory." In *Herodotus and His World: Essays from a Conference in Memory of George Forrest*. 319–36. Edited by Peter Derow and Robert Parker. Oxford: Oxford University Press, 2003.

Descartes, Rene. *Discourse On the Method*. Translated by Robert Stoothoff. In *The Philosophical Writings of Descartes*. Volume 1. Edited and translated by John Cottingham, Robert Stoothoff, and Dugold Murdoch. Cambridge: Cambridge University Press, 1985.

Dewald, Carolyn. "'I Didn't Give My Own Genealogy': Herodotus and the Authorial Persona." In *Brill's Companion to Herodotus*. 267–90. Edited by Egbert J. Bakker, Irene J. F. De Jong, Hans Van Wees. Leiden: Brill, 2002.

Euben, Peter J. "The Battle of Salamis and the Origins of Political Theory." *Political Theory* 14, no. 3 (1986): 359–90.

Evans, J. A. S. *Herodotus, Explorer of the Past*. Princeton: Princeton University Press, 1991.

Ferguson, Niall. "Think Again: Power." *Foreign Policy* 134 (January/February 2003): 18–22, 24.

Flory, Stewart. *The Archaic Smile of Herodotus*. Detroit: Wayne State University Press, 1987.

Forde, Steven. *The Ambition to Rule: Alcibiades and the Politics of Imperialism in Thucydides*. Ithaca: Cornell University Press, 1989.

Fornara, Charles W. *Herodotus: An Interpretive Essay*. Oxford: Oxford University Press, 1971.

Forsdyke, Sara. "Herodotus, Political History and Political Thought." In *The Cambridge Companion to Herodotus*. 224–41. Edited by Carolyn Dewald and John Marincola. Cambridge: Cambridge University Press, 2006.

———. "Athenian Democratic Ideology and Herodotus' *Histories*." *American Journal of Philology* 122, no. 3 (2001): 329–58.

Fowler, Robert. "Herodotus and His Prose Predecessors." In *The Cambridge Companion to Herodotus*. 29–45. Edited by Carolyn Dewald and John Marincola. Cambridge: Cambridge University Press, 2006.

Franck, Thomas, et al. "Iraq and the 'Bush Doctrine' of Pre-Emptive Self-Defence." In "Crimes of War Project." http://www.crimesofwar.org/print/expert/bush-introBush-print.html (updated August 20, 2002; accessed August 12, 2007).

Gould, John. *Herodotus*. London: Wiedenfeld & Nicholson, 1989.

Griffin, Jasper, "Herodotus and Tragedy." In *The Cambridge Companion to Herodotus*. 46–59. Edited by Carolyn Dewald and John Marincola. Cambridge: Cambridge University Press, 2006.

Griffiths, Alan. "Stories and Storytelling in Herodotus." In *The Cambridge Companion to Herodotus*. 130–44. Edited by Carolyn Dewald and John Marincola. Cambridge: Cambridge University Press, 2006.

Harrison, Thomas. "Prophecy in Reverse? Herodotus and the Origins of History." In *Herodotus and His World: Essays from a Conference in Memory of George Forrest*. 237–55. Edited by Peter Derow and Robert Parker. Oxford: Oxford University Press, 2003.

———. "The Persian Invasions." In *Brill's Companion to Herodotus*. 551–78. Edited by Egbert J. Bakker, Irene J. F. De Jong, Hans Van Wees. Leiden: Brill, 2002.

———. *Divinity and History: The Religion of Herodotus*. Oxford: Oxford University Press, 2000.

Hart, John. *Herodotus and Greek History*. New York: St. Martin's Press, 1982.

Hartog, Francois. *The Mirror of Herodotus: The Representation of the Other in the Writing of History*. Translated by Janet Lloyd. Berkeley: University of California Press, 1978.

Havelock, Eric A. *The Greek Concept of Justice: From Its Shadow in Homer to Its Substance in Plato*. Cambridge: Harvard University Press, 1978.

Hegel, G. W. F. *The Philosophy of History*. New York: Dover Publications, 1956.

Herodotus. *The Histories*. Translated by A. D. Godley. Cambridge: Harvard University Press, 1920.

———. *The History*. Translated by David Grene. Chicago: University of Chicago Press, 1987.

Hesiod. *Aegimius*. Translated by Hugh G. Evelyn-White. Cambridge: Harvard University Press, 1914.

———. *Catalogues of Women and Eoiae*. Translated by Hugh G. Evelyn-White. Cambridge: Harvard University Press, 1914.

Hobbes, Thomas. *Leviathan*. Edited by Edwin Curly. Indianapolis: Hackett Publishing, 1994.

How, W. W., and J. Wells. *Commentary on Herodotus*. Oxford: Oxford University Press, 1912.

Howland, Jacob. *Kierkegaard and Socrates: A Study in Philosophy and Faith*. Cambridge: Cambridge University Press, 2006.

Hunter, Virginia. *Past and Process in Herodotus and Thucydides*. Princeton: Princeton University Press, 1982.

Immerwahr, Henry R. *Form and Thought in Herodotus*. Cleveland: Press of Western Reserve University, 1966.

Johnson, Laurie M. *Thucydides, Hobbes, and the Interpretation of Realism*. DeKalb: Northern Illinois University Press, 1993.

Kass, Leon. *Toward a More Natural Science: Biology and Human Affairs*. New York: Free Press, 1985.

Keith, Sidney. "Herodotus: The First Political Scientist." Ph.D. Dissertation. University of Toronto, 1989.

Kristol, William, John Lewis Gaddis, Barton Gellman, and Dennis Ross. "Analyses 1992: First Draft of a Grand Strategy." In "Frontline: The War Behind Closed Doors." http://www.pbs.org/wgbh/pages/frontline/Shows/iraq/themes/1992.html (last updated January 2003; accessed August 12, 2007).

Lateiner, Donald. *The Historical Method of Herodotus*. Toronto: University of Toronto Press, 1989.

Lefkowitz, Mary. *Not out of Africa: How Afrocentrism Became an Excuse to Teach Myth as History*. New York: Basic Books, 1996.

Liddell, Henry George, and Russell Scott. *Greek-English Lexicon: Abridged Edition*. Oxford: Oxford University Press, 1997.

Linforth, Ivan M. "Greek and Egyptian Gods (Herodotus II.50 and 52)." *Classical Philology* 35, no. 3 (1940): 300–01.

Lloyd, Alan B. *Herodotus, Book II: Introduction*. Leiden: Brill, 1975.

Lopez, George. "Just? Unjust?" *Sojourner's Magazine*, online at http://www.sojo.net/index.cfm?action&mode=printerfriendly&issue=soj (last updated May 2004; accessed May 5, 2008).

Marincola, John. "Herodotus and the Poetry of the Past." In *The Cambridge Companion to Herodotus*. 13–28. Edited by Carolyn Dewald and John Marincola. Cambridge: Cambridge University Press, 2006.

McGlew, James F. *Tyranny and Political Culture in Ancient Greece*. Ithaca: Cornell University Press, 1993.

Merry, Robert W. *Sands of Empire: Missionary Zeal, American Foreign Policy, and the Hazards of Global Ambition*. New York: Simon & Schuster, 2005.

Mikalson, Jon D. "Religion in Herodotus." In *Brill's Companion to Herodotus*. 187–98. Edited by Egbert J. Bakker, Irene J. F. De Jong, and Hans Van Wees. Leiden: Brill, 2002.

Moles, John. "Herodotus and Athens." In *Brill's Companion to Herodotus*. 187–98. Edited by Egbert J. Bakker, Irene J. F. De Jong, and Hans Van Wees. Leiden: Brill, 2002.

Munson, Rosaria Vignolo. *Black Doves Speak: Herodotus and the Languages of Barbarians*. Cambridge: Harvard University Press, 2005.

———. *Telling Wonders: Ethnographic and Political Discourse in the Work of Herodotus*. Ann Arbor: University of Michigan Press, 2001.

The National Security Strategy of the United States of America, September, 2002. http://www.whitehouse.gov/nsc/nss.html (accessed March 5, 2008).

Nichols, Mary P. *Citizens and Statesmen: A Study of Aristotle's Politics*. Lanham, Md.: Rowman & Littlefield, 1992.

———. *Socrates and the Political Community: An Ancient Debate*. Albany: State University of New York Press, 1987.

Nye, Joseph S. Jr. *The Paradox of American Power: Why the World's Only Superpower Can't Go It Alone*. Oxford: Oxford University Press, 2002.

———. *Soft Power: The Means to Success in World Politics*. New York: Public Affairs, 2004.

Orwin, Clifford. *The Humanity of Thucydides*. Princeton: Princeton University Press, 1994.

Osborne, Robin. "Archaic Greek History." In *Brill's Companion to Herodotus*. 497–520. Edited by Egbert J. Bakker, Irene J. F. De Jong, and Hans Van Wees. Leiden: Brill, 2002.

Ostwald, Martin. *Nomos and the Beginnings of the Athenian Democracy*. Oxford: Oxford University Press, 1969.

Page, Carl. "Thumos and Thermopylae: Herodotus vii: 238." *Ancient Philosophy* 16, no. 2 (1996): 301–31.

Palmer, Michael. *Love of Glory and the Common Good: Aspects of the Political Thought of Thucydides*. Lanham, Md.: Rowman & Littlefield, 1992.

Palter, Robert. "Black Athena, Afro-Centrism, and the History of Science." *History of Science* 31, no. 93 (1993): 227–87.

Pangle, Thomas L. "Introduction." In Leo Strauss, *Studies in Platonic Political Philosophy*. Chicago: University of Chicago Press, 1983.

Pelling, Christopher. "Speech and Narrative in the *Histories*." In *The Cambridge Companion to Herodotus*. 103–21. Edited by Carolyn Dewald and John Marincola. Cambridge: Cambridge University Press, 2006.

———. "Speech and Action: Herodotus' Debate on the Constitutions." *Proceedings of the Cambridge Philological Society* 48 (2002): 123–58.

Plato. *Republic*. Translated by Allan Bloom. New York: Basic Books, 1968.

———. *Minos*. Translated by Thomas L. Pangle. In *The Roots of Political Philosophy: Ten Forgotten Socratic Dialogues*. 53–66. Edited by Thomas L. Pangle. Ithaca: Cornell University Press, 1987.

Plutarch. "Of Herodotus' Malice." In *Plutarch's Essays and Miscellanies*. Volume 4. 331–71. Edited by Arthur Hugh Clough and William Watson Goodwin. New York: The Colonial Company, 1905.

———. "Of Isis and Osiris, Or of the Ancient Religion and Philosophy of Egypt." In *Plutarch's Essays and Miscellanies*. Volume 4. 65–139. Edited by Arthur Hugh Clough and William Watson Goodwin. New York: The Colonial Company, 1905.

———. "Lycurgus." Translated by John Dryden. In *Plutarch: The Lives of the Noble Grecians and Romans*. 49–74. Edited by Arthur Hugh Clough. New York: The Modern Library, 1905.

———. "Solon." Translated by John Dryden. In *Plutarch: The Lives of the Noble Grecians and Romans*. 97–117. Edited by Arthur Hugh Clough. New York: The Modern Library, 1905.

Powell, Colin L. "Remarks on the Occasion of George Kennan's Centenary Birthday," http://www.state.gov/secretary/rm/29683.htm (last updated February 20, 2004; accessed August 12, 2007).

———. "Remarks at the Elliot School of International Affairs," http://www.state.gov/secretary/rm/2003/2386.htm (last updated September 5, 2003; accessed August 12, 2007).

Raaflaub, Kurt. *The Discovery of Freedom in Ancient Greece*. Chicago: University of Chicago Press, 2004.

Riley, Jack. "Freedom and Empire: The Politics of Athenian Imperialism." In *Thucydides' Theory of International Relations: A Lasting Possession*. 117–50. Edited by Lowell S. Gustafson. Baton Rouge: Louisiana State University Press, 2000.

Robertson, Noel. "The True Meaning of the 'Wooden Wall.'" *Classical Philology* 82, no. 1 (1987): 1–20.

Romm, James. "Herodotus and the Natural World." In *The Cambridge Companion to Herodotus*. 178–91. Edited by Carolyn Dewald and John Marincola. Cambridge: Cambridge University Press, 2006.

Rood, Tim. "Herodotus and Foreign Lands." In *The Cambridge Companion to Herodotus*. 290–305. Edited by Carolyn Dewald and John Marincola. Cambridge: Cambridge University Press, 2006.

Rosen, Stanley. *The Quarrel Between Philosophy and Poetry*. New York: Routledge, 1988.

Sancisi-Weerdenberg, Heleen. "The Personality of Xerxes." In *Brill's Companion to Herodotus*. 579–90. Edited by Egbert J. Bakker, Irene J. F. De Jong, and Hans Van Wees. Leiden: Brill, 2002.

Saxonhouse, Arlene W. *Free Speech and Democracy in Ancient Athens*. Cambridge: Cambridge University Press, 2006.

———. *Athenian Democracy: Modern Mythmakers and Ancient Theorists*. Notre Dame: University of Notre Dame Press, 1996.

Scullion, Scott. "Herodotus and Greek Religion." In *The Cambridge Companion to Herodotus*. 192–208. Edited by Carolyn Dewald and John Marincola. Cambridge: Cambridge University Press, 2006.

Shah, Anup. "Military Expansion: The Bush Doctrine of Pre-Emptive Strikes; A Global Pax Americana," http://www.globalissues.org/Geopolitics/Empire/Bush.asp?p=1 (last updated April 24, 2004; accessed August 12, 2007).

Shimron, Binyamin. *Politics and Belief in Herodotus*. Stuttgart: Franz Steiner Verlag Wiesbaden GMBH, 1989.

Sourvinou-Inwood, Christiane. "Herodotus (and others) on Pelasgians: Some Perceptions of Ethnicity." In *Herodotus and His World: Essays from a Conference in Memory of George Forrest*. 103–44. Edited by Peter Derow and Robert Parker. Oxford: Oxford University Press, 2003.

Stadter, Phillip. "Herodotus and the Cities of Mainland Greece." In *The Cambridge Companion to Herodotus*. 242–56. Edited by Carolyn Dewald and John Marincola. Cambridge: Cambridge University Press, 2006.

Strauss, Leo. *Natural Right and History*. Chicago: University of Chicago Press, 1953.

———. "On Thucydides' War of the Peloponnesians and the Athenians." In *The City and Man*. Chicago: University of Chicago Press, 1964.

———. "Liberal Education and Responsibility." In *An Introduction to Political Philosophy: Ten Essays by Leo Strauss*. 321–48. Edited by Hilail Gilden. Detroit: Wayne State University Press, 1989.

Taylor, Flagg. "What Makes a Scythian a Scythian? Book IV of *The History*." Spring, 1999 (unpublished).

Thomas, Rosalind. "The Intellectual Milieu of Herodotus." In *The Cambridge Companion to Herodotus*. 60–75. Edited by Carolyn Dewald and John Marincola. Cambridge: Cambridge University Press, 2006.

———. *Herodotus in Context: Ethnography, Science and the Art of Persuasion*. Cambridge: Cambridge University Press, 2000.

Thompson, Norma. *Herodotus and the Origins of the Political Community: Arion's Leap*. New Haven: Yale University Press, 1996.

Thucydides. *History of the Peloponnesian War*. Translated by Rex Warner. New York: Penguin Books, 1954.

———. *History of the Peloponnesian War*. Translated by Richard Crawley. New York: Free Press, 1996.

Tigerstedt, E. N. *The Legend of Sparta in Classical Antiquity*. Stockholm: Almquist & Wiksell, 1965.

Tritle, Lawrence. "Warfare in Herodotus." In *The Cambridge Companion to Herodotus*. 209–23. Edited by Carolyn Dewald and John Marincola. Cambridge: Cambridge University Press, 2006.

Vasunia, Phiroze. *The Gift of the Nile: Hellenizing Egypt from Aeschylus to Alexander*. Berkeley: University of California Press, 2001.

Vlastos, Gregory. *Platonic Studies*. Princeton: Princeton University Press, 1973.

Ward, Ann. "Self-reflection, Egyptian Beliefs, Scythians and 'Greek Ideas': Reconsidering Greeks and Barbarians in Herodotus." *The European Legacy: Toward New Paradigms* 11, no. 1 (2006): 1–19.

Waters, Kenneth H. *Herodotus on Tyrants and Despots: A Study in Objectivity*. Wiesbaden: Franz Steiner Verlag, 1971.

Wolfowitz, Paul. "Defense Planning Guidance." In "Frontline: The War Behind Closed Doors," http://www.pbs.org/wgbh/pages/frontline/shows/iraq/etc.wolf.html (last updated August 12, 2007; accessed August 12, 2007).

———. "Frontline: Missile Wars: Interview: Paul Wolfowitz," http://www.pbs.org/wgbh/pages/frontline/shows/missile/interviews/wolfowitz.html (last updated June 12, 2002; accessed August 12, 2007).

Xenophon. *Cyropaedia*. Translated by Walter Miller. Cambridge: Harvard University Press, 1965.

Index